My Music Is My Flag

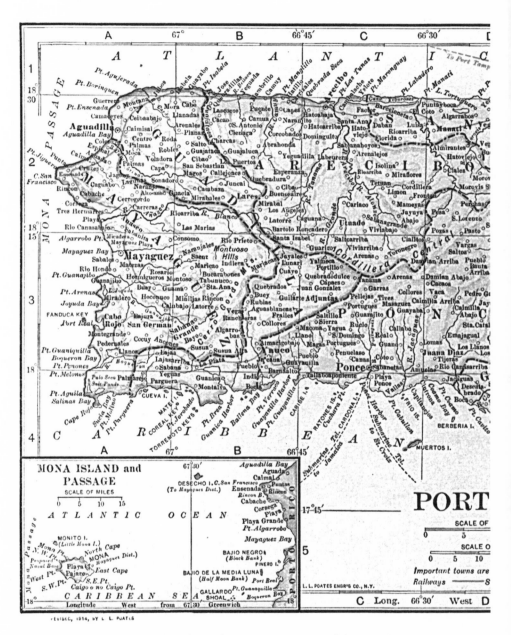

Puerto Rico, 1914. From *World Atlas and Gazetteer.* Courtesy of the Map Section, Centro de Estudios Puertorriqueños, Hunter College, CUNY.

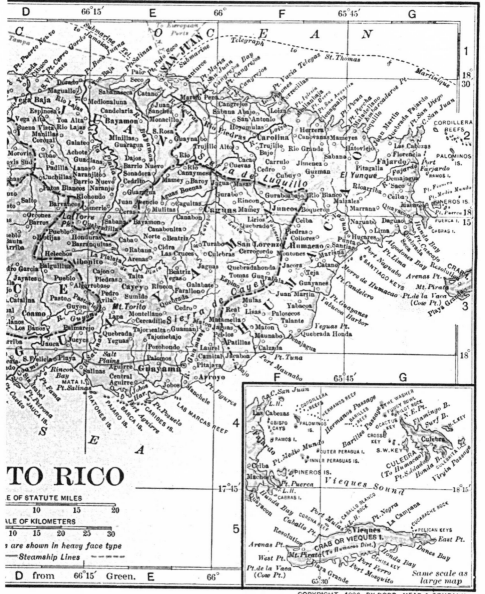

My Music Is My Flag

Puerto Rican Musicians and Their New York Communities, 1917–1940

Ruth Glasser

UNIVERSITY OF CALIFORNIA PRESS
Berkeley · Los Angeles · London

University of California Press
Berkeley and Los Angeles, California

University of California Press, Ltd.
London, England

© 1995 by
The Regents of the University of California

First Paperback Printing 1997

Library of Congress Cataloging-in-Publication Data

Glasser, Ruth.
    My music is my flag : Puerto Rican musicians and their New York communities, 1917–1940/
    Ruth Glasser.
      p.   cm.
    Includes bibliographical references (p.   ), discography (p.   ), and index.
    ISBN 0-520-20890-0
    1. Puerto Ricans—New York (N.Y.)—Music—History and criticism.   2. Popular music—New
    York (N.Y.)—History and criticism.   3. Popular music—Puerto Rico—History and criticism.
    4. Puerto Ricans—New York (N.Y.)—Ethnic identity.   I. Title.
    ML3481.053   1995
    780'.8968729507471.—dc20   94-9015
                                                       CIP
                                                        MN

Printed in the United States of America
9 8 7 6 5 4 3 2 1

Dedicado a la memoria de Antonio Pérez Temazatzi
(1929–1991)

and to
Genoveva Rodríguez
(1923–1992)

and
Ida Peretz Glasser
(1900–1993),

who knew no ethnic boundaries

Que lejos estoy de mi Borinquén
Que lejos estoy de mi tierra
La que el mundo mira con desdén
Porque no tiene bandera.
    Davilita (Pedro Ortíz Dávila)

Contents

Illustrations

Frontispiece. Puerto Rico, 1914

Following Page 128

1. Dance card, 1923
2. Aguadilla school band at the turn of the century
3. Orquesta Happy Hills, San Germán, Puerto Rico, early 1930s
4. Rafael and Jesús "Pocholo" Hernández as soldiers during World War I
5. Francisco "El Paisa" Quiñones
6. James Reese Europe and his band en route to France, December 1917
7. Augusto Coen and his Golden Casino Orchestra, New York, 1930s
8. Flyer for Columbus Day dance, 1932
9. Performers in the nightclub El Chico, 1946
10. Mother's Day celebration in Brooklyn at a Puerto Rican branch of the International Workers' Order, 1937
11. Puerto Rican and Hispanic League, Brooklyn section, ca. 1920s
12. Lower East Side Hispanic Drum and Bugle Corps, New York City, 1937

Preface

What's a nice Jewish girl from Brooklyn doing studying Puerto Rican music? Since embarking on my study several years ago, I have been asked countless versions of this question by a wide variety of people. I believe that one's choice of research reveals a somewhat autobiographical agenda, a working out of questions that are meaningful on a level that goes much deeper than the intellectual. I would like, therefore, to answer this question in both personal and more general terms.

This book began as a dissertation that was hatched sometime between 1986 and 1988, although in the tidiness of hindsight I could easily point to dozens of life experiences that influenced my choice. In the interest of getting to the subject at hand, I will stick approximately to the present. By the mid-1980s I had one foot in the academic world and one in community organizing. I was also straddling the fence between these spheres in doing public-oriented history projects. The most influential of these was the Waterbury (Connecticut) Ethnic Music Project (1985–86), directed by Jeremy Brecher.

Jeremy, I, and the others associated with this project haunted the lives of the mainly working-class people in this deindustrializing Connecticut city. We spent months going to masses, dances, gospel afternoons, national independence celebrations, and people's homes. We recorded the music of more than fifteen ethnic groups and spoke to people about how that music and its performance context had been, and continued to be, meaningful in their lives.

In the process, we became interested in a series of larger questions.

Or perhaps it would be more accurate to say that we were thrown into the middle of community debates that showed us that what were theoretical issues for us were important concerns in the day-to-day lives of the people we were studying. We looked at and thought about the relationship between a changing economic and social landscape and the evolution of musical forms. We saw these concretely expressed in Waterbury in many ways. People debated how to keep community cultural institutions alive, while jobs disappeared and the younger generation moved on to other areas. They debated whether to use traditional song forms with English lyrics in order to reach out to that younger generation and to those outside the ethnic group. We found ourselves constantly bumping up against questions of authenticity as members of ethnic groups kept saying that they would tell us what they could but that so-and-so over there was the "real thing." No matter how comprehensive our efforts were, the "real thing" always seemed to be somewhere else, just beyond our reach.

As we planned the first live showcase of the music we had come upon, the Waterbury Traditional Music Festival, our group had to confront the ongoing power of ethnic expression and ethnic divisions within an economically troubled community. We found that people of different ethnic groups who had lived practically side by side for years often did not know anything about each other's music. Some of them, particularly those from racially distinct groups, felt an actual aversion to performing together on the same program. Conversely, we found a great deal of sharing and borrowing between some groups, particularly groups that had migrated to Waterbury at about the same time or groups that shared a white ethnic or minority background. Musicians and audiences were also quite eclectic in their musical tastes, not necessarily making distinctions between folk, popular, and art music. At the same time, we learned that there were indeed debates over cultural authenticity not only among ourselves but also among members of the various ethnic communities. Far from being the naïve "folk" portrayed in much scholarship of "traditional" music, our interviewees were often cultural activists who consciously strove to pass on certain musical forms and to revive others. Rather than being a process of unconscious transmission, cultural preservation involved energy, intelligence, and just plain work, much of it tedious and difficult. All of this had to be taken into account as we planned a multiethnic festival designed to represent the best of each community back to itself and to the other groups in the city.

It would of course be Pollyannaish to suggest that our festival solved inter- and intra-ethnic problems in Waterbury, thus paving the way for cooperative and creative solutions to the city's economic woes. Nevertheless, I think that it and the ensuing five festivals have been steps in the right direction. The festivals have provided a forum for celebrating the ongoing cultural vitality of a city recently given low livability ratings by a magazine directed to yuppie readers. The festivals have showcased local groups and honored the work of cultural activists who usually work behind the scenes. They have exposed different ethnic communities to each others' musical expressions and have actually helped to promote collaborations between members of these groups, at least on the cultural level.

While our ethnic music investigations and activities raised some of the large questions and observations that have guided the writing of this book, the project also sent me in a specific direction. As the only member of the project with even a limited knowledge of Spanish, I was delegated to conduct the interviews and collect the music in the fast-growing Puerto Rican community of Waterbury. This community tended to be cavalierly dismissed by those outside it as at best closed or hard to get into or at worst "no good" or "all on welfare." However, despite my inadequate Spanish and almost complete ignorance of Puerto Rican music and culture, I had no problems penetrating this supposedly clannish group. I found that Puerto Rican musicians and cultural activists were all too aware of the negative stereotypes with which others framed their ethnic community. Consequently, they were generally delighted that a cultural outsider was interested in studying their music and bringing it to a more general audience.

Throughout this investigation I was exposed to a richer variety of music than I had envisioned. I fell in love with the Puerto Rican forms most generally regarded as folkloric, such as the *seis,* the *aguinaldo,* the *bomba,* and the *plena.* However, just as in the other ethnic communities, I discovered mixes, borrowings, and popularizations with deep historical roots and personal meaning. Musicians played the supposedly Central European *valses* (waltzes) and mazurkas as staples of their folkloric repertoire. They composed gospel songs and *plenas* with modern themes. And they worshipped contemporary or relatively recent Latin American composers of *tangos, boleros,* and *sones.*

Among those composers was Rafael Hernández. The first time I ever heard of him was on May 2, 1986, when Pedro Vélez of Waterbury told me that "in Puerto Rico we think he's the greatest. Because the meaning of his songs, it came from the heart. He would sing mostly to the country people, to Puerto Rico. He's gone, but you can ask anybody who was Rafael Hernández, they'll tell you. They talk about him as though he was alive."

By the end of 1986 I knew that I wanted to write a dissertation that combined some of the concerns raised by community members in my first important foray into public history and cultural programming. And the name Rafael Hernández kept sticking in my mind. I could find very little information on him in English, but there was a persistent and haunting image of him in the scant literature. It was an image of Hernández in the 1930s, sitting in a chair in front of his sister's record store at Madison Avenue and 113th Street in El Barrio, New York City, strumming his guitar and composing Puerto Rican songs. What was Hernández doing in my hometown before World War II? I wondered. Why did he persist in singing about Puerto Rico? And, I asked, with the almost inevitable *yanqui* arrogance creeping in, if he was so wonderful, why hadn't I or any of the other English speakers I knew ever heard of him or of his songs?

The Hernández tableau nagged at me so much that I had to find the answers to these questions. I did not know whether there would even be enough material to write an article, much less a book-length essay. Other obstacles seemed nearly insurmountable. My Spanish needed a great deal of work, and my musical training was minimal. And despite my positive experiences in Waterbury, my status as an ethnic outsider worried me. I still remember those first few days that I crept around the Centro de Estudios Puertorriqueños at Hunter College, wondering if someone was going to challenge my interest or my credentials. My worst fears of imposterhood were realized when I met with an ethnomusicology professor specializing in Latin and Caribbean music. She had a number of harsh things to say to me. First of all, she would not share her unpublished work on Latin music with me. Moreover, she warned that those Latinos whom she knew to be working in the field of Latin music would probably be hostile and uncooperative with me since Puerto Ricans hated Jews because of the landlord-tenant relationship that had existed between them in New York (she had not asked me about my ethnicity beforehand). Furthermore, she observed, Latinos were resentful of non-Latinos who constantly siphoned off their culture, leaving them with nothing. It is worth noting that she herself was neither Puerto Rican nor Latina. Perhaps only those who come later than oneself are to be considered exploiters, cultural imperialists.

After the initial pain of the encounter, I was able to recognize the professor's anti-Semitism and excessive academic competitiveness. At the same time, I could not entirely discount her words. Precisely because of my concerns about the process of researching and writing history, and my recognition that it always has a contemporary social and political context, I worried that there might be some truth to her charges of cultural rip-off. I thought about all the white artists who had made money from African-American music, while the originators of the music stayed poor, about all the "outsiders" involved in collecting and presenting Third World music and culture. I wondered if it would be better to stay away and leave the research to those on the "inside." I thought about the ways in which such cultural inequities are often analogous to economic, political, and social power imbalances and about how common it is, even when one has the best intentions, to think that he or she knows best what members of another culture should preserve and how they should go about doing it. Finally, I realized that although I found the professor's description of Jewish-Latino relationships stereotyped and offensive, it might well reflect the feelings of many of New York's Puerto Ricans. I had seen enough casual anti-Latino prejudice among my own white ethnic contacts, particularly among the children of immigrants. Not coincidentally, their negative feelings were often cloaked in hostility toward programs of cultural preservation such as bilingual education in the public schools because they had had to learn "the hard way." Many dismissed *all* contemporary Latin American music as "that noisy stuff the Hispanic neighbors are always playing till four o'clock in the morning." From my own experience, I realized how pervasive seemingly irrational and unfair interethnic attitudes are and how operational they are in the lives of many people.

I continued poking around various New York collections looking for a feasible related dissertation topic, but I held myself in reserve from consultations with the Puerto Rican or Cuban–New Yorker *sabios* of music until I had considered my own motives and consulted with other outsiders involved in Latin music. I realized that such introspection and networking would be never-ending, an apparent weakness that could be turned into a strength in doing sensitive work. As an ethnic outsider, I would always need to think about the relationship between my personal life, my work, and those I was writing about. I had constantly to remind myself that my prior research, writing, and programming in Waterbury had brought a mutual sense of discovery and delight between me and

the subjects of my work, many of whom were now my friends. It heart-
ened me that my desire to base my dissertation on an area of Puerto
Rican musical history was a source of pride to them.

On the more academic side, I noted that although there seemed to be
a plethora of books and articles on, for example, Mexican-American
musical and cultural history, there seemed to be no equivalent for Puerto
Ricans in the continental United States. They had been explained ad
nauseum in sociological, anthropological, and political science treatises,
which dealt mainly with the post–World War II migration process and
its ill effects on the community, the proliferation of crime, drugs, poverty, and so forth, but little had been done to indicate that "Puerto Rican" is not just another term for post–World War II urban pathology.
Fortunately, that had begun to change through the Herculean labors of
the Centro de Estudios Puertorriqueños in New York, a valuable research center whose members have done a wonderful job collecting oral
histories, restoring important historical documents, and writing many
provocative articles about aspects of Puerto Rican communities in different parts of the United States before and after World War II. The
publication of Virginia Sánchez-Korrol's *From Colonia to Community*
(1983) was another important step in the right direction. On the cultural
side, however, more remained to be done.

Speaking to a variety of mostly white, Jewish, male researchers and
programmers of Latin music, I was reassured that it was possible to step
outside one's own culture to do research and cultural organizing that
would be appreciated by members of the ethnic group that was one's
subject. If properly produced, such materials could even be used as am-
munition toward furthering a group's goals of community pride and
self-empowerment. Politically speaking, I also felt that it would be more
valuable for me to cross cultural lines. I could try both to understand
another ethnic group in more depth, always sharing my tentative interpretations with them, and to bring some inkling of their cultural wealth
to those who had contemptuously dismissed them as a body. I resolved
always to find ways to give back the results of the research to the people
I was researching, to present them not only in a dissertation but also in
a format accessible to both Hispanic and non-Hispanic general readers.

I also began to see that it would be both logically faulty and politically counterproductive to stay within "my own" community in my research. Such a strategy disintegrates as one scrutinizes it. By rights,
should I be exploring only, say, Ashkenazic Jewish cradle songs and how
they had changed from the Old World to the New? What made this my
own community and culture to research? After all, I did not grow up

with such music. The religious Eastern European Jews who might call this music their own would probably consider me an ethnic outsider, if not an apostate.

Mulling over these issues did not dissuade me from my goals, but it did influence the format of my research. I was determined to explore these very questions of who would be a cultural group insider and who would be an outsider. One could not take for granted physical ethnic group unity or in-group conceptions of criteria for ethnic membership. These might change not only from person to person but also from situation to situation. Manuel "Canario" Jiménez, for example, a musician whose life and work I explore in this book, was the most famous exponent of a Puerto Rican music with which he did not grow up. Was he a cultural insider or an outsider? It depended upon the context, as well as the point of view of individual Puerto Ricans, non–Puerto Rican listeners, and contemporary members of the music industry. Drastic changes in historical situations could also alter ethnic identity. Referring to my own example, although I might be regarded by Orthodox Jews as a defector in religious or cultural terms, a political and social crisis such as another Holocaust would temporarily make us a more unified body, the result of both external conceptions of who is Jewish and our collective need to take action for our very survival. To a large extent, it is memories of that horrific past that bind us together, although we would undoubtedly have different opinions on the meaning of that history.

On a day-to-day level, however, another subjective phenomenon operates. It is sometimes easier to be what Jeremy Brecher calls a "pet outsider"[1] than it is to be a person with even slender claims to insidership. Any Newyorican for whom Spanish does not come easily knows what I mean. As someone who voluntarily struggled to learn more of the language and culture of Puerto Rico and its migrants, I get more credit from those born on the island than a Puerto Rican who also has struggled to speak good Spanish.

As I work, I try to be aware of such contradictions and to analyze them, and I sometimes reap their benefits. I have found that as I have "done my homework" about music and musicians and forced improvement in my Spanish, I have gained a deeper sense that a well-informed outsider may have a place among members of an ethnic group. And the strongest reaction I have received to date is a sort of bemusement at the novelty of a young Jewish woman studying old Puerto Rican music. One elderly musician actually told me that I had the memory of an eighty-year-old!

After spending several months in Puerto Rico and then doing subsequent research, I am unembarrassed by this apparent oddity. Rather than minimizing my differences from the collectors, elderly musicians, and their families, I have learned to accept and even enjoy the novelty status people usually accord me. Allowing the conversation to turn to my Jewishness has often brought about welcome dialogues on the subject of ethnic identity and interethnic contact. The perennial question how I became interested in learning Spanish and studying Puerto Rican music allows me to talk about my feelings about cultural sharing and the possibilities of mutually beneficial exchange between scholars and community people. It also brings up informants' own concerns about the preservation of what they perceive as their cultural heritage.

At the same time, many informants and I have experienced a mutually appreciative exchange. Just as I have been thrilled to receive firsthand information about Latin Americans making music in New York City fifty or more years ago, some of the veterans of this experience have been at first cautious or shocked and then excited by my interest. After my first hour and a half with the late professor, guitarist, and *cuatro* player don Paquito López Cruz, he said to me brightly, "Well, I'm sure now I've answered all your questions." When I just as cheerfully answered him, wondering at the same time whether I was being too pushy, "No, señor, I am very *preguntona* [inquisitive]," don Paquito laughed. Before I knew it he was promising me all the interviews I could wish for, expecting me to be at his concerts, and introducing me to his friends as the *muchacha* from Yale who was doing a study of an important historical experience in which he had been included. When I brought him and veteran singer Johnny Rodríguez copies of Richard Spottswood's wonderful, computerized list of pre-1942 Latin American recordings made in the United States, I saw history come alive as they scanned the lists of recordings they had participated in making and told me stories about recording sessions and band personnel. I also saw these men moved by an in-print rendering of at least some of what they had accomplished in their lives. Much of this documentation was not readily available to anyone outside the purview of academics or record collectors. Ironically, but somewhat typically (that is, these types of ironies always seem to occur), I brought tapes of old 78s to Augusto Coen's stepson Ray and to Rafael Hernández's sister Victoria.

The very accessibility of these elderly musicians to a graduate student and their pleasure at being recognized in however obscure a context underscore their typical position on the margins of mainstream American popular music. Similarly, the past and present economic difficulties that many of them share speak to their status as members of a working class, people who could rarely leave their day jobs behind and pursue music full-time. Both as workers and as cultural workers of the past, they deserve to be recognized, chronicled, and celebrated by Puerto Rican and non–Puerto Rican audiences, Spanish and English speakers alike.

Having, I hope, answered the question with which I opened this preface, I would like to thank the many people who have been influential in shaping this work. Jeremy Brecher has been, and continues to be, a mentor and colleague with whom I can discuss everything from politics and theory to the vagaries of interviewing, writing proposals, and designing public programs. José Luis Rodríguez and Alejandro López have been ongoing sources of inspiration, always reminding me what this is all for. Rina Benmayor, at the Centro de Estudios Puertorriqueños, has been supportive and helpful toward my work from the beginning. Others associated with the Centro who have helped immeasurably include Félix Cortés, Nelly V. Cruz, Juan Flores, Ana Juarbe, Nélida Pérez, Félix Rivera, Carlos Sanabria, Amílcar Tirado, and Blanca Vázquez. My dissertation adviser, David Montgomery, and the other members of my dissertation committee, Martin Bresnick and Micaela di Leonardo, gave me invaluable perspectives from their respective disciplines, history, music, and anthropology. Edgardo Díaz Díaz has given me new insights into Puerto Rican music, and with Donald Thompson I have shared many delightful hours of historical detective work. I would also like to thank Bernadette Moore of the Radio Corporation of America Archives, the staffs of the New York Municipal Archives, the Rodgers and Hammerstein Collection of the New York Public Library, the Schomburg Collection of the New York Public Library, the Library of Congress, the Historical Sound Recordings Collection at Yale University, the National Library of Canada, the Instituto de Cultura of Puerto Rico, the University of Puerto Rico, Río Piedras, and Peer International Corporation of New York and Puerto Rico. Others who contributed in many different ways to this research and writing process include Noel Allende, Luis Alvarez, Mike Amadeo, Angel Armada, Reid Badger, Gustavo Batista, David Brown, David Calderón, Héctor Campos Parsi, David Carp, Micaela Castillo and her family, Roberto Colón and Teresa Soto, Bill Cronon, Jill Cutler, Ovidio Dávila and Gladys Rosario, James Reese Europe, Jr., Ann Fabian, José Arturo Fernández, Jay Gitlin, Irving and Estelle Glasser, Paul Glasser, Penina and Myron Glazer, Jorge Javariz, Terry Lichtash, Ana López, Jesús López, René López, Pedro Malavet

Vega, Rafael Marcano, Morton Marks, Félix Matos, Henry Medina, Dolores Mercado, Juan Mora Bosch, Jesse Moskowitz, Louis Núñez, José Ortíz, Angel Quintero, Nina Quirindongo and La Casa Alonso, Norberto Rivas, José Angel Rodríguez, Max Salazar, César Salgado, Harry Sepúlveda, Roberta Singer, Alberto Soto, Richard Spottswood, Lisa Tiersten, Carlos Torre, Pedro Vélez, and Sarah Wilson.

Many thanks also to the Mellon Fellowship for the Humanities of the Woodrow Wilson Foundation for a dissertation-year fellowship and to the musicians I have interviewed for this book, who are mentioned throughout the work and listed in the bibliography. Unless otherwise noted, translations of their words and of other Spanish texts are my own. Transcriptions of song lyrics are also my own work. Finally, I would like to make special mention of those who helped and inspired me but, sadly, did not live to see the completion of this project: Sol Armada, Bobby Capó, Tito Henríquez, Francisco López Cruz, Rafael Portela, José Salinas, Efraín Vaz, and Ernesto Vigoreaux.

I am grateful to Peer International Corporation for permission to cite lyrics from the following. International copyright secured. All rights reserved.

By Pedro Flores: "Amor Perdido" © 1940; "El Ultimo Adiós" © 1941; "Sin Bandera" © 1975.

By Rafael Hernández: "El Chismoso," "Linda Quisqueya," "Menéalo Que Se Empelota," and "Pura Flama" © 1928; "Mi Guagua" and "Temporal, Temporal" © 1929; "Lamento Borincano" © 1932; "Perfume de Gardenias" © 1936; "Preciosa" © 1948; "Los Carreteros" © 1958; "El Buen Borincano" and "Cuchifritos" © 1961.

By Manuel Jiménez: "Arizona" © 1929; "Cuando las Mujeres Quieren a los Hombres" © 1930; "Cortaron a Elena" and "Qué Tabaco Malo" © 1959; "Santa María" © 1960; "Héroes de Borinquén" © 1974.

By Flor Morales Ramos: "Tintorera del Mar" © 1978.

I also thank Southern Music Publishing Co., Inc., for permission to cite lyrics from Manuel Jiménez, "Llegó de Roma (El Obispo)" © 1959.

Introduction

Buscando Ambiente

> People and their cultures perish in isolation, but they are
> born or reborn in contact with other men and women, with
> men and women of another culture, another creed, another
> race. If we do not recognize our humanity in others, we shall
> not recognize it in ourselves.
>
> *Carlos Fuentes*

On July 14, 1930, the *New York Times* reported that the country's rate
of unemployment was at least 20 percent and rising fast. On this day,
eight and a half months after the stock market crash, the newspaper also
showed that over the past year Prohibition had cost the U.S. government
$960 million in enforcement proceedings and loss of alcohol tax rev-
enues.

Just as Americans continued to drink during Prohibition, those who
could afford it continued to seek amusement during the Great Depression. Singer and bandleader Cab Calloway remembered that

> there were breadlines everywhere and near riots in New York. Everybody
> was angry with poor old Herbert Hoover. Everybody except people in the
> entertainment world, I guess. It's a funny thing, when things get really bad,
> when the bottom falls out of the economy, that's when people really need
> entertainment. . . . Jazz was swinging, the theaters on Broadway were clean-
> ing up, and in Harlem the nightclubs, speakeasies and jazz spots were packed
> every night.[1]

Calloway was in a good position to know. Newly installed in Harlem's Cotton Club, he was earning about fifty thousand dollars a year.
Variety reported that the club itself was the most profitable in New York

City, having netted a clear four hundred thousand dollars in the previous season.

That summer the entertainment emanating from New York City seemed boundless. Three Rudy Vallee orchestras were playing on each Cunard cruise ship, while the famous crooner himself had just acquired the first sponsored network radio show. Composer Cole Porter's "Love for Sale" had been banned from the airwaves for its overt references to prostitution, but many of his other songs were skyrocketing to popularity on Broadway. Vaudevillian Molly Picon was the headliner at the Palace theater. And with a flip of the dial, highbrow New Yorkers could hear some of the first live broadcasts of full-scale operas.

On July 14, 1930, still another musical event was taking place in a Manhattan recording studio. While this event would never be noticed by most of the U. S. population, it would prove momentous to speakers of Spanish in New York and Latin America. On that day a Puerto Rican group led by Manuel "Canario" Jiménez recorded Rafael Hernández's "Lamento Borincano." Canario, his two guitarists, and his *maracas* and *clave* players received about twelve dollars apiece for their efforts.

The modest fee notwithstanding, this song had a value that extended far beyond its monetary value. Just as Gorney and Harburg's "Brother, Can You Spare a Dime?" (1932) became a virtual theme song for the Depression, such was "Lamento Borincano" for Puerto Ricans and other Spanish speakers. More than any other song, this inexpensively made, apparently simple *bolero* would embody the essence of this era and the hard times it brought for many Latin Americans in both the United States and their homelands. Though it was composed and recorded in New York, "Lamento Borincano" also became a lasting, hugely popular anthem for Puerto Rico, an island with an ambiguous national status.

It is these hidden, quietly heroic, and often ironic cultural moments that I chronicle in this book. Amazingly, Puerto Rican musical production remains nearly as invisible to North American audiences today as it did in the 1930s. Just as Puerto Rico exists in the minds of North Americans, when they think of the island at all, as a kind of netherworld, not quite Latin America but not quite part of the United States, people in the English-speaking world have generally given little thought to the immense cultural wealth produced by Puerto Ricans. Indeed, they have had little opportunity, for while innumerable books and articles in English dissect social problems among Puerto Ricans, few describe their history or artistic expressions.[2] Puerto Ricans in general, and Puerto Rican migrants in particular, are found more often in the pages of crisis-oriented contemporary studies than in those of historical works. In fact, scholars casting backward for an explanation for the persistently low socioeconomic status of many Puerto Ricans have often blamed this problem on an ostensible cultural deficit within the group itself. Glazer and Moynihan's 1963 contention that the Puerto Rican heritage is "weak in folk arts, unsure in its cultural traditions, [and] without a powerful faith" still finds its adherents thirty years later.[3] Indeed, as problems multiply in North American inner cities, there has been a recent academic and popular revival of this blaming-the-victim approach.[4]

Ironically, works by ethnomusicologists and music critics on Latin popular music often reinforce this impression. They take Puerto Rican music out of its historical context, a context that properly includes an explanation of what happens to cultural expression within a colonial society. Unwittingly, such writers make Puerto Rican music the loser in an ahistorical Darwinian scheme that closely parallels social science condemnations of Puerto Ricans as a failed ethnic group. To them, Cuban music survived and flourished because it was the fittest. It is as if there were no political or cultural hierarchies between colonies and neo-colonies organized first by Spain, later by the United States. It is as if there were no shared history to explain the similar development of musical forms in different parts of Latin America, or the dominance of one set of sounds over another.

With both colonial and migration history unexamined, it has become a truism that popular Latin music in New York equals Cuban music, even though Puerto Ricans have for many years been among the field's most prolific performers and composers. Many popular and scholarly assessments suggest that Puerto Rican musicians have left their own ostensibly meager musical resources behind and "merely" adopted Cuban sounds. Puerto Rican musicians in New York City during the 1930s "imported" Cuban music and were "strong in the hybridizing wing." Their own music becomes more or less a footnote to the history of the *rumba* and to subsequently popular Cuban genres. A description of the collection of contemporary Latin sounds known as *salsa,* for example, asserts that "stylistically its backbone consists of Cuban dance music."[5]

When it comes to Puerto Rican sounds, then, I know of no in-depth histories of such popular music and its practitioners and audiences for any period. And yet the music and history of composers such as Rafael Hernández and groups such as Canario's are fascinating in their own right, as is the interwar period, when such artists wrote and played many songs of lasting beauty—within the context of the massive displacement and migration of their compatriots.

This book is intended to fill these narrative and conceptual gaps within the history and culture of the Puerto Rican migration experience. It is also meant to encourage the reader to reevaluate the structure of ethnic history in general and the place of ethnic cultural expression within it. For contemporary writings about Puerto Ricans and other ethnic North Americans, whether negative or positive, often reflect or rebel against the paradigms set up by earlier thinkers. Thus, they do not get outside of previous models to consider other possibilities.

Scholars such as Oscar Handlin, for example, writing before the 1960s, portrayed American ethnic communities as disorganized and unhealthy settlements reflecting the abrupt uprooting of Old World, rural peoples. Their problems, he felt, were solved within a few generations through assimilation and the dissolution of the ethnic enclave. In contrast, the subsequent work of historians such as Sánchez-Korrol, Yans-McLaughlin, Vecoli, Bodnar, and others has argued that these ethnic communities were highly organized environments in which family and community life reflected a coherent set of values, though not necessarily the stereotypical American ones of individualism and economic success through upward mobility.[6] Portraits in recent ethnic monographs show music taking place in intimate gatherings within a strictly ethnically based community setting. Their depictions of closely knit settlements utilizing cultural activities for both ethnic and economic sustenance constitute a reaction against their predecessors' work.

Such recent contributions have been crucial to a more three-dimensional portrait of ethnic life, especially for Puerto Ricans and other groups that have been ranked low on what Micaela di Leonardo calls "the ethnic report card system."[7] However, while such approaches bring us important new information and insights, they are also problematic. Just as Handlin praised the pastoral paradises the immigrants had ostensibly left behind, modern historians romantically recreate such utopias in urban areas in the United States. Contemporary monographs that apparently argue against Handlin frequently follow him in presuming that "healthy" ethnic communities preserve an unspoiled and uniform Old World folk culture, exist within bounded geographical territories, and have little interaction with members of other groups. Moreover, they suggest that consensus means stability and that disagreements, divisions, and change within a group of ethnic Americans indicate a community in crisis.

Evidence from both the Old World and the New World, however, suggests that such assumptions lead to serious distortions of the ethnic experience, with implications not only for the past but for contemporary societies as well. In recent years, for example, scholars have rejected simplistic rural-to-urban migration paradigms, acknowledging the variety of regional and class backgrounds of ethnic Americans. Historians such as Rudolph Vecoli tell us that Italians, for example, thought of themselves as Genoese or Calabrian back in the Old Country and only merged under one national umbrella in the United States. Such an observation would seem to be a promising beginning for a study of the subjectivity and plasticity of ethnic identity and its cultural components. Unfortunately, while ethnic historians have begun to recognize the fragmented and constantly changing nature of the ethnic experience in economic, political, and social terms, they frequently draw the same tired conclusions in the cultural realm. John Bodnar's *The Transplanted,* for example, an otherwise fine synthesis of much of the recent monographic work on immigrant communities, presents an unreflective interpretation of ethnic cultural life:

> Almost no dimension of the traditional life immigrants knew remained unaffected by the new order which confronted them. At the same time most newcomers did not hesitate to exploit or draw upon past belief and practice if it in some way would facilitate and render intelligible their new life and condition. . . . Consider their use of the rich repository of song, dance, and folktales which nearly all groups brought to the American city. . . . While these traditions had already begun to recede in the premigration lands in the face of modern explanations of an individual's plight which were tied to science, industry and technology . . . folk culture could serve to reinforce group identity in the face of meeting new groups, inform outsiders about immigrants and who they were, and even provide explanations of their lowly status which all newcomers could understand.[8]

Historians now acknowledge the multifaceted and ever-evolving economic, social, and political reasons for immigrant and migrant movements but persist in viewing music of the ethnics' homelands as an unmediated and uncontroversial folk sound shared by the entire community, faithfully reproduced in the United States. They do not try to find out whether the variety of regional, class, political, religious, and other backgrounds of ethnics from the same national entity might affect their perceptions of national identity or their construction and use of forms of cultural expression such as music. Historians are generally content to take both ethnicity and ethnic cultural expression as givens, as the by-products of a common national identity, the automatic offshoots of the economic and social spheres presumably underlying them. Uncritically adopting the nostalgia of their informants, for example, chroniclers of Latino music in New York City often evoke a mythically cohesive community that preserves and produces authentic music. Within such a framework, constant infusions of "genuine" music made by "real" ethnics in their own neighborhoods are ultimately diluted and commercialized by musicians catering to non-Latino audiences in the "Anglo" sections of the city. As in many other portraits of ethnic cultural life, Latinos within this framework had two choices: to remain "ethnic" (i.e., "Latin," in itself a dubious category) or to become "Americanized."[9]

Such unquestioned assumptions not only rewrite the ethnic experience within history but impose value-laden models on contemporary ethnic life as well. People in the United States, and indeed all over the world, are constantly being told that to avoid internal or external conflicts and to be economically and socially successful they must ally themselves with one racial or ethnic category. They must choose between assimilation and cultural preservation. As the Yugoslav writer Bogdan Denitch recently pointed out, however, the culprits in interethnic strife are not multiculturalism or overlapping identities themselves but strategies of "ethnic cleansing," which are "forcing the creation of new identities that 'are so much narrower, more parochial, and less flexible.'"[10] Moreover, it is apparent that economic difficulties often provoke conflicts between peoples who previously coexisted peacefully.

Anthropologists Fredrik Barth and Micaela di Leonardo, historian David Whisnant, ethnomusicologist Adelaida Reyes-Schramm, and sociologist Felix Padilla suggest, however, that rather than indicating the deterioration of a community and its cultural practices, the constant evolutions of ethnic identity and spheres such as music are normal historical processes. Within any living society ongoing intra- and interethnic negotiation and reshaping of cultural forms in dialogue with material conditions are the stuff of which national and ethnic identities are made and remade.[11]

Puerto Ricans on the island and the mainland did not adopt Cuban music wholesale to the detriment of their own traditions but incorporated it into an ever-evolving repertoire of available cultural materials. Indeed, I concur with Eric Hobsbawm and Terence Ranger's contention that tradition itself often amounts to a set of conventions from a variety of sources, agreed upon by a self-defined group of people, that are frequently redefined in moments of rapid social transformation.[12] In New York, where Puerto Ricans lived among a constellation of constantly changing ethnic groups within a protean social environment, this process accelerated and perhaps became more acutely meaningful. The diverse collection of Puerto Rican migrants who found themselves living in New York City, sometimes together and sometimes apart, did not unite behind a common ethnic identity represented by agreed-upon institutions and cultural symbols. Instead, they formed a range of organizations and debated over appropriate cultural programs and representative repertoires. They exchanged forms of entertainment and ideas about its purpose among themselves as well as with members of other ethnic groups. Puerto Rican communities in New York were neither ethnically inviolable nor disintegrating, and their cultural choices were far broader than an "ethnic" or an "American" identity.

Indeed, I attempt to demonstrate that musical subcultures can exist side by side or within a dominant culture with varying degrees of exchange and mutual influence. Examples of the complex dynamics inherent in such diffuse expression quickly emerge when one scrutinizes musical production. Mark Slobin and Richard Spottswood, for example, analyze the eclectic career of an early-twentieth-century Jewish musician, noting his not untypical "inter-ethnic popular culture contact" and "fluency in two parallel, related, yet complementary ethnic styles."[13] As Charles Keil concurs with his study of polkas among Polish and Mexican-Americans in Milwaukee, different ethnic groups can play and dance to very similar musical forms without even knowing it, while maintaining a socially antagonistic relationship to one another.[14] Indeed, all sorts of combinations are possible, depending upon the conditions in which cultural forms and social, political, and economic relations have developed. North Americans between the world wars were usually totally oblivious to the rich Spanish-language musical production going on right under their noses, unless it was danceable. Most Puerto Ricans, however, were conversant in the popular mainstream styles and artists of the period and even used them as a point of reference for their own. A 1930 ad in New York's major Spanish newspaper, La Prensa, for example, billed the popular Cuban singer Antonio Machín as "El Rudy Vallee cubano," that is, the Cuban Rudy Vallee.[15] Clearly, imbalanced power relations between groups and countries can have subtle cultural correlatives, though musical expression is not just reducible to this interpretation.

In fact, music is simultaneously a material and a symbolic phenome-

non. As Raymond Williams and William Roseberry suggest, cultural ob-
jects are embedded in a process of creation and reception such that "cultural creation is itself a form of material production, [so] that the
abstract distinction between material base and ideal superstructure dis-
solves in the face of a material social process through which both 'material' and 'ideal' are constantly created and recreated." [16] Songs such as
"Lamento Borincano" or, for that matter, "Love for Sale" are, concretely speaking, the mediated products of the entertainment industry.
Musicians are workers producing tangible products, and music itself often follows trade routes and is made up of concrete mixes that we can
trace. A musical analysis of "Lamento Borincano," for example, would
show the influences of Italian opera, Puerto Rican mountain music, and
Cuban popular sounds.

And yet music is not reducible to its commercial and genealogical
dimensions. By musicological standards, there was nothing particularly
Puerto Rican or folkloric about "Lamento Borincano." Nevertheless,
many Puerto Ricans immortalized it as a profound expression of national consciousness. Thus, a major aim of this work is to reexamine
the causal relationship between music and the social, political, and economic conditions intersecting with it. Though musical production is dependent upon the conditions of what I hesitatingly call this larger setting, it also possesses its own internal dynamics. The lives of musicians
are simultaneously based in economics and aesthetics, and their production is both symbolic and concrete. They span both sides of this traditional causal divide and thus provide a significant case study with which
we can reevaluate our preconceptions of what produces what. I take
pains to show the ways in which musical forms actually serve to articulate and even define social distinctions, a point nicely illustrated in Manuel Peña's study of music among Mexican-Americans in Texas. [17] At the
same time, I demonstrate the unpredictability of music, which can often
transcend social, economic, and political conditions and class, racial,
ethnic, and geographic barriers that its audiences cannot.

There are many ways in which Puerto Rican music, or indeed any
ethnic music, both relates to other spheres and yet creates its own. For
example, while tens of thousands of Puerto Ricans settled in New York
prior to World War II, this migration in no way equaled the one following the war. And yet it was precisely this period between the world wars
that produced the most fervently patriotic Puerto Rican music by the
most beloved Puerto Rican popular composers of this century.

There were ironies in this music's relationship to other ethnic sounds, which seemed mainstream by comparison. During economically desperate times, as we have seen, Cab Calloway was earning a thousand dollars a week. But Calloway's theory regarding the direct relationship between hard times and entertainment is foiled when one remembers that Canario and many other artists were probably earning thirty dollars or less in the same week that Calloway pocketed his thousand. In any given time, as well as over time, ethnic musical production is multilayered and subject to a range of influences. The songs created by Rafael Hernández, for example, were as embedded as those of Cole Porter in the record and publishing industries' organization of production and distribution, and yet they were marketed to vastly different audiences and yielded very disparate rewards to their composers.

The way Puerto Ricans made meaning of their music and musicians and how they decided what was an authentic or traditional expression varied between social groups as well as between individuals, always in a dialectic with the concrete conditions under which the music was produced. Music in Puerto Rico was subject to foreign and commercial influences as well as to differences in race, class, and regional development, and in New York it continued to be protean, shaped according to situation and evolving through time. Rather than serving as a unifying force in a dividing or dissolving American ethnic community, music itself was an ongoing source of diverse definitions for Puerto Rican ethnic identity and an arena of contention. Just as the music they created and were exposed to was complex and mediated, so were the responses to it of people with varying and ever-evolving ideas about their cultural identity and Puerto Rican or Latin music's relation to it. On the island blacks and whites, upper and lower classes, danced to the same mixes of Spanish, Cuban, Puerto Rican, European, and North American ballroom music—in separate clubs. Both there and in New York they argued about whether the *plena,* of black "lowlife" origins, was a fitting national music. Some celebrated their Latino identity and the wealth of musical forms it embraced, whereas others, as Puerto Ricans, members of the working or elite classes, blacks or whites, or some combination of the above, bemoaned the lack of a music representing their particular perceived condition.

Throughout the 1920s and 1930s there were disputes and disagreements among ethnic musicians, audiences, and industry personnel over what was authentic Puerto Rican music and what ought to be recorded and played at live events. In this work I try to demonstrate the often highly subjective nature of the ethnic cultural experience, an experience within which ethnic peoples individually mold their collective identities, drawing from a broad repertoire of cultural forms.[18] This experience draws upon the ongoing contact between the old country and the new, a phenomenon that historians often overlook. It is particularly vital, of course, in the case of Puerto Ricans, for political, economic, and geographical reasons.

Throughout this book, I present these arguments through individual portraits within a general consideration of the diversity of Puerto Rican music and the people who helped to bring it into concrete form: composers, performers, audiences, local merchants and club owners, record company executives, and that most elusive of all figures, the ethnic intermediary, who will be explored in his or her various guises throughout this work. In general, I try to capture the complex collaborative though not necessarily cooperative process involved in the creation and reception of musical expression. As Howard S. Becker and other sociologists of cultural production would put it, art is a social activity, and "whether we speak of the collective acts of a few people . . . or those of a much larger number . . . we always need to ask who is acting together to create what events."[19]

The narrative concerns I deal with in the following chapters are of course inseparable from the analytical ones, which are intentionally embedded in the very format of the work, with its thematic rather than chronological chapters and its treatment of issues of causality. For example, in my organization of the narrative I try to reorient the reader's sense of cause and effect, base and superstructure. Instead of providing background chapters on Puerto Rican and New York political, economic, and social history before going on to the music, which would imply that such information is the hidden layer underlying cultural activities, I let the introduction of the lives of musicians and other musical personnel, audiences, and the songs motivate the exploration of other issues. Thus, for example, the examination in chapter 1 of Puerto Rican music's multiple influences and the myriad experiences of musicians leads to a discussion of regional, multinational, and colonial capitalism issues. A look in chapter 2 at the difficult residential and vocational choices facing black Puerto Rican musicians reveals struggles over racial and ethnic identity among Puerto Rican and other Latino settlers in New York. Chapter 4 suggests that songs such as Hernández's "Lamento Borincano" were simultaneously the concrete production of a commercial recording industry, articulators of ethnic identity, and a form of sublimated political protest during a trying period.

In a deeper thematic way, I grapple throughout these chapters with the causal relations between the production and consumption of Puerto Rican music and the social, economic, and political conditions of a particular time and place. I show that Puerto Rican music, like any living cultural form, was always subject to a mix of influences on the island as well as in New York City. North American and Puerto Rican musicians, for example, have for a long time been aware of the existence of each others' music, and neither they nor their audiences have been as reluctant to accept its hybridization as ethnic histories generally lead us to believe. At the same time, many of the forces producing such new and diverse combinations of music, including economic pressures upon musicians and a North American near monopoly of the production of commercial entertainment, have been anything but benign or in the hands of Puerto Ricans. Throughout this book I demonstrate that Puerto Ricans worked within a music business they did not control. At the same time, musicians and audiences made choices that reflected their own intertwined economic and aesthetic motives and musical and social relationships. Puerto Rican composers and performers crafted their own words to these "foreign" musical genres and prided themselves on their ability to please a wide variety of dancers and listeners. Likewise, audiences were proud of their musical *compatriotas* who were successful in their careers. Rather than feeling a sense of anger and ethnic betrayal when Puerto Rican musicians began to play with the Catalan Xavier Cugat or the North American Paul Whiteman, their compatriots, who generally lived in the same neighborhoods and worked in the same daytime jobs, felt that they were bringing credit to the group as a whole, along with money and new sounds into the community. Canario's musicians did not despise him because he adopted the style and songs of others and was not as talented as they were. They were glad his hustling abilities brought them work.

Musical production had its own nuances in the more technical spheres. Influenced by economic downturns or international conditions that cut off supplies of materials and artists, record production was also tremendously affected by changes within the medium itself. Ethnic recording had its own particularities. During the Depression, for example, when other types of record sales plummeted, sales of Spanish-language and other discs stayed steady and even flourished. Never a source of dramatic sales for companies even in the best of times, ethnic records continued to do what they had always done: they provided a means for manufacturers to sell phonographs to homesick U.S. migrants and immigrants. The rise of radio, which drastically affected mainstream record sales from the mid-1920s, had little effect on those ethnic groups toward whom few programs were geared at that time.

The history of Puerto Rican music in New York City is thus a history of infinite crossovers and variations on a theme. It is a history that reflects the conditions surrounding it and yet escapes them. Puerto Ricans have defied scholars' longstanding categories by popularizing folk music and folklorizing popular music. To chart some of these fascinating variations and examine their significance is the purpose of this book.

CHAPTER ONE

"In Our House, Music Was Eaten for Breakfast"

One spring day in 1931 a delegation of some of Puerto Rico's most out-standing musicians went to Viejo San Juan to see the then governor of Puerto Rico, Theodore Roosevelt, Jr.[1] Empowered by a resolution in the Puerto Rican Senate, they desired to establish a conservatory of music on the island. With the blessings of Governor Roosevelt, the committee hoped to institutionalize classes in theory, piano, and string instruments. Their academy would also host a concert orchestra, a string quartet, a trio, and a choral group, all firmly within Western classical music traditions.

At 9:00 A.M. the delegation was cordially received by the governor at La Fortaleza, his official residence. As the musicians outlined their plan, Roosevelt smoked his pipe and waxed enthusiastic. "Oh yes," he said. "I think that support for your unrefined music *[la música brava]*, that is, the *tiple*, the *güiro*, the *cuatro* and all those native instruments, is commendable."

"But Governor," the musicians politely protested, "that's not what the law provides for or what we desire: we want to establish a music school where Puerto Ricans can develop their artistic talents, in the highest sense, and according to the standards established in foreign con-servatories. We have come seeking your approval of this law."

The repeated explanations were in vain. Throughout the meeting, Governor Roosevelt amiably insisted that the delegation should found an institution to promote "native" music. Although the conservatory project had been approved by both the Puerto Rican House of Represen-tatives and the Senate, Roosevelt ultimately vetoed the bill.[2]

Nevertheless, after more than three decades of U.S. political domination of Puerto Rico, Roosevelt was considered by many island residents to be a sympathetic governor. After all, the Rough Rider's son was one of the few of the North Americans appointed to the post who had bothered to learn Spanish or to take any interest in the island's culture. And as Roosevelt mentioned repeatedly to the delegation, he loved the *música jíbara*, country music developed over several centuries in the mountains of Puerto Rico. Indeed, the governor was an informal patron of this music himself, bringing rural *tríos* and *cuartetos* to perform before distinguished guests at La Fortaleza.

The cultural miscommunication between the North American governor and these illustrious Puerto Rican musicians was thus fraught with irony.[3] It had subtle long-term implications in addition to its immediate political consequences. It is ironic that this North American should have been defending indigenous genres and instruments, while a delegation of Puerto Rican cultural leaders was arguing for formal support of music within a European-based art tradition. This apparent contradiction underlines the complexity of the history of cultural development in a colonial context. Clearly, a case study of music within the Puerto Rican setting is not a simplistic morality play in which a hegemonic metropolitan power imposed its own music on a populace valiantly struggling to preserve its folkloric forms. And yet the starkness of the power relation is apparent enough. As governor of the island, Roosevelt and the North American political muscle he represented could override any decision made by the branches of the Puerto Rican legislature. The governor had the power to officially mandate his particular vision of musical preservation in Puerto Rico, with or without the consent of the island's inhabitants.

It was within such a constrained context that twentieth-century Puerto Rican music did (and did not) develop. There were many forms of extra-official musical activity on the island that went far beyond the two poles represented by European art music and *música jíbara*. Nevertheless, their evolution was inevitably affected by the political and economic circumstances of North American domination. Thus, Roosevelt successfully blocked the umpteenth Puerto Rican plan to establish the conservatory, while many other countries, including Cuba, had had one for a long time. At the same time, economic and political structures over which Puerto Ricans had little control allowed North American enterprises to set the parameters for most commercial music development on the island. It is perhaps no coincidence that the delegation that visited Roosevelt planned to raise funds for the conservatory through a tax on records, radio, and the new sound cinema, which they felt were responsible for the decline in local music and jobs for musicians. It is also no accident that such a plan would be vetoed, given that these media were dominated by North American companies.

It is through an unraveling of such interconnected political, economic, and cultural situations that we can begin to comprehend the lives of Puerto Rican musicians on the island. The contours of musical activity in Puerto Rico show why so many of these artists, like thousands of their nonmusical compatriots, opted for migration to New York as a strategy for survival. In turn, this migration would have cultural consequences for *boricuas* (Puerto Ricans) on both sides of the ocean.[4] In order to understand this migration and its effects, then, it is vital to explore the context out of which the musicians came, the settings within which they worked, the musical repertoires within which they composed and played, and the symbolic meanings of such music for both themselves and the other diverse residents of a colonial territory struggling to define itself as a nation.

"THERE'S NO THERE THERE"

> Amanece, amanece,
> ya se escucha de los jilgueros la alegre diana.
> Amanece, amanece,
> y el rocío se va secando sobre la grama.
>
> Y las flores van despertando
> y por la sierra los carreteros se oyen cantando . . .
>
> ——————
>
> Day breaks, day breaks,
> from the linnets is heard the happy wakeup call.
> Day breaks, day breaks,
> And the dew is drying upon the grass.
>
> And the flowers are waking
> And in the mountains the cartdrivers are heard singing . . .

If one were to listen uncritically to the lyrics of the beautiful songs penned by homesick migrants, the Puerto Rico they had left behind was a pastoral paradise of singing small farmers. In its rhythms and harmonies, "Los Carreteros" recalls an era when cartdrivers sang along with the tempo of the wheels of their oxcarts in order to break the monotony of long trips.[5] But "Los Carreteros" is a song about a past experience,

written by Rafael Hernández in New York and recorded by Canario y
Su Grupo in that same city in 1931. In fact, dozens of songs written and
recorded in New York during the Great Depression were imbued with
longing for a bucolic Borinquén, or Puerto Rico. These tunes were as
much a staple of the Puerto Rican migrant repertoire as were the nostalgic songs of their European and Asian immigrant counterparts.

This musical retrospection, however, filtered out some of the more
prosaic realities of the migration.[6] Even when the members of the migrant group were not persecuted for their religion, politics, or skin color,
conditions of profound suffering and hardship impelled people to leave
their rural homes. For European, Asian, and Latin American small farmers the nineteenth century was a time when many lost their land or their
ability to make a living from it. In the short term, they were victims
of taxes, title laws, and credit policies that favored larger landowners,
merchants, and manufacturers. In the longer term, they were casualties
of global trends toward capitalist production, characterized both by the
rise of the factory and by large-scale export-oriented agriculture.

As a result of these trends, the pastoral paradise was generally a more
distant memory than many migrants' songs might lead the listener to
believe. Small farmers displaced from their lands went to work on large
plantations or in increasingly urban areas. As historians of the immigrant experience have recently demonstrated, those who crossed the Atlantic or the Pacific to work in the United States generally did so as a
last resort, the final step in a series of migrations.[7] In a process that
might take one generation or several, many migrants sojourned in the
urban areas of their regions or countries before embarking on boats that
would take them far away from their homelands.

Nevertheless, historical studies of migration that turn a critical eye
toward these social, economic, and political processes are not always
attuned to the cultural changes that accompanied them.[8] By focusing on
music produced by humble people, they imply a sort of unspoiled cultural democracy of unmediated folk forms, "corrupted" in the twentieth
century by both migration and a monolithic music industry. In hindsight, it is all too easy for scholars to take the attitude of Governor Roosevelt and insist that the future migrants were all simple peasants listening to rustic, homegrown musical forms. But the reality was of course
much more complicated.

Puerto Rico *was* the home of some distinctive genres. These were
linked to relatively discrete economies and geographical regions and to
the ethnic origins of the people in those areas.[9] But Puerto Rico was no

exception to the general trends of displacement and serial migration of agricultural workers. Indeed these trends were exacerbated and accelerated by colonial political and economic development first under Spain and then, after 1898, under the United States. Throughout the nineteenth and early twentieth centuries, enormous changes in the island's agricultural economy provoked massive alterations in its population distribution and occupational structure. In turn, these dislocations would profoundly affect the musicians and the context and quality of their music making, even before many of them, or their children, migrated to the United States.

Thus, the colonial Puerto Rico of several centuries was not just the land of the mountain-bred *seis* and *aguinaldo* or of the *bomba* and *plena* of the coastal plains. Music of many genres and origins both reflected and articulated the ongoing social, economic, political, and cultural changes on the island. As workers journeyed from one region or economic situation to another, they took their music with them and were exposed to new forms. And it was not just the content of the music that changed: the context, the very structural conditions of entertainment, changed as well. Migrants might still produce their own songs, for example, but as they moved to ever more urban settings they encountered the world of impresarios and professional musicians.

While Puerto Rican music, like music in any living culture, was constantly changing, during the nineteenth century a variety of musical entertainment became particularly widespread throughout the island. In small towns as well as cities, municipal bands played eclectic, semiclassical musical programs before diverse audiences. European opera companies and instrumentalists appeared in provincial theaters and sometimes remained to teach and entertain people from a spectrum of social groups. Both *mulato* artisans and "purebred" Spaniards danced waltzes and one-steps in their respective clubs. And long before radio came to Puerto Rico, island dwellers heard bands play advertisements set to music. Decades before the phonograph was even invented, touring circus and theatrical companies acquainted Puerto Rican audiences with the latest Cuban, Spanish, and Italian music.

It is true that the twentieth century, in which the development of the mass media coincided with U.S. sovereignty over Puerto Rico, promoted more rapid and more pervasive diffusion of popular music, particularly that from Cuba, Mexico, Argentina, and the United States. And as more and more Puerto Ricans migrated to the "Iron Babel," New York City, those island-mainland ties became all the more direct and had an enormous influence on Puerto Rican popular culture. But there were long-standing precedents for musical eclecticism, professionalization, and commercialization in Puerto Rico. The homeland's music was anything but a timeless "folk" repertoire. The music that migrants carried with them as a treasured part of their heritage was constantly changing in dialogue with social, economic, and political forces. In Puerto Rico music embodied contours of class, region, and race and yet had its own unique dimensions, which transcended these categories.

CROPS AND *CANCIONES*

During five centuries of Spanish rule, Puerto Rico's distinctive geographical zones became sites of relatively self-contained agricultural economies. The configurations of this agriculture, its scale of production, and the relationship of producers to the process were variable, changing, and far too complicated to explain in detail here.[10] A few broad strokes, however, will help to fill in the economic context of musical development.

By the nineteenth century Puerto Rico had been transformed from a largely subsistence economy to a producer of cash crops. While sugar and tobacco were the main products of the coastal plains of Puerto Rico's perimeter, the mountainous areas in the center of the island were primarily dedicated to coffee cultivation. These products were exchanged for manufactured goods from a number of industrialized nations, including the United States. Consequently, coastal ports that concentrated on importing and exporting these goods developed in tandem with this large-scale agriculture. These agricultural niches and trade routes had their counterparts in local musical production, cultural imports, and their distribution throughout the island.

The coastal regions, dominated by large sugar plantations and *centrales* for grinding the cane, depended upon the labor of thousands of African slaves. While these slaves never constituted more than 15 percent of the population, and less than half of that by abolition in 1873, their proportions in sugar-producing areas were much greater.[11] It is not surprising that these regions would nurture distinctive musical forms with recognizably African components.

Nevertheless, the complex of music and dances known as the *bomba* were not simple transplantations but a synthesis of cultural forms. The captives brought over the course of centuries to work in Puerto Rico came from a spectrum of western, central, and northern African societies. Some of them had been transplanted from the plantations of nearby islands, particularly those of French and English colonization. Working together cultivating sugar, these slaves and, after 1873, *jornaleros* (day laborers) managed to weave together threads of their distinctive musical forms into the multicultural *bomba*.

The *bomba* was characterized by its namesake, a drum that varied in size and construction according to available materials. Supplemented by other percussion instruments, the *bomba* was generally polyrhythmic and featured a complex interaction between drummers and dancers. It was characterized by an African-derived call-and-response vocal style, in which a lead singer was answered by a chorus singing in unison. Lyrics were generally secondary to the rhythms and vocal textures produced by singing words or syllables.[12]

Then as now, musicians with few economic resources made creative use of whatever was on hand to construct their instruments. *Bomba* drums were made of empty rum, nail, or lard barrels. A goatskin head was stretched over the cask, and a system of ropes or screws was added for tuning the drum by changing the tension on the head. Other percussion instruments of varying sizes and sounds were made of hollowed-out tree trunks or other available cylindrical materials.[13]

These instruments were constantly evolving not just as a result of cultural synthesis and the raw materials available in a changing society but also because of the fears of colonial authorities. Local Spanish officials nervously watched slave celebrations involving drum-based music, for they were convinced that they were occasions for planning and carrying out revolts. Throughout the eighteenth and nineteenth centuries, on the heels of such revolts, they outlawed these "talking drums," forcing African descendants to either hide their festivities or invent new instruments and musical forms to circumvent the laws.[14]

The *bomba* was not the only instrument or dance heard and utilized by these Afro–Puerto Ricans.[15] Slaves and their descendants reinvented African instruments, and the new instruments were gradually incorporated into a range of Puerto Rican musical groups. One example was the *marímbula*, a descendant of the African *mbira*, or thumb piano. The *marímbula* was typically a large wooden box with a sound hole cut in the front. Tongues made from metal rum cask hoops or clock or phonograph springs were placed halfway over the hole. The instrument served as a homemade bass, and like the drums, it was found, with variations, in all the areas of the African diaspora.[16]

Afro–Puerto Ricans also became adept at performing the music of their oppressors. As in other parts of the Caribbean, a large number of these slaves and freed blacks became artisans, exercising skills considered demeaning for whites to perform. One of these was music making. From the times before emancipation dated a tradition that would last far beyond, namely, the tradition of the black or *mulato* artisan/musician performing the songs and dances of his masters on European instruments. The slave owners themselves brought a variety of musical traditions from their culturally distinct regions of Spain, Italy, Germany, France, or Ireland. Among their ranks were also planters from other parts of Latin America or the Caribbean who were fleeing revolutions and slave rebellions in their homelands. Thus, Afro–Puerto Rican musicians became adept at a range of European and Creole genres, including *contradanza, pasodoble, rigodón, lancero, minué* (minuet), *vals* (waltz), polka, and *chotis* (schottische). They incorporated these dances into their own repertoires, just as they infused European forms with elements of their own traditions.

In the island's interior small independent farmers, *jornaleros,* and *agregados* (sharecroppers) cultivated their own musical forms along with coffee, fruit, tobacco, and subsistence crops. While the *jíbaro* culture developed in the mountains has been celebrated for its independence, it always had a relationship, however tenuous, to other sectors of Puerto Rican society. Within a counterculture developed in opposition to the Spanish colonial government in San Juan and its extensions throughout the island, surviving members of preconquest indigenous societies, escaped slaves, and Spanish settlers fleeing plantation work to strike out on their own mingled in the mountains and established their own farms.[17] Not surprisingly, while the *jíbaro* culture that developed was based primarily on that of the Spanish settlers, it also incorporated elements of other local groups to create a rich and varied musical repertoire. Instruments commonly found in *jíbaro* music, such as the *maracas* (gourd rattles) and the *güiro* (a gourd scraper), had antecedents in both African and local indigenous cultures. These combined with the Spanish guitar and the *cuatro* (a variation on the guitar that originally had four strings but later had five double strings) to create a music that reflected both its diverse ethnic roots and the socioeconomic conditions of the mountainous regions.

The most popular song-and-dance form among the *jíbaros* was the *seis,* a dance incorporating six couples in its configuration. The genre preserved melodies and verse forms found in Spain during the time of the conquest. Like much Latin American music, it was permeated by melodic and harmonic elements of southern Spain, which themselves bore a strong Moorish influence. The *seis* and the related *aguinaldo* made frequent use of harmonic minor scales and the progression of descending chords known as the "Andalusian cadence" (e.g., A minor–G major–F major–E major).[18] One of the most popular strophic forms within the *seis* was the *décima*, a ten-line verse, also of Spanish provenance, with a precise meter and rhyme scheme. At the same time, these forms incorporated rhythmic elements developed in all the areas of Afro-Hispanic encounter. Most notable among these was what came to be known as the *habanera*, a syncopated rhythm scheme upon which many genres of popular music were based. Subtle disjunctures between the singer's voice and the instrumental accompaniment also created a poly-rhythmic effect characteristic of many African-derived musics.

Within the *seis con décima* Puerto Rican peasants, many of whom could not read, preserved their history, transmitted the contents of the Bible down through the generations, and commented on life around them. Over the centuries, variations of the *seis* developed that were closely identified with particular functions, regions, and composers.[19]

While the mountain culture has often been portrayed as in itself time-less and enduring, it was also subject to great changes throughout the century. The mountains continued to receive escapees from large-scale, primarily coastal agriculture until well into the nineteenth century. At the same time, these interior areas were in a state of constant flux be-cause of encroachments by merchants and large landowners looking for more territory and additional laborers. Aided by a series of property and antivagrancy laws passed by the colonial government in the nineteenth century, *hacendados* (estate owners) increasingly consolidated their landholdings at the expense of smaller farmers and forced displaced peasants to come to work for them. Inevitably, this changed patterns of leisure and music making as well as work, as the local and insular governments tried to limit fiesta days and compel peasants to work within a stricter routine.[20]

As the nineteenth century wore on, slaves and freed blacks increas-ingly worked side by side with the peasants of primarily Spanish descent who were displaced from their own small mountain and coastal land-holdings. In the coastal areas new forms of music developed at the inter-sections of the old. toward the end of the century, for example, the *plena* developed among a lower-class, primarily *mulato* population on Puerto Rico's southern coast, later spreading throughout the island with the workers from these communities. The *plena* combined the narrative

verse structure found in Spanish music with the call and response, suc-
cinct topicality, and percussive emphasis of African music. *Plenas* were
often satirical and reflected the difficulties of life among the poor in
urban and sugar-producing areas.

URBAN SOUNDS

While the majority of Puerto Rico's population lived in rural areas until
well into the twentieth century, an increasing number of artisans, laborers, professionals, and merchants lived in the large port cities and small
towns of the island. During the Spanish colonial period, urban and
small town musical life had a fair amount in common. Each town or
city had a central church, which usually sponsored organists, musical
ensembles, and compositional activity. In a colonial society where
church and state were intertwined, so were sacred and secular occasions,
events in the metropolis and in its colonial outposts. Thus, Spanish royal
marriages and births, local patron saint days or more generalized Catholic holidays, all became occasions for frequent concerts and dances as
well as religious processions and masses.

There were military as well as church underpinnings to much music
in Puerto Rico. Following the early-nineteenth-century wars for independence by its colonies in South and Central America, the Spanish government carefully reinforced its hold on its remaining Caribbean colonies. The additional regiments sent to keep the peace in Puerto Rico,
as in Cuba, became important incubators of musical activities. Army-
sponsored bands utilized the talents of local musicians, giving Puerto
Ricans of different classes, races, and regions both musical training and
performance opportunities. Army bands played not just for military but
also for civilian functions, including open-air concerts and dances. Indeed, their instrumentation and rhythms had an enormous influence on
contemporary and ensuing ballroom genres. These ensembles were also
the precursors of publicly supported municipal, school, police, and
firefighters' bands, which became ubiquitous throughout the island during the late nineteenth and early twentieth centuries.

During the nineteenth century, more secular and even commercialized
forms of musical entertainment developed in the large and small towns
throughout the island. By the 1830s, Puerto Rican port cities, coffee,
sugar, and tobacco processing centers, had founded their own theaters,
artistic circles, and private musical academies. In the very biggest cities
there were also large annual fairs, which were important showcases for

island music, featuring band and orchestra concerts and contests and dances.[21] Stage shows from outside Puerto Rico followed established trade routes to become another important island import. Spanish and Italian opera companies came to Ponce and San Germán, on the southern coast, and toured the island, touching upon Mayagüez and Aguadilla in the west, San Juan in the north, and Humacao on the east coast. From Cuba came the *bufos cubanos,* a type of light theater, which introduced new genres and songs into all sectors of Puerto Rican society.[22] The *bufos* and other itinerant Cuban entertainment ensembles introduced into Puerto Rico a number of genres that became staples of both the island and the New York repertoire.[23]

One such genre, the *guaracha,* was closely related to another important Cuban dance music, the *son.* Both were duple-meter forms that emphasized percussion instruments such as the *marímbula,* the *tres* (a modified guitar with three double or triple strings) or guitar, the *clave* or *palitos* (sticks), and the *güiro.* Both featured a bass line where the first beat was displaced or tied to the second, and the accent tended to fall toward the end of the measure, creating a syncopated effect. But whereas the *guaracha* kept strictly to a four-line verse structure and tended to be very fast, the slower *son* usually featured almost infinitely expandable *montuno* sections, in which a lead singer improvised, answered by a chorus repeating a refrain.

The *rumba,* a complex of African-derived sounds, also used numerous percussion instruments, among which *claves* and differently pitched *conga* drums were prominent. Like many Latino musical forms of African ancestry, it consisted of a series of short instrumental and sung sections, often including a *montuno.* It usually featured a variation of the rhythm known as the *clave.*

Like the *rumba, guaracha,* and *son,* the *bolero* also had a duple meter. A slower ballad form, its basic rhythm did not have the displaced accents of the other genres. Its consistent bass pattern of a half note followed by two quarter notes, however, was often varied and complicated by additional percussion instruments. *Boleros* tended to have long, flowing melody lines rather than the short phrases of the other genres. Performers within the genre generally stressed virtuoso singing and guitar playing over prominent percussion or improvisation.

Such genres were by no means impermeable, but lent themselves to both mixing and outside influences. The compatible meters and the successive, almost self-contained thematic sections in many Latin American genres often led to combinations of the forms within one song. More-

over, within their strong, identifiable rhythm schemes, Puerto Rican artists were able to incorporate different instruments and song phrases
from classical, foreign, or indigenous sources, creating their own significant musical collages. In turn, these genres had specific social connotations that long outlasted their original performance contexts.

The *bufos* themselves, for example, were burlesques that bore more
than a passing resemblance to North American minstrel shows. Like
their counterparts in el Norte, they incorporated African-descended
forms into their repertoires. Making liberal use of blackface, they carica-
tured the sources of this music. Both the *guaracha* and the *rumba,* genres
strongly associated with the *bufos,* used lighthearted lyrics that depicted
people (often *negritos* or *mulatos*) in humorous or ridiculous situations.
By contrast, the slower *bolero* usually had poetic words describing the
anguish of love for the *patria* (homeland) or for an unattainable woman.
The social taxonomy of these forms was established by the late nineteenth century and lasted well into the twentieth: the *guaracha* and the
rumba were associated with the picaresque, the overtly sexual, the *negro;* the *bolero,* with the lyrical, the sanctified, the white.[24] Indeed, popular Puerto Rican singers in New York City were often typecast as *guar-
acheros* (*guaracha* singers) or *boleristas* (*bolero* singers) and sometimes
had difficulty breaking out of these stereotyped roles.[25]

In its musicians, venues, and genres, music in nineteenth-century
Puerto Rican towns and cities articulated and transcended issues of
class, race, gender, and national identity in complicated and ever-
changing ways. As more sectors of Puerto Rican society came to and
mingled in its cities, cultural forms articulated class and racial boundaries, only to violate or transform them. The genesis and creation of the
danza, a popular genre of dance music in the late nineteenth century,
reflected the complexities of race, class, and nationality in Puerto Rican
society. The form itself was the product of multiple migrations, with
roots in the English "country dance," the *contradanza* of Spain and
Cuba, and the *contredanses* brought to Puerto Rico by French planters
fleeing the Haitian revolution.

A stately dance of promenading couples moving to the sounds of European instruments, the *danza* is usually regarded as a wholly European-
based music of the upper classes. But its context of creation and performance reveals something else. Since music making was not a respectable
occupation for the primarily white elite, it continued even after abolition
to be the province of *mulato* artisans. In addition to their primary skilled

trades, these artisans played in and led municipal bands and often gave music lessons as well. Craftspeople made shoes or cabinets by day and music by night, for their peers or for the upper classes. Policemen, fire-fighters, and cigar makers composed the *danzas* to which the upper classes moved. And musically, they created a new synthesis that reflected African and *jíbaro* as well as European elements. Thus the *danza* was both "an authentically popular musical expression" and one that bore "the mark of the *hacendados'* hegemony."[26] The *danza,* like its Cuban cousin, the *danzón,* was a multisectioned music that made use of the lilting *habanera* rhythm. Like some of the forms described above, it was expandable and often made liberal use of "quotes" from other musical pieces. Typically, a *paseo,* or introduction, was followed by a melodic section known as a *merengue.* A contrasting melodic section usually fol-lowed, and the piece closed with the original *merengue.* The orchestras playing the *danza* usually bore a strong martial influence, consisting of brass instruments sometimes overlaid with piano, flutes, violins, and *güiro.*

Dances and other popular entertainments were occasions at which class and color differences were manifest. A writer observing the festivi-ties in honor of Ponce's patron saint in 1875 noted that the elite danced in the main hall of the Teatro La Perla, the artisans in a room on the second floor, and the lower classes, in the city's public market.[27] During the latter half of the nineteenth century the residents of Puerto Rico's cities formed their own *casinos españoles,* social clubs where only elites of proven Spanish birth or descent could come to dance. Soon a multitiered set of casinos developed in the towns throughout the island. "Second-class" casinos were formed and frequented by the typically *mu-lato* artisans, and when money permitted, common laborers and the very dark-skinned might even form "third-class" clubs.

Despite this strict geographical and social segregation, however, the *danza* and other forms of popular music pervaded all sectors of society. Just as black and *mulato* artisans performed for the upper as well as the lower classes, they tended to play the same mixture of European and Caribbean forms for all sectors. In a tropical climate where much of life was lived in public, music wafted across social boundaries in less formal ways as well. The *señorita* of the urban monied classes, taking her de rigueur piano lessons, had only to pause at her instrument and pay at-tention to the streets outside, where a sonic democracy reigned. When they were not banned, the "African" drums of the *bomba* were audible

for miles. By day the young woman could hear the cries and songs of the
street vendors, by night the string trios that brought *serenatas* (romantic
serenades) to her windows and those of her neighbors.[28]

During the nineteenth century, as before and after, eclecticism in the
music itself was the rule. Variety was promoted by the struggle of musicians to find gainful employment, as well as the lack of clear boundaries
between sacred and secular, classical and popular music. Small ensembles sometimes played religious music for church ceremonies, for example, and immediately after assembled outside to perform operatic
overtures and classical symphonies for secular entertainment.[29] The lyric
and comic theater companies that came to the island from Spain, Italy,
and Cuba provided sporadic jobs for local orchestral musicians. They
also brought new genres of music, which performers in turn would bring
to the dance bands that were fixtures of the various class, racial, and
social groups on the island. This "infiltration" was, however, complex,
syncretic, multifaceted, and ever-changing. Puerto Rico, a Caribbean
transit stop between Spain and the colonies of the Central and South
American mainlands, received not only new song genres and dances
from Spain but those from other parts of Latin America on the way back
to the Old World.[30]

Not only was this foreign influence mutual but it extended beyond
the strictly urban realm, illustrating the mobility and permeability of
music among island groups of vastly different social and economic backgrounds. Occasionally, for example, even *jíbaros* would go to the nearest
towns to attend dances and other musical functions, and they would
pick up the newest styles. It is likely that in this way the *vals*, the ma-
zurka, and other European dances penetrated much of the Puerto Rican
countryside and were absorbed, with some modifications, into the *jíbaro*
repertoire.[31] Likewise, the *seis* became a favored form among urban
composers and was often used as the *despedida*, or final piece, at *casino* dances.

Music also played a vital role in shoring up the nationalist impulses
sporadically given form within the nineteenth century and continuing
with the change of sovereignty in 1898. As *hacendados* and merchants
struggled for greater control of the island's political and economic development, they became increasingly concerned with the components of
their national identity. Music was an important part of the cultural arse-
nal that made these rebels feel they had the right to claim an identity
that was not just not-Spanish by some accident of geography, but af-
firmatively Puerto Rican.

Although there were certainly a variety of distinct musical forms developing throughout the centuries in colonial Puerto Rico, the upper-class rebels singled out the refined-sounding *danza* as the most important national music. During the era of the 1868 Grito de Lares, the most famous revolution attempt of the nineteenth century, composers began to write words to the originally instrumental *danzas*. Just a few months before the abortive rebellion, a *danza* known as "La Borinqueña" encapsulated growing revolutionary and nationalistic sentiments.[32]

Even during times of apparent political quiescence, music remained a means for Puerto Ricans to maintain a sense of national identity. When the mayor of Ponce outlawed the playing of "La Borinqueña" in 1892, a huge public outcry followed.[33] After the American invasion, Puerto Rican intellectuals enshrined the *danza* and decided that *jíbaro* music constituted a genuine national expression. Lacking political power, island thinkers and cultural leaders drew cultural boundaries by acting defensively against the onslaught of music from the United States and Cuba. Ignoring the *bomba* and the *plena,* they used music to define Puerto Rican culture as white and Spanish-derived. In the meantime, working-class musicians continued to play a constellation of national and international sounds.

PUERTO RICAN MUSIC IN A NEW CENTURY

The musicians who migrated to New York City in the years between the world wars were born in a transitional era. They were the inheritors of older traditions and practices and the beneficiaries of some new ones. During their youth, these musicians might perform with nineteenth-century-style public bands one day and make records in primitive studios the next. Those who played in cinema orchestras accompanied the new silent films with both *danzas* written on the island in the 1860s and the new fox-trots coming from the United States.

Puerto Rican musicians floated on the same historical tides that carried many of their compatriots to other parts of the island and, finally, to New York City. Usually members of the laboring classes, they were affected by the extreme social, economic, and political changes taking place within a relatively short time in Puerto Rico. Musicians were also at the mercy of a fickle and poorly paid occupation. Their professional prospects reflected both the larger changes taking place on their island and the peculiar dynamics of their trade. For numerous musical and extramusical reasons, these artists were confronted by a range of constantly changing homegrown and commercially mediated musical forms. And it was with the rise and demise of old and new musical forms and venues that their own fortunes were shaped.

Wherever budding musicians lived and roamed, they kept their ears open and took advantage of local opportunities for musical development. The early experiences of the great variety of musicians who would migrate to the United States reveal the importance of region, class, race, and, generally by omission, gender on their artistic formation. By looking at musical and extramusical changes in early-twentieth-century Puerto Rico, interlaced with musicians' personal testimony, we can begin to understand their artistic evolutions and migrations in both an individual and a collective sense.

The U.S. invasion of Puerto Rico brought enormous economic changes to all regions of the island. Within a few years North American investors, aided by tariff protection, had virtually taken over the island's sugar production and made it the predominant local industry. Large U.S. tobacco concerns also began to control the cultivating and processing of this valuable leaf. Coffee farming, which received no government protection and little outside investment, was experiencing a sharp decline. Those who grew up in the small coffee towns in the interior, therefore, witnessed and participated in a population exodus to the sugar- and tobacco-processing areas. Those who lived in large towns and cities saw their communities grow, their populations transform. Inevitably, as in the case of the *plena,* this would mean the decline of some older musical forms and the creation of new fusions.

Variations in life situations, the "infiltration" of non-native types of music, and the influence of mechanically reproduced cultural forms all assured that these musicians, as well as their audiences, were anything but peasants coming down from the hills, with folk traditions intact, to face urban life and popular culture for the first time in the mainland setting. For Puerto Rican musicians and audiences, as undoubtedly for most or all ethnic groups, musical awareness and activity took the form of an ever-evolving collage in which distinctions between folk, fine, and art music were often blurry or unimportant. For the musicians, this eclecticism continued to have an economic urgency. Only the most versatile of performers could even begin to think about earning a living within this difficult profession. Thus, many musicians got their start in mass media and even "high-culture" milieux. Performers who in New

York would become purveyors of "popular" or "folkloric" music began performing in Puerto Rico in cinema orchestras, dance ensembles, on the radio and occasionally on records, if not as classically trained musicians in government-sponsored bands.

But Puerto Rican areas of settlement and the individuals within them did not all experience these changes at the same pace or in exactly the same way. The diverse backgrounds of these budding musicians, combined with parental and larger social attitudes toward their musicianship, led them to have quite different experiences and opportunities in their early musical careers. Guitarist and composer Francisco "Paquito" López Cruz (1907–88), for example, grew up in Naranjito. A small mountain town where people raised coffee and tobacco along with livestock, fruits, and vegetables, in López Cruz's eyes it was a paradise of *música típica:* "I want to tell you that I've been a musician from childhood because I was born in a town with a lot of music. *Jíbaro* music, folkloric music. And from childhood, I had the luck to listen to so much *jíbaro* music, from the country people of my town. And the town itself was almost the country, it didn't have more than two little streets."

The people of the cities considered those from *la isla,* or the interior, mountainous regions, to be culturally as well as socially and economically backward. Indeed, as the 1931 encounter between Governor Roosevelt and the delegation of musicians indicates, cultured urbanites often had ambivalent or negative feelings toward the music López Cruz praised. And yet despite this class- and region-based stereotyping, in many rural areas that was not the only music found. The recollections of country musicians indicate both the idiosyncrasies of individual life experiences and subtle variations in the cultural formation of even these little towns.[34] Differences in roadbuilding and transportation, trade routes, and patterns of labor migration, for example, created myriad variations in musical experience, which we can only begin to suggest.

Singer and guitarist Pepito Arvelo (b. 1917), the son of a small farmer and vendor, grew up in Lares. His town in western Puerto Rico was famous for both its coffee production and its abortive independence attempt in 1868. For years, coffee farmers in Lares had shipped their crops through the port in Aguadilla. As was true in many areas, the *jíbaros* routinely came down from their mountain settlements not only for trade but to participate in seasonal festivities, such as the annual celebration held in honor of San Carlos, Aguadilla's patron saint. Through such conduits, peasants learned the latest dance and musical styles, and they took them back to their small settlements. Arvelo remembers the instruments traditionally associated with the *jíbaro* music, for example, but some genres played were Spanish-, European-, and Cuban-derived:

> In that countryside *[esos campos]*, what they made were little house parties. The *cuatro*, the guitar, the *güiro* were used. *Pasodobles, valses,* and *boleros* were played. Simple music—they almost didn't know how to play. No one sang, everything was instrumental. And violin—very rare *[muy difícil]*. Only in the towns could you hear it.
>
> I didn't hear much *jíbaro* music. *Jíbaro* music belongs to towns like Vega Alta.[35]

In the impoverished Lares of Arvelo's childhood, musicians were exposed to a variety of musical forms but were constrained by lack of instruments and teachers. But they were by no means ignorant of the musical changes going on around them. Revealingly, Arvelo comments on the lack of popular and commercial musical resources but suggests that they were not unknown. By the time he was ten, in 1927, the only phonograph he had seen was a windup Edison on the back of a truck that took merchandise to the town's central marketplace. With no electricity, radios were scarce well after the medium arrived on the island, in 1922. Expensive instruments such as pianos or modern ones such as saxophones were rare.

Both the region and the economic status of musicians' families helped determine whether instruments and mechanically transmitted music were available to them. Violinist, saxophonist, and composer Francisco "Paquito" López Vidal (b. 1908) grew up in Cayey. Although the town was located in the island's interior, almost due south of San Juan, it had been a base for Spanish troops for many years, as well as a center for growing and processing tobacco since the nineteenth century. By 1915 it boasted theaters, cinemas, city bands, many official fiestas involving music, and electricity. López Vidal's recollections come from this ambiance, as well as a family background in which his father was a professional, a construction engineer. López Vidal remembers: "In the houses of Cayey it was common to have a piano. The people in the house played piano, Puerto Rican *danzas* above all. In many places there were little orchestras as well. Mostly bad ones, because the good orchestras were in San Juan. This was a little interior town."[36]

When parents approved of and even participated in music themselves, these conditions were propitious for producing whole families of fine musicians. This was especially true in the island's more multicultural coastal cities. Manuel Peña, born in the first years of the twentieth century, grew up in the eastern Puerto Rico town of Humacao, a port and commercial center with a well-developed theatrical and musical scene. Peña was virtually born into musicianship: "My father [Juan Peña Reyes] was the director of the municipal band of Humacao, a band of forty musicians. . . . My father was who taught us. The whole family are musicians. Trumpet was my instrument. My preparation was in serious music, classical music." [37]

An even bigger port town in Puerto Rico's northwestern corner, Aguadilla, produced an impressive collection of outstanding musicians, not a few of whom made their mark in New York City. A sizable population that included African slaves and free blacks, Spanish merchants, Haitian and Latin American landowners fleeing revolutions, and infusions of French, Irish, German, Dutch, and Italian settlers made the city extremely cosmopolitan by the end of the nineteenth century.

Rafael Hernández (1891–1965), the son of poor Afro–Puerto Rican tobacco workers, was among the many talented artists who grew up in Aguadilla. Hernández, his sister Victoria, and his brother Jesús all became accomplished musicians. As Victoria Hernández describes it, "We are musicians since birth. In our house music was breathed in the morning, it was eaten for breakfast." [38]

The Hernándezes were raised by their grandmother, who strongly encouraged their musical careers. For blacks and *mulatos* from an impoverished background, music could be a means of upward mobility. While Rafael learned to play cornet, violin, guitar, *bombardino,* and trombone,[39] Victoria became adept at violin, cello, and, when the family could finally afford to own an instrument, piano. But according to Victoria, the man who would become Puerto Rico's best-known and most prolific twentieth-century popular composer at first tried to escape his destiny. Her brother Rafael resisted family pressures:

> He didn't want to be a musician. He wanted to be a cigar maker, he wanted to be anything except a musician. In Aguadilla, there was a belief that all who played cornet died of tuberculosis, they discharged blood from their mouths. And the first instrument he played was cornet in a Good Friday procession. Well, so he played and nothing happened to him. So you know what he did to my grandmother? She was the one who brought us up, who hit us. [Rafael] took a pin, and he began to extract blood from his molar. Then he spit: "On account of you I'm tubercular. Look at the blood!" [40]

Hernández won the battle but not the war. He was allowed to switch from cornet to violin, but his musical training continued uninterrupted.

In general, family attitudes greatly influenced the careers of the future musicians. While López Cruz did not grow up in a formal, institutionally musical community like Humacao or Aguadilla, he did feel that he was immersed in a musical and supportive ambiance within his family:

> In the house there was a musical atmosphere. My uncle was a very good musician. My father liked to sing, and my mother as well. So in the house they would get together at night, as there were no movies, there was no television, there was nothing. Some female neighbors [vecinas] would get together at the house, and mamá rehearsed with them, some church songs. And I went along [yo iba] listening to all that.[41]

Others, however, were not so fortunate. Parents had a range of ambivalent and even contradictory responses to their children's talent. They worried about their offsprings' ability to make money as musicians and about the status of their chosen profession. As in the nineteenth century, the white and more affluent populations, who had access to more career opportunities than blacks did, did not see music as a step up the social or the economic ladder. Parents often regarded musicians as hard-drinking *bohemios,* incapable of earning a decent living for themselves and their families.

While negative publicity often made it difficult for boys to follow a career in popular music, it was all but impossible for girls. The rigid gender roles found in Puerto Rican society, particularly among whites and the upper class, extended even to choice of instrument. As late as 1935 an upper-class resident of Comerío, a tobacco-growing town south of San Juan, was heard remarking that "the piano was a woman's instrument, but . . . the guitar was for men."[42] True to this belief, a few women, generally from municipal band families, excelled at piano or voice. These women usually performed within domestic, church, or classical concert settings; occasionally they had jobs as accompanists for silent films.[43] Prior to World War II, though, Puerto Rican women who participated in popular music usually did so as behind-the-scenes composers, teachers, or mothers raising families of musical children. The life of the roving, free-spirited guitarist was not for them.

Some parents who did procure music lessons for their children became upset when their children took the classes too seriously. When Francisco López Vidal was eight years old his father made a special trip to San Juan to purchase a mandolin for him in time for Three Kings' Day. Proud of his talent, López's parents showed him off at various houses. By the age of twelve the boy was taking violin lessons in San Juan, with their blessings. But when he began four years later to play violin and then saxophone in the orchestra of a silent movie theater, they became alarmed. López Vidal explains, "My father didn't want me to be a musician, because he was from a proud family."[44] While López Vidal stubbornly held to music, he did capitulate to his father's wish that he study engineering as well.

Some parents reacted more strongly, even when they were musical themselves. Johnny Rodríguez fondly remembers his Cuban-born mother singing *guajiras,* his father accompanying her with guitar and harmonies. But his father, who wanted Johnny to become a lawyer, was adamantly opposed to the idea of his son singing or playing an instrument.[45]

An uncle of Rodríguez's taught him his first song, and his father, ever on the alert for signs of his offspring's undoubtedly inherited musical talent, soundly scolded the unfortunate relative when he heard Johnny singing a few bars. Shortly thereafter another surreptitious musical action immersed Johnny in hot water: "I bought a guitar, and he found it under the bed . . . he put it on top [and said,] 'I don't want to have a drunkard *[borrachón]* here; one is enough in the family.' And I didn't drink, nor did I know anything about that, but my father, since he was the son of Spaniards, he had that drastic temperament *[carácter drástico].*"[46]

Rodríguez persisted. When his parents went to bed at eight or nine o'clock at night, he would climb out a window and join some friends. Using a banjo in place of the guitar his father had broken, Johnny and his friends sang the latest popular songs on street corners or in the *serenatas* young men would commission to court their love interests.

Not surprisingly, much of the teaching and early experience of the musicians reflects the level of urbanization and affluence of the areas in which they grew up. In his small town, Pepito Arvelo got his first performance opportunity at a traditional religious gathering: "Me with my little guitar *[guitarrita],* at eleven, twelve years old, the first little dance that I played they gave me twenty cents. It was what's called in Puerto Rico the Fiesta de Cruz. Rosaries are sung, and there's dancing in the house, and you're still playing at daybreak *[uno amanece tocando].*"[47] Arvelo taught himself on guitar, learning by observing the music and musicians around him. López Cruz described a similar early experience: "I would go to dances to watch the musicians. I learned the *cuatro* and the guitar by ear without knowing music."[48]

While Arvelo remained isolated in the country, López Cruz had an opportunity to refine his musical knowledge and broaden his experience when his family moved to areas more urbanized than Naranjito. After eighth grade, López Cruz had to leave the town where he had been born because it had no high school. The youngster found Bayamón, his new home, a musical as well as educational mecca. There, he says, thanks to contacts made while performing in high school, "in a short time I became a musician, and the professional singers called me to play *serenatas* and such things."[49] Bayamón, a small city west of San Juan, also had two theaters with live orchestras.

López Cruz's move to Comerío a year later proved even more propitious: "In Comerío there was a school band, beautiful music, a municipal band, and an orchestra. In Comerío now I had two teachers who showed me how to play clarinet, with music. Comerío was for me something very big *[bien grande]*, because there was a musical atmosphere, music in every corner."[50]

MUNICIPAL BANDS AND DANCE *ORQUESTAS*

"The pride of each town was to have a good band," remembers Miguelito Miranda of Manatí.[51] Indeed, public bands and their leaders were the hub of most of a town's musical life and teaching opportunities. Local government and school-sponsored bands were magnets for musicians from outlying areas and important training grounds for the popular and classical musicians who would later migrate to the United States.

Taking the military bands of the Spanish colonial regime as their models, musical leaders, who were often talented composers and performers, organized bands of brass, woodwind, and percussion players. They trained groups of as many as sixty schoolchildren or adults to entertain in town plazas, tour the island, and participate in festivals and contests. During the early twentieth century Juan Peña founded the municipal band of Humacao, Jesús Figueroa, the firemen's band of Aguadilla, and Manuel Tizol, the firemen's band of San Juan, later the city's municipal band. Most of these municipal bandleaders and composers were also prolific parents, raising large families that literally became in-house ensembles. The Tizols, Peñas, and Figueroas, along with the Duchesnes of Cayey and Fajardo, the Maderas of Mayagüez and Guayama, and numerous others, reared virtual dynasties of musicians and bandleaders who became famous throughout the island and in New York City.

Even when the bandleader was one's father or a close family friend, the training was rigorous. Instructors used a rigid European-based system in which students had to spend several years learning basic theory and *solfeo*, a sight-singing method, before they were allowed to concentrate on their instruments.[52] In Puerto Rico, band musicians were reading musicians. They might be skilled at several instruments as well.

Even poor children had access to this formal training. Rafael Hernández studied with Pepe Ruellán Lequerica, a famed Aguadillan teacher, before going on to play in Lequerica's Banda Escolar (School Band) and Tizol's San Juan municipal band. Lequerica, who was noted for taking poor but talented students under his wing for little or no money, may have been as responsible as Aguadilla's cosmopolitan ambiance for the bumper crop of musicians the city produced.

In an atmosphere in which musical training and performance were valued almost as a public service, even people without families could find training and encouragement and borrow instruments. In an anonymous interview, a Puerto Rican trumpeter describes how he was orphaned at the age of ten, shortly before World War I. Sent to a public orphanage in Santurce, he learned both shoemaking and trumpet.[53] It was the musical trade that helped this unnamed trumpeter when he left Puerto Rico as a young adult. He found himself, along with many young Duchesnes, Maderas, Peñas, Tizols, and scores of other Puerto Rican musicians, looking for ways to use his reading and playing skills in the New York City of the 1920s and 1930s.

The changing circumstances of musical production in Puerto Rico motivated this apparently giant leap between cultures and continents in the course of one generation. The occupational difficulties of municipal bandleaders and their disciples during the early twentieth century illustrate many of the cultural changes taking place in Puerto Rico. Musicians had always struggled to piece together a living on the island, but the structure and content of that struggle had changed according to the political and economic context. The change in sovereignty, for example, curtailed the power of the Catholic Church and its sponsorship of composers and ensembles. With the U.S. takeover of the island, its regimental bands also became a thing of the past. The formation of municipal bands represents the struggle of musicians to find another institutional form within which to continue their composing, performing, and training of future generations.

Post-1898 changes in the Puerto Rican economic structure also affected town musicians in a variety of ways. Many of the organizers of municipal bands had been born in the late nineteenth century to predominantly *mulato* families of artisan-musicians. As always, it was a

rare musician who did not have to take up another trade to survive.
Manuel Peña remembers that when he belonged to his father's municipal
band in Humacao the pay was terrible: "We rehearsed three times a
week, and we played a concert every Sunday in the public plaza. They
paid us a pittance [miseria], thirty dollars a month."[54] Prospects were
no better for those who played at dances; if anything, they were even
more unpredictable. Trumpeter Máximo González Negrón's description
of San Germán might have been about other parts of the island as well:

> No musician knew how much he was going to get paid, he didn't know when
> he was going to get paid; it could be in one or two days or in a week. More-
> over, at times he didn't even know when he'd have a playing date, since he
> was advised a little while before beginning the work. . . . In that time the
> musical dates were few and one was almost always available. . . .
>   The number of musicians [for a performance] always depended upon the
> number that there were. . . . But all of us musicians were companions and
> . . . all of us . . . participated in whatever was brought to us.[55]

González remembers that he and his *compañeros* were happy to find
fifty cents or a dollar and a half in their pockets at the end of a performance, which meant, especially for dances, playing for "as long as couples stayed dancing and applauding."[56] In many cases there was also a
pay hierarchy, percussionists receiving less than those playing European
brass, woodwind, or string instruments.[57]

Even the most illustrious figures in the music world had to work at
other jobs. Jesús Figueroa's talents might have been well known
throughout the island, but he worked as a police officer as well. Manuel
Tizol was descended from generations of artisan-musicians. Efraín Vaz's
father, a typical municipal bandleader developing the musical abilities
of his offspring and other youth of Aguadilla, was also an instrument
maker and a tailor, and he passed those skills on to his son. Many musicians had a strong sense of class consciousness, developing guilds for
musicians as well as for those in other trades.[58]

After the Spanish-American War, U.S. manufacturers flooded Puerto
Rico with cheap factory-made goods that rendered local skilled artisans
obsolete. Many artisan-musicians could no longer earn enough to live
on in the primary trades they practiced. Where possible, musicians held
on to steady jobs and small businesses that in effect subsidized their
music making. Tito Henríquez's job with a San Juan bus company
brought him in contact with Ernesto Vigoreaux, who was an expert
mechanic as well as a trumpeter and composer. Others in Vigoreaux's

Santurce dance orchestra were plumbers, automobile painters, and masons.[59]

Other artisan-musicians, such as the *tabaqueros* (cigar makers), fought a constant battle against the mechanization of their craft as U.S. factories with branches on the island increasingly set the terms of production. For such tradespeople, mixing nonmusical trades with their lives as entertainers not only meant survival but could provide important organizational tactics. Among the most highly organized and politicized members of the working class, *tabaqueros,* many of whom also sang, played, and composed, were in a good position to formulate collective strategies for their fellow musicians.[60] San Juan trumpet player Juanchin Ramírez, for example, worked with his half brothers, the Lumbanos, a group of *tabaquero*-musicians who worked as promoters for local movie theaters, circuses, zarzuelas, and other events in the 1920s.[61] The Lumbanos also helped San Juan musicians to get bookings, functioning as an unofficial union years before Puerto Rico developed its own branch of the American Federation of Musicians.[62]

Musicians found that the terms of production were taken out of their hands in the performance sphere as well as in their nonmusical trades. The U.S.-appointed insular officials, for example, pressured Puerto Rican municipal and school bands to change their calendars and their repertoires to conform with American holidays and patriotic songs. While these groups continued the tradition of weekly concerts and participation in patron saints' festivals and other longstanding religious celebrations, U.S. holidays such as Flag Day and Washington's Birthday were added to the roster. By 1903, songs such as "America" were sung in public schools throughout the island.[63]

There were some bright spots, however, even within this bleak scenario of narrowing musical and nonmusical options. The economic urgency of bandleaders ensured a rich and varied local musical life and gave the future New York performers a taste in versatility. Bandleaders were usually energetic organizers who did far more than conduct their public bands in weekly *retretas* (open-air concerts) or parades. Manuel Tizol organized chamber groups and cultural societies for the San Juan elite. Tizol and most other bandleaders had their own dance *orquestas* as well. Even the smaller towns of Puerto Rico had energetic musical leaders. Trumpeter Máximo González Negrón remembers the undisputed musical "czar" of San Germán in the 1920s, Francisco Nazario Quevedo, a man who "completely dominated the musical atmosphere of my town." Nazario had an orchestra for dances and for more formal functions, as well as a school band. He supplied musicians for religious processions, circuses, burials, and announcements for upcoming events at the local cinema.[64] Nazario also owned a barbershop, which probably provided him with both a living and an invaluable source of potential clients for his musicians. From San Juan to Ponce, Mayagüez to Humacao, the youth of municipal bands learned to play popular music in ensembles often led by the very same conductors. Indeed, the core of many dance bands were the same brass, woodwind, and percussion instruments, played by reading musicians, with string instruments added to the basic configuration.[65]

From the novice musicians's point of view, such groups and their leaders provided invaluable contacts and training. The genre mixing typical of musical events also trained these young musicians to be versatile. A city parks concert, for example, might include zarzuela and opera selections, *danzas,* American patriotic songs, and compositions by both European composers and the band director himself.[66] Composers often took pride in themselves, and were proudly regarded by others, for their ability to compose not only popular songs but also light classical pieces and more "serious" classical works, or a combination of various forms. The class divisions usually associated with classical and popular music were ambiguous in Puerto Rico. Not only was such genre mixing common but audiences as well as the majority of performers came from the working classes.

The popular music played at dances was also eclectic. Touring companies, styles Puerto Rican musicians who had gone abroad brought back with them, sheet music, and eventually movies, records, and radio all assured an ongoing and ever-evolving infusion of new dance styles. And political and economic changes indirectly affected musical styles. The invading American troops, for example, brought not only U.S. sovereignty but also one-steps, two-steps, and rags. In turn, local composers invented their own songs in accordance with these models or combined them with older forms such as the *danza.* In the 1920s, ongoing political and economic as well as artistic connections with other countries assured music from a variety of sources: romantic Cuban and Colombian songs, current North American jazz styles, the Argentine *tango,* and the fox-trot, all of which competed for attention and to some extent displaced earlier styles.[67]

As always, dance groups arose in a variety of contexts, both connected to and independent of municipal bandleaders. From isolated mountain towns to the dense settlements of workers in the coastal plains to the elegant urban salons of the upper class, all had at least occasional celebrations featuring popular music. Not surprisingly, the type and frequency of dances often depended upon income and class as well as the vagaries of production in a particular region. In the 1920s, Taso Zayas and other caneworkers on the southern coast of Puerto Rico could attend weekly dances held in a private house. The family that ran the dances did so to earn money, and the fee fluctuated depending upon the current economic situation of the workers who attended. By the light of kerosene lamps, poor people of all colors danced or played cards while a small band made up of accordion, *güiro*, guitar, and tambourine played *plenas*, fox-trots, *boleros*, and Charlestons.[68]

As with municipal bands and musical genres, the evolving circumstances of dance orchestras were a testimony to larger island upheavals. In sugar-producing areas the number and elaborateness of festivities increased during the harvest season and decreased during the *tiempo muerto* (literally, dead time), when many were unemployed. Similarly, in tobacco-producing towns like Comerío, entertainment bore a direct relationship to the quality of the harvest during a particular year, even for the upper class.

Changes in transportation and communication also had an effect on popular ensembles. Throughout the early twentieth century, for example, the new insular government improved railroads and built new roads throughout Puerto Rico to facilitate the export of cash crops and the import of manufactured goods. In the twenties and thirties it became easier for band and orchestra leaders to recruit members from other parts of the island. Efraín Vaz remembers his father building up an orchestra in Aguadilla with musicians from other towns in the western and northern coasts of the island. Vaz and the other musicians in his father's orchestra were also able to travel to other towns and alternate with other ensembles hired for private parties of the wealthy and public festivals. Greater interpenetration between towns would inevitably lead to musical mixtures transcending regionalisms.[69]

This mobility worked against musicians and bandleaders as well as for them. Members of the wealthier classes who could afford to bring in musicians from other towns for their parties did so, to the detriment of local musicians. Moreover, many members of this class equated North American music with Puerto Rico's economic and social progress. Such ideas about musical quality would have a direct influence on the employment of musicians and the preservation of musical forms. In Comerío in the thirties, for example, for a dance for the children of prominent townspeople

> an eight-piece orchestra, costing sixty dollars, was brought from San Juan for the occasion. Local dance orchestras using native instruments are not sophisticated enough for casino dances, although they may be used in house dances of the upper class. With the exception of two native instruments used for keeping time, the instruments used were the same as those found in a typical American dance orchestra. . . . There was a mixture of American and Latin-American music with the former predominating.[70]

Even the names of popular orchestras reflected these changes. The 1920s and 1930s yielded Augusto Rodríguez's Midnight Serenaders, the Orquesta Jolly Kings of Mayagüez, Vigoreaux's Santurce Serenaders, and the Orquesta Happy Hills of San Germán. The groups' arrangements and combinations of instruments, the genres they played, and the experiences of their members all testified to the ongoing influence of North American cultural forms and their increasing transmission through movies, records, and radio, as well as through instrument sales and sheet music.

Even in the best of times music was not a stable profession in Puerto Rico. In the period between the world wars profound economic, technological, and cultural changes meant that musicians were constantly searching for new jobs. As the twentieth century wore on, Puerto Rican musicians found that both their musical and nonmusical occupational options were narrowing. In many ways, the conditions of music making during this period were analogous to those of other trades. Performance conditions and even band configurations were increasingly set by those contracting the musicians rather than by the artists themselves.

In a country in which control of the mechanical media, such as the movies, radio, and records, was in foreign hands the situation was especially difficult. Musicians found jobs in the new, mostly U.S.-dominated mass media, particularly cinema and radio. As in other commercial media, such as the recording industry, Puerto Ricans were at the bottom of a complex colonial and neocolonial hierarchy. This affected the development of Puerto Rican musical tastes, since the island experienced a virtually one-way flow of mass media products from outside the island. At the same time, political and economic decisions made by the U.S. government helped to hasten the death of the older forms these mass media forms were replacing.

Scholarships abroad for talented musicians, which had been available in the nineteenth century, became increasingly scarce in the twentieth. So did insular government and municipal funds for public-oriented live music in general. Lacking government support, the municipal bands themselves began a decline that became a death rattle with the onset of the Depression. In 1934 the Puerto Rican Reconstruction Administration (PRRA), the island's equivalent of a New Deal agency, included a program to create new town-based bands throughout Puerto Rico. Musicians such as Luis R. Miranda, a clarinetist who had played in and directed military bands since the late nineteenth century, gained a temporary respite from joblessness. For the most part, however, these bands disappeared with the end of the New Deal.[71] Even the prestigious Luis Miranda, who was musical director of the PRRA, migrated to the United States once the agency closed down.[72]

As the class-conscious, guildlike municipal bands began to disappear, musicians resorted to increasingly privatized and commercial avenues of music making. Commercial links were not new, however. Many musicians had earned at least part of their living making public announcements and composing songs or jingles on behalf of various companies for years. Indeed, embedded in the municipal bands' *retretas* in the days before radio were sporadic musical "commercials" created for local and, increasingly, foreign companies who had the money to pay for such advertising.[73] But now these commercial jobs were linked to the promotion of U.S. products or, often, to homegrown Puerto Rican products processed with U.S. capital. Musicians now composed jingles dedicated to North American cigarettes, advertised records produced locally or imported by the Victor Talking Machine Company, or incorporated references to specific brands of soap into their songs.[74]

The decline of the municipal bands created a ripple effect in the musical life of the island. Small towns lost local free entertainment, which was replaced increasingly by U.S.-controlled or influenced mass media and private bands. Bandleaders who for generations had served as music teachers migrated to San Juan in search of work. With them disappeared the route by which many young students became apprentices to this trade without resorting to expensive schooling or private lessons. Just as musicians experienced a sort of proletarianization in their working conditions, so did the very nature of training become more class-based. When the numbers of local teachers waned, only wealthy families could afford to send their children to San Juan to take music lessons.[75] They did so, of course, with "culture" and not vocational skills in mind.

Virtually no aspect of music making on the island was unaffected by the U.S. political and economic presence. Puerto Rican instrument makers and department stores that had sold pianos for decades now found themselves outdone by U.S. mail-order firms or local subsidiaries of mainland companies doing a brisk business with the latest in "jazz" instruments—saxophones, ukuleles, and banjos.[76] The new jazz craze filtering into Puerto Rico was undoubtedly influenced largely by the strong presence of the U.S. film industry.

CINEMA

The first rudimentary filmmaking and exhibition apparatuses found their way to all of Latin America by the 1890s. For the entire region, and indeed throughout the world, the United States quickly became the leading developer and exporter of cinema-related technology, as well as the dominant force in the production and distribution of films. Within that structure of control, however, a few Latin American countries, most notably Mexico, Argentina, and Brazil, began to develop their own national cinemas. Puerto Rico, on the other hand, was a colony without the economic and political resources with which to nurture its own film industry. Moreover, under the auspices of the United States and its control over distribution of the world's cinema, Puerto Rico became a captive market for films from the mainland as well as those the United States distributed from the fledgling national cinemas of Mexico and Argentina.

After 1898 most facets of local movie distribution and exhibition were controlled by U.S. entrepreneurs. Cinema was slow to spread throughout the island, thus once again showing the importance of regional contexts as well as the pace of an industry developed from the outside. Even in culturally sophisticated Cayey the cinema was at first a makeshift affair located in a tent in the plaza. In Peñuelas, a coffee-growing and sugar-processing area in the island's southern interior, the movies were brought first by Protestant missionaries and later by the circus. Passed from institution to institution, it was not until 1919 that cinematic entertainment was housed in a building set aside expressly for that purpose.

Moviegoing in Puerto Rico developed within quite a different social context than in the United States. Early cinema in the United States was seen by the upper and middle classes as vulgar entertainment for the primarily immigrant working classes and even became a target of reformers' zeal.[77] The class connotations of the movies in Puerto Rico were completely different. On the poverty-stricken island, workers who earned a few dollars a week could not afford to go to the movies on a regular basis. A form of entertainment that cost ten or fifteen cents for a matinee and more during evenings and weekends was clearly not aimed at the poorer classes.[78] Moreover, as a North American invention, cinema had a certain cachet of novelty and modernity for the middle and upper classes. Thus, even before moviegoing became respectable for the middle classes of the United States it was a somewhat fashionable pursuit for the elite in Puerto Rico. San Juan had its first cinema by 1910, and by 1920 cinemas were common at least in the major cities.[79]

For the working classes, however, the cinema had still another significance: it was a source of employment. Many theater managers and owners were themselves municipal bandleaders. They turned to this new medium much as they had turned to skilled trades in an almost-bygone era. As the cinema became a fixture in most of the small towns as well as the larger cities of Puerto Rico, theater owners hired musicians to accompany the silent films and to play between the film showings. By the second decade of the twentieth century the cinema had become an important source of employment for musicians. Musicians who played for occasional zarzuelas and live theater performances, New Year's parties and patron saint festivals, might also maintain a "difficult dignity" by supplementing their income with cinema work.[80]

For the accompaniment of silent films owners of island cinemas hired anywhere from a lone piano player to an entire ensemble of clarinets, flutes, violins, piano, percussion, bass, and brass instruments. Once again, regional variations determined the instruments and the music. In López Cruz's Comerío, where there was no movie house until 1925, popular as well as folkloric sounds influenced this impressionable youth: "It was Saturdays and Sundays, nothing more. The music that they played, it was *cuatro,* guitar, and *güiro.* During the film. It didn't matter if it were something very agitated; the *cuatro* and guitar music continued with a sentimental, romantic waltz, and the people, well, they didn't notice. But this entered my ear, my spirit, my body, and all of this went into my formation as a musician."[81]

The charms of such sounds notwithstanding, musicians in interior towns were likely to move to more cosmopolitan areas, where an abundance of theaters and more elaborate orchestras offered more hope of employment. In city theaters musicians might play six or seven evenings a week and receive from $1.00 to $2.50 per evening for their services. Even women and minors might be found playing in these cinemas, further reinforcing the wholesome and refined connotation of moviegoing in Puerto Rico. Carmen Sanabia, pianist and mother of the famous Figueroa clan of classical musicians, played in San Juan movie houses for years, as did some of her children.[82] As a young girl in Cayey, Angélica Duchesne played piano in the movie theater founded by her father, the town's municipal bandleader. So did several of her brothers. The cinema could be an important rite of passage, both a training ground for young musicians and a transition to more Americanized music, arrangements, and instruments. Francisco López Vidal was only sixteen when he began to play in Duchesne's movie theater:

> In those times the silent films had programs where they indicated the different scenes, for example, of horses running or of unrequited love [amor triste]. And the music was in accord with those films. In the orchestra I played violin, there was another who played saxophone, trumpet, and everything, and the director played saxophone. And he said to me, "Paquito, why don't you buy yourself a saxophone and I'll teach you.". . .
>
> In those music books the saxophone pairings were like American music, it sounds better than with violin. I didn't say anything to him. I went to the instrument store and I bought a saxophone, I bought the method. And nobody taught me the saxophone. I learned by myself. . . .
>
> About three months later I presented myself in the theater with the saxophone and with the violin. And then [the director] said to me, "Ah, I'm glad because now I can teach you," and I said to him, "No, give me the music and I'm going to play." What happened? In those times there were orchestras. So as I played both violin and saxophone, now I was more needed.[83]

The repertoire of urban cinema music was varied, but as López Vidal's memories indicate, North American sounds and arrangements often formed an important part. In many cases musical scores were included with the films sent from the United States. American-style fox-trots and waltzes formed an important part of this silent film repertoire and filtered their way into popular dances and even public band concerts. And yet the audiences in the silent movie theaters were often lively and participatory, insisting upon certain types of Latin music at appropriate moments. Angélica Duchesne remembers that when there was a chase scene in cowboy movies the people in the balcony screamed "Pasodoble!" and the orchestra had to play one instantly. The music could even supersede the film. "When my brother played 'El Manisero' [The Peanut Vendor]," remembers Duchesne, "the people got quiet as if they were in Mass. When we finished, they applauded and forgot about the movie."[84]

The role of the cinema musician usually extended out into the street, where another set of musical conventions reigned. Duchesne's father would hire a bus to take the musicians around town to announce the movies. The pieces were like a coded musical clock, echoing the sequence of the *carnets,* cards used at *casino* dances to give the order of the pieces for the evening. They also told people when showtime was:

> On the corner of the plaza we would play a piece at about seven at night. The show began at eight o'clock sharp. Then we would go up [to the cinema] with a *pasodoble,* "Las Corsarias." We got up to the theater, and when it was almost time for the show we went down to the corner and played the *seis de Andino.* The people knew: "Listen, they're playing the *seis,* now they're going to begin [the film]." It was a matter of establishing the custom, you see.[85]

The careers of cinema musicians were usually strongly linked to the commercialism that preceded the establishment of movie houses in Puerto Rico and later extended into the realms of radio, recording, and live performance. In the silent film era musicians such as trumpeter Ernesto Vigoreaux played with their *conjuntos* after the silent films, mixing musical message from firms such as the Puerto Rican–American Tobacco Company, for example, with *danzones* and *danzonetes.*[86]

By 1928 there were more than one hundred cinemas throughout Puerto Rico. But the *cine* did not provide a stable living for either its owners or its resident musicians. By the late 1920s a series of crises had gravely undermined this important venue. In 1928 the hurricane San Felipe destroyed or seriously damaged movie houses throughout the island. If and when owners were able to rebuild, many rewired their theaters to accommodate the new "talking pictures."[87] As in the United States, the advent of sound cinema proved catastrophic for local musicians, who were no longer needed as musical accompaniment for the films. The onset of the Depression brought economic pressures upon theater owners, who drastically reduced their prices from ten, fifteen, and twenty-five cents to as little as three cents or five cents. During hard times cinema owners had to be imaginative in order to attract an audience experiencing economic difficulties. At times an empty deposit bottle was an acceptable substitute for the price of admission.[88] Many movie houses closed as well.

Under such circumstances elaborate orchestras became more and more of a superfluous luxury even in the cinemas in the big cities. Displaced musicians tried to get additional work as cafe performers or to break into the new radio field. Others migrated to the United States or other parts of Latin America in search of musical employment.[89] Some gave up on music altogether. Vigoreaux remembers at least two cinema violinists who dedicated themselves to new careers: one became a milk-man, and the other sold gasoline.[90]

The conversion of the cinemas also had important effects on the musical tastes of audiences. North American movies featuring jazz and the films of Argentine *tango* singer Carlos Gardel were among the first sound movies to come to Puerto Rico. Avid moviegoers began to demand that musicians add jazz and *tango* to their musical repertoires. When Mexican movies flooded Puerto Rico shortly thereafter, *corridos* and *rancheras* also became popular favorites.

It was in great part these twin specters of unemployed musicians and the "decline" of musical taste that the 1931 visitors to Governor Roosevelt were fighting. But they were dealing with a complex set of issues. Puerto Rican cultural leaders argued that the sound cinema displaced musicians, competed with locally available live theater and opera, and adulterated Puerto Rican musical culture. North American distributors and exhibitors, however, insisted that the movies represented the democratization of culture, making it affordable for the masses for the first time.[91]

Ironically, some of these very same cultural leaders utilized another primarily North American medium, radio, in order to preserve jobs for musicians and homegrown musical forms. Radio became a means to preserve *danzas* and *jíbaro* music, although removed from their dancing and celebratory contexts, as well as to bring in the latest fox-trots and *guarachas*. It would not be the last time a mass medium would enshrine a cultural form it had helped to render obsolete.[92]

RADIO

Puerto Rico's first official use of the airwaves was in the fall of 1922, a scant few months after broadcasting commenced in the United States and Cuba. Despite its early beginnings, radio developed slowly in Puerto Rico in comparison with its development in the mainland United States and other parts of Latin America. After WKAQ was licensed in San Juan by a subsidiary of the American Telephone and Telegraph Company, it would be fully twelve years before Puerto Rico possessed another radio station. In 1940 Puerto Rico still had only 5 operating stations. By contrast, Cuba had at least 24 radio stations by 1924 and 85 by 1939. By that same year Mexico had 119.

As with cinema, the history of radio in Puerto Rico reveals the power of a mass media controlled largely by outsiders in shaping the experiences and expectations of musicians and their audiences. In the early years of radio many musicians did not take the medium seriously. Ernesto Vigoreaux, mechanic, composer, trumpeter, and bandleader during radio's nascent years, commented, "Do you know why we didn't want to go to the radio? Because there wasn't a Puerto Rican who owned a radio."[93] If Vigoreaux's testimony is to be believed, only wealthy Americans in San Juan's tourist district, the Condado, had radios.

Whether or not only English speakers had radios, it is true that few people on the island could afford to own one. The population of Puerto Rico was still primarily poor and agricultural, with many experiencing actual declines in wages and hours of work. Most could not buy luxuries such as the radios imported from the United States. In 1930 there were still only four thousand radios on the island and an estimated audience of about twenty-five thousand people out of a total population of over 1.5 million.[94] By contrast, by the mid-1930s 70 percent of all homes in the United States had a radio.[95]

Local radio personalities worked hard to make radio an appropriate local medium. In the 1920s people in San Juan, at least, could gather to listen to live broadcasts from local restaurants and cinemas. By 1930 the radio had become an important advertising medium for U.S. companies, and its programming hours expanded accordingly.

In the 1930s radio became an outlet for those who formed orchestras in the wake of the decline of silent cinema and municipal bands, as well as for what was actually the second wave of musicians who later migrated to the United States. Showcasing the talents of hopefuls on their way out of Puerto Rico as well as those returning triumphant and famous from New York City, the medium became a sort of appendage to the recording industry. Singers Bobby Capó and Johnny Rodríguez, for example, who came to New York toward the end of the 1930s, became professionals through their radio experience. Thus, their entry into music was qualitatively different from that of those who had begun in municipal bands and their offshoots or cinema orchestras, many of whom were already struggling to make it in New York City. In a country in which the older institutions were in decline and the activities of local record companies were sporadic and insubstantial, radio became an important local outlet as well as a channel toward recording contracts and live work in New York.

Johnny Rodríguez's first truly professional experience began with radio in a rather serendipitous way. As he grew into adolescence, his secret nocturnal adventures involved not just singing on street corners but also performing *serenatas* for the current love interests of his friends. One fateful day he was singing with a talented instrumentalist from Barrio Obrero (literally, Workers' Neighborhood, a part of Santurce), Teodocio, in an elegant San Juan neighborhood:

> One day Teddy took me to Hato Rey to give a serenade in Floral Park and I was singing, "Marta, capullito de rosa" (Marta, little rosebud). It was to the servant who lived in the back, "Marta, del jardín linda flor" (Marta, beautiful garden flower), and suddenly the lights went on in the house, and I ran because, you know, they would throw you in jail. And so Teddy went behind me. . . . I jumped the fence, and I said, "Jump however you can and dump the guitar and let's go." And then the *señor* came out in a bathrobe, it was don Félix Muñiz, may he rest in peace, and he says to us, "Listen, don't go, you with the guitar, don't go because I want to talk business with you." And [Teddy] says, "Business?" And me, standing on that corner, I heard what they said. "Juanito, come here . . . you're going on the radio." And I said, "Look, this old man, what he wants is to call the police." And [Muñiz] said, "You're a young boy. I thought you were older, but how well you sing. I'm going to put you on the radio, on the noon program of the West Indies Advertising Company." And I said to him, "I'm in school. I can't go. I also look for a buck at night." And he said, "Yes, I'm going to pay you."[96]

At the age of sixteen Rodríguez began to appear on the noon show of the West Indies Advertising Company, an important sponsor of early radio. Both personal ambition and his position as the oldest child in a large family led him to sacrifice school and take the job. Not surprisingly, Johnny's father had no idea of his truancy or his new career until an acquaintance congratulated him for having a son who was a radio star.

Both of Rodríguez's parents died around this time, and Muñiz, the owner of the West Indies Advertising Company, took Johnny under his wing and showed a keen interest in his orphaned family and their financial situation. He also helped Rodríguez make the transition from the instrumentation, repertoire, and performance style of a street performer to that of a more polished professional, providing an important bridge between Johnny's past and future. "Don Félix told me, 'Well, what you have to do is come to the studio tomorrow morning at nine or nine-thirty to see if you can sing with the orchestra.' . . . Forget it, I had never sung with an orchestra or with anyone. I had sung with one of those washtubs and with Teddy's guitar."[97] In this way, Johnny began to sing professionally, rehearsing for his daily midday show with an orchestra of eight or nine musicians. Muñiz organized well-publicized tours around the island for his protégé. Eventually Johnny's increasing radio fame led to a request by the Victor Talking Machine Company for him to come to New York to record, a more concrete incentive for migration than his predecessors and most of his contemporaries had had.

While scouts for North American record companies grabbed those artists who were attracting attention on the radio, radio personnel themselves reached back within the resources of the island to recruit potential artists. Tito Henríquez remembers an important scout from his youth in the 1930s, "La Abuelita Borinqueña" (the Puerto Rican grandmother): "When I was in the eighth grade with little groups and things, a *señora* would go look for talent in all the public schools, 'La Abuelita Borinqueña.' She had a radio program on WKAQ on Sunday afternoons, and she brought professional artists to the schools, like Johnny Rodríguez and his Cuarteto Borincano."[98]

Radio stations used earlier radio-made artists in a campaign to search for other youthful performers and to help them start their careers, often with musicians already established in New York. Another important scout and show host, Rafael Quiñones Vidal, discovered Bobby Capó through his high-school searches. Picked up by Rafael Hernández's Cuarteto Victoria in 1939, Capó toured with the group for several months before going on to a long and productive career as a singer and composer in New York.

The experience of radio in the 1930s shows once again how people in poor countries under different cultural conditions adapted the U.S.-produced media. By the end of the decade even poor people in Puerto Rico's small towns and rural areas found ways to listen to their favorite artists on the radio. At a time when "the only ones who had radio were the rich, the stores, and those poor devils who dared to invest the $22 to $40 from the little they possessed," the youths in towns like Corozal would get together in the local *cafetines* at the lunch hour to listen to the daily broadcast of Cuarteto Mayarí, among the lucky few to become famous through recording in New York.[99] The children would slowly lick penny *limbers* bought to appease the *cafetín* owner, as they listened attentively to the *guarachas* and *boleros* of this popular group.[100] One of these youths, Antonio Moreno Caldero, remembers losing track of time: "When it was two minutes to 1:00 P.M. and the chords of the *cuarteto*'s closing theme began with 'Mayarí, Mayarí,' we ran toward school, because at 1:00 the bell rang, and if you entered a minute late to the classroom the teacher would tan your hide [*pelarte*], with the permission and encouragement of your parents."[101]

INCENTIVES FOR MIGRATION

Given Puerto Rican musicians' apparent flexibility in adapting to changing circumstances, why did so many migrate to New York City? Part of
the answer is to be found, of course, in the larger internal changes taking
place in Puerto Rico. These musicians, so many of whom had some un-
related primary employment, were as affected as other working people
on the island by phenomena such as the mechanization of the tobacco
industry and the decline of the small coffee farm and the coffee export
trade, culminating in the disastrous hurricane San Felipe in 1928. Such
occurrences, along with the takeover of large tracts of land by primarily
U.S.-owned sugar companies, were largely shaped by the strong U.S. economic and political dominance of Puerto Rico starting in 1898. The
development of a monocultural, sugar-based economy in the late nineteenth and the early twentieth century displaced many workers from
other areas of agriculture. Moreover, even before the Great Depression
hit the United States, workers confronted decreasing wages and seasonal
layoffs in the island's burgeoning sugar and needlework industries.
Meanwhile, prices of the now largely imported foodstuffs were soaring.

Like many of their *compatriotas,* Puerto Rican musicians experienced the need to migrate from rural regions to increasingly urbanized
and coastal areas within Puerto Rico, following the flow of jobs, as
workers in "primary" fields. As workers in "secondary" fields such as
entertainment, they were also dependent upon the fluctuating densities
of various settlements. For performers, the shape and particular circumstances of urbanization determined which areas were most populous
and thus likely to have the most entertainment opportunities or potential. From small towns in which they played, alone or in small ensembles,
at family gatherings or local parties, musicians migrated to larger cities
in search of work in theaters, dance bands, and municipal orchestras.

Puerto Rican musicians and their audiences were also at the mercy
of music-industry structures and processes that paralleled other types
of U.S.-dominated island development. U.S. government and corporate
strategies played a major role in determining the musical world of island
musicians and audiences and in shaping the opportunities available to
musicians in Puerto Rico and New York. Within the fledgling record,
radio, and cinema industries outsiders increasingly set the terms for musical production. U.S. record companies, for example, virtually ignored
Puerto Rico as a recording site but flooded it with discs made by Puerto
Ricans living in New York. This strategy both encouraged ambitious

musicians to migrate and hindered the development of an island-based recorded repertoire for audiences to enjoy. Even local radio became a means to siphon off the island's most popular artists for show-business careers on the mainland.

Whether or not they were musically inclined, working-class Puerto Ricans saw their circles of migration expand. For musicians, however, the migration to New York City had its own particular set of meanings. Not only was New York City the site of the largest Puerto Rican settlement on the mainland but it was the hub of the entertainment industry for the world's population. There Puerto Ricans would mingle on bandstands and in recording studios with aspiring musicians of many nationalities.

In the meantime, the ever-changing musical activities of the island provided a constant point of reference and artistic exchange for *compatriotas* on the mainland. Musicians based in New York City went to Puerto Rico on tours or for family visits, while *boricuas* who could not bear or afford to leave the island for long spent a few days at a time making records on the mainland. And on both sides of the ocean, musicians eagerly watched for and made changes in musical styles and performance opportunities.

CHAPTER TWO

From "Indianola" to "Ño Colá"

The Strange Career of the
Afro–Puerto Rican Musician

"Jazz Won the War!" declared the genre's most ardent fans at the end of 1918.[1] Beneath this rallying cry's apparent flippancy were layers of potent meaning. For the Allied victory of World War I owed a great deal to the efforts of nearly four hundred thousand African-American soldiers, among whose ranks were numerous bands and singing groups that had charmed their way through France. Christened with regiment nicknames, the "Hellfighters" of the 369th, the 350th Field Artillery Band, the "Buffaloes" of the 367th, and the "Black Devils" of the 370th put ragtime, vaudeville tunes, spirituals, and southern melodies on France's musical map.[2] Their musical conquests both symbolized the importance of American blacks in the Great War and presaged significant cultural innovations for the United States and Europe in the decades to come.

But the layers of meaning went still deeper. Within the ranks of these black soldiers was still another subculture, Puerto Rican brass and reed players who contributed their considerable talents and lung power to this musical and military effort. These men, recruited directly from Puerto Rico, were among the pioneers who introduced jazz to France. They were also among the first Puerto Rican musicians to sojourn in the mainland United States, exchanging musical ideas with their erstwhile companions and bringing new sounds back to the island.

Within the context of World War I began a process of migration and a cultural exchange between two groups, African-Americans and Puerto Ricans, that would last for many years. In the shadows of a later world war encounters between Cuban and black American musicians would influence bebop and produce Latin jazz and the *mambo*. But decades before that, Puerto Ricans and other Latinos played trumpets and tubas and composed and arranged for some of the best-known black and white jazz orchestras in the United States. In turn, they brought jazz orchestrations and harmonies back to Latino ensembles. In many respects World War I was the kickoff point for a creative intermingling that was often invisible to outsiders.

BATTLING *BORICUAS*

That Puerto Ricans formed part of African-American military bands was the result of the confluence of two significant historical events: Congress's passage of the Jones Act, which made Puerto Ricans citizens of the United States, in March 1917;[3] and, just one month later, Congress's declaration of war with Germany and the U.S. entry into World War I. In the flurry of registration that followed, over 236,000 Puerto Rican men were declared eligible for the draft. Nearly 18,000 of these were mustered into the U.S. armed forces. Some 4,000 soldiers were sent to guard the Panama Canal, and the rest trained in Puerto Rico.

The thousands of Puerto Rican men who donned the uniform of the United States Army for the first time undoubtedly got more than they expected, for along with that uniform came a new and potent identity, that of the black man in the United States. Even men who trained for the war on their own island were put into racially segregated camps. Although this was standard policy within the U.S. military, it was a new configuration for the Puerto Rican soldiers in training. Puerto Rican society was not devoid of color consciousness or prejudice, but racial categories were different than in the United States. Not only did Puerto Rico have a greater degree of racial mixing than its northern colonizer but its racial classification scheme comprised fluid and diverse categories that were typical for most Latin American countries.[4] Unlike their North American neighbors, according to whom people were either black or white, Puerto Ricans defined themselves and each other on a continuum from white to black, with facial features, hair texture, and even wealth or occupation helping to determine how a person was classified.[5] For these new soldiers in the American army, the "white" and "Negro" camps in which they were placed represented an alien social experience.

No Puerto Rican soldier, however, had an experience as acutely bittersweet as that of those members of the African-American regimental bands who played and fought overseas. In artistic terms, to be a Negro meant to be in the vanguard of popular music; however, in social terms, it counted for innumerable abuses in the lives of these soldiers. Within just a few months these new recruits felt the sting of racism in northern and southern training camps, as well as the adulation and apparent colorblindness of the French. They were abruptly thrust into the cultures of Harlem and southern-born African-Americans. A white world that saw all people of color as essentially alike expected these Puerto Ricans to identify themselves with this new ethnic group both socially and musically.

As musicians and soldiers, moreover, Puerto Ricans were asked to be emissaries of that adopted culture, as well as to put their best feet forward as overseas representatives of the United States. Part of regiments whose members the outside world labeled American Negroes, these men had to absorb new musical forms and make them their own. Within this linked renegotiation of their ethnic and musical identities, Puerto Rican military musicians were swept into a maelstrom of racial and national problems far beyond their prior experience. As they were initiated into new modes of musical expression, they learned firsthand the extramusical implications of this apparently innocent entertainment. As best they could, they interpreted their position in the midst of some of the social, political, and economic difficulties plaguing African-Americans in the United States in the years before and after World War I.

Since the *boricuas* who played and fought in the regiment are not alive to tell their stories, we must turn to the written and oral accounts of numerous participants and observers. Based on this evidence, as well as the later New York careers of various Afro-Latino musicians, we can speculate on how these men experienced their new racial and cultural context.

HISTORIC ENCOUNTERS

The musicians brought to the mainland from San Juan were actually among only a handful of Puerto Ricans who fought the war in France and were part of explicitly "American" regiments. Although relatively few in number, these Puerto Ricans formed a particularly prominent part of the United States Army's most famous musical ensemble, the 369th Infantry "Hellfighters" Band, led by Lieutenant James Reese Europe. Europe himself recruited some eighteen musicians from San Juan's bands and orchestras and probably from advertisements placed in Puerto Rican newspapers.

Victoria Hernández still remembers the "americano de color" who arrived in Puerto Rico looking for army musicians. It was May of 1917. Her brother Rafael had left Aguadilla and toured the island with a Japanese circus, and then, like many of his peers, he had gone to San Juan in search of more musical opportunities. Now he was playing violin in the Orquesta Sinfónica of San Juan and trombone in Manuel Tizol's municipal band. He had also organized his own orchestra of a dozen musicians, which played at dances and baseball games and accompanied the silent movies in the Cine Tres Banderas.[6]

For a North American bandleader who had stepped off the boat in San Juan and was conducting a hurried search for instrumentalists, Hernández and his colleagues must have seemed a godsend. With centuries of connections to the colonial military, public bands like Tizol's were decidedly martial in instruments and orchestration. The musicians within both the band and the orchestra were adept at reading sheet music, and most could play several instruments. Europe grabbed Rafael Hernández, his brother Jesús, and sixteen more musicians and took the next boat back to New York.[7]

To date it is still a mystery how James Reese Europe found out that Puerto Rico could supply good musicians for his band. It is possible that he knew about the musicians because they had already been "discovered" by North Americans, a little over a year before. At the beginning of 1917 agents for the Victor Talking Machine Company had stopped off in San Juan as part of a recording tour of South America and the Caribbean. Several numbers by both Tizol's band and an orchestra led by Rafael Hernández ended up on their acetates.[8] Jim Europe had himself been recording for Victor since 1914 and would have had good connections with company personnel.

However James Reese Europe found out that Puerto Rico was a mecca for musicians, this recruitment brought about a significant encounter between two groups whose histories had telling differences as well as striking intersections and similarities. The coming together of African-American and Puerto Rican musicians in the context of World War I and their interactions in the ensuing decades were conditioned by these parallels, overlaps, and differences. Indeed, the careers of recruiter and recruited, the basis upon which the Puerto Rican trip was initiated and the band formed, tell us a great deal about the two groups and the worlds they came from.

The life history of the man who scouted for Puerto Rican instrumentalists itself testifies to the heights a talented and ambitious black musician, composer, and conductor could reach in the United States, as well as the restrictions a socially constructed racial identity placed upon him. As versatile as the municipal bandleaders in Puerto Rico, he worked within vastly different parameters. Born in Mobile, Alabama, in 1881, James Reese Europe was a highly trained musician who spent years in New York City as a writer and orchestra leader with black musical shows. But the opportunities for African-Americans in a white-dominated entertainment industry were often transient and dependent on prevailing racial attitudes and the charisma of individual black talents. By the beginning of the second decade of the twentieth century the deaths of several of the great black Broadway performers, composers, and writers ended a brief era of black participation on the aptly titled Great White Way, a circumstance that sent Jim Europe and many of his peers to the society dance bands. A talented organizer and advocate for African-American musicians, Europe founded the Clef Club in 1910. Much more than a gathering place for musicians, the club functioned as a union and booking agency for New York City's African-American artists, who were all but ignored by the American Federation of Musicians. Thanks to Europe's protective organizing and his position as the leader of a society orchestra with seemingly endless spinoffs and branches, he was able to get employment for many black musicians in hotels, cabarets, and private parties for the wealthy. Europe directed the Clef Club's enormous orchestra of more than one hundred musicians. Featuring an unusual combination of instruments, including many mandolins, banjos, and pianos, the ensemble played marches, rags, pop, and musical theater and classical pieces. Their appearance in Carnegie Hall in 1912 marked the first time a black orchestra had ever appeared on that stage and the first time anyone had made the hallowed auditorium resonate with popular tunes. Subsequently, Europe worked with Vernon and Irene Castle, the famous dancing couple, and recorded with the Victor Talking Machine Company. It was the first time an African-American orchestra had received a recording contract.[9]

James Reese Europe's accomplishments are a credit to his personal abilities and underscore his anomalous position as a black composer and orchestra leader. In carving out a role for himself and his musicians, the bandleader was forever exploring new frontiers and reconquering old ones. No doubt it was this pioneering ability, as well as his organizational and musical skills, that led Colonel William Hayward to ask Europe to form an army band.

When Jim Europe enlisted in the Fifteenth Infantry of the New York National Guard in 1917, he was stepping into a recently formed Negro regiment that already had a troubled history. It was only because of pressure from local black leaders and the efforts of Colonel William Hayward that skeptical government and army officials had grudgingly conceded that "the great colored population of New York" could yield soldier-worthy material.[10] Under these circumstances, the gestation of the regimental band was itself laden with significance and points to the multiple motives of its organizers. Colonel Hayward, the regiment's white commander, begged Europe to organize "the best damn brass band in the United States Army," undoubtedly to give the beleaguered regiment some prestige.[11] In his turn, Europe hoped that this increased visibility for black performers would raise their status within the United States and lead to funding for his personal dream, a black symphony orchestra. In the meantime, Europe informed Hayward that he needed to go farther afield than the continental United States in order to recruit superior musicians for this current effort. Hayward solicited money for the project from an American millionaire, and Europe was on his way to Puerto Rico, while his drum major, Noble Sissle, a vocalist, composer, and arranger in civilian life, auditioned musicians back in New York.

Thus, the conditions under which James Reese Europe recruited the Puerto Ricans were themselves filled with significance. Whatever his pipeline to Puerto Rico, it is clear that he knew that island blacks and *mulatos* had access to the type of training many of their counterparts could not get in the United States. Jim Europe's Puerto Rican "finds" included a variety of clarinetists, valve trombonists, saxophonists, and tuba, French horn, bassoon, and *bombardino* players in their teens and twenties. Whether they were first-generation musicians "from the island," like Rafael Hernández and his brother Jesús, or the scions of illustrious musical families, all could read music and play in a wide variety of social and musical contexts.[12] Those who came from generations of musicians had additional vocational and moral support. Rafael Duchesne, who became a band sergeant and first clarinetist in Europe's band, was the son of Francisco Duchesne, a barber, flutist, and orchestra director in his native Fajardo. His uncle Casimiro Duchesne was a clari-

netist, composer, and conductor of San Juan bands and orchestras.
Angel Duchesne, the municipal band conductor and cinema owner of
Cayey, was also a member of this prolific family.

In both the United States and Puerto Rico a mixing of cultures in
relationships of unequal power resulted in class stratifications that were
at least partly based on color. But while both places provided socially
restrictive environments for blacks, the particular nature of each society's racism channeled their development as artists. On both sides of the
ocean, music was one of the few careers open to people of color. In both
places distinct musical cultures often developed within the context of
black or *mulato* people's working-class trades. Whereas in Comerío or
Cayey *tabaqueros* sang, played, and composed together as they worked,
in black barbershops in New Orleans or New York proprietors, employ-
ees, and patrons experimented with new types of vocal harmony.[13]

In Puerto Rico, however, where perceptions of race were partially
based on the amount of money and education a person possessed,
working-class people of color could utilize music for social mobility and
added prestige. Additionally, there was a degree of solidarity among
working-class Puerto Ricans, regardless of color, that was not to be
found in the United States. In Puerto Rico music as a career choice was
most commonly the province of black and *mulato* members of the working class. But whatever the complexion of the musician, once he had
chosen this career, he experienced a rough equality in training, genres
played, and performance opportunities, at least up until the 1930s.[14]
The whites-only policy within Puerto Rican popular entertainment applied just to the upper-class casinos. Moreover, musicians of color entertained even in those places where they were excluded as guests.

Musicians in Puerto Rico had to be creative to cope with the constantly changing circumstances within the entertainment world. But
these struggles were quite different from those experienced by their
African-American colleagues. For African-American musicians a more
pointed racism was overlaid upon the basic instability of the profession.
They were part of a trade that was integrated only in the most general
sense, and only to their detriment. Unlike in Puerto Rico, there was no
racial stigma attached to music making in the United States. Indeed, for
a succession of ethnic groups arriving to the country in the nineteenth
and early twentieth centuries, music provided an honorable form of rec-
reation, cultural preservation, and, occasionally, social and economic
mobility. Rather than hiring people of color to do their composing and
performing on a contractual basis, enterprising whites had thoroughly

organized and commercialized virtually all aspects of musical training, performance, and distribution by the late nineteenth century.

Within such an atmosphere, those African-Americans who were fortunate enough to get training often did so almost inadvertently, through army, orphanage, and other publicly supported bands. Needless to say, these bands were segregated, and African-American musicians usually had less access to decent instruments and funding than their white counterparts. In the realm of popular music, African-American musicians played in black theaters within segregated circuits, generally controlled by whites. With the lines between classical and popular music more strictly drawn in the United States than in Puerto Rico, even the most qualified African-American musician would more likely be found in a minstrel show than in a symphony orchestra. Given such circumstances, it is easy to see why Europe would go abroad to recruit musicians.

Even the way Europe justified his trip to Puerto Rico to a sympathetic white officer points to the peculiar social positioning of African-Americans and their cultural forms within the United States. Colonel Hayward later recounted to a group of his fellow officers that

> Jim Europe one day explained to me that the reed instruments, that is, clarinets, flutes, saxophones, and one or two other instruments, served the same purpose in a military band that string instruments serve in a symphony orchestra, and he said there was a great scarcity of reed instrument players in the United States among the colored people. He explained that the difficulty had something to do with the lips of the colored man—I don't know whether it was thick lips or thin lips—but Jim Europe knew, and I asked him what the answer was. He said the answer was Porto Rico. When I got over my astonishment over that answer, he explained to me that there were a lot of really good reed instrument musicians in Porto Rico, that their lips were all right, and that they were all well educated; that he had corresponded and found out about it, and then he unfolded a most amazingly ambitious plan. . . .
>
> Europe suggested that if we could give him proper orders to go to Porto Rico and enlist musicians for his band, that he could get the pick of the crop and build the best band in the army, if I would permit him to pay some bonuses where needed for the key men for each set of instruments.[15]

That he chose to explain it to his white superiors in a way that he felt would make sense to them tells a great deal about perceptions of black musicians within the white United States. White ideas about black musical abilities had a life of their own within the North American context. African-Americans were supposed to be natural and spontaneous musicians. Even a group as dignified as the Clef Club Band, whose uniformed and serious musicians represented a marked contrast to the stereotypes of black minstrels prevalent in most contemporary entertainment, was not immune. Contemporary newspaper descriptions of the Clef Club and their Carnegie Hall concert reinforce white assumptions about "natural" black musical ability, assumptions that would later haunt Puerto Rican musicians both in African-American orchestras and on their own:

> Most of these Clef Club men play by ear; two-thirds of them could not read a note when they first joined the organization. They have "picked up" the ability to play an instrument, and like the Hungarians and the gypsies, when they have caught the melody they are quick to catch by ear their own orchestral parts also. . . .
> Yet . . . many of them [are] waiters, porters, elevator boys, barbers, employees and tradesmen of different kinds. Even as the Negroes in the South sing naturally in four-part harmonies at their work in field or factory, so too these Negroes in the North, almost equally untrained musically, play and sing by virtue of sheer natural ability.[16]

The Puerto Rican performers in Jim Europe's band were recruited precisely because of their outstanding musicianship, but the image white America had of black artistry worked against their training. It must have been extremely difficult for the "Porto Ricans," taught to read and display their craft openly in island orchestras and small groups, to come to a country where the very qualities they were recruited for had to be concealed, to get used to being "Negroes" with an instinct for music rather than a painstakingly labored skill and a generations-old guildsman's pride. These *boricuas* had to learn to adapt to the stereotypes of blacks as natural musicians. This translated into working without sheet music. Classically trained, they were sometimes unfavorably judged by audiences and colleagues alike as technicians without improvisational abilities.

In addition to these concerns, the Puerto Rican musicians had to adjust to daily life within the black regiment. Contemporary accounts suggest that Rafael and Jesús Hernández, Rafael Duchesne, and the other musicians who joined the Fifteenth Infantry of the National Guard (later renamed the 369th U.S. Infantry Regiment), did indeed have to struggle to adapt to their role within this black regiment. Noble Sissle's memoirs of the regiment's experience in the war make mention of the Puerto Rican musicians, although not as individuals. He portrays the "Porto Ricans" as a collective and childlike unit, pathetic, demanding, although ultimately loyal. This portrait is ironic, given the not dissimilar white depictions of blacks in contemporary minstrel shows and popular literature. Nevertheless, Sissle gives us some insight into the process of adjustment faced by these musicians who came to New York: "Their Palm Beach suits were not only of many faded colors, but the trousers were too long for short ones and were too short for long ones. The poor little fellows with the East winds whipping around the edges of their sieve-like clothes, I fear made their first night in New York far from being a comfortable one. But Jim was just like a father to them. In fact, everyone did all they could to make them comfortable." [17]

The language barrier made it difficult for the musicians to communicate, especially in the beginning. Although to external appearances this was a "colored" regiment, it represented a historic, probably first-time interaction between African-American and Puerto Rican musicians. Just before the regiment left for its first training camp, at Fort Whitman, New York, Sissle complained,

> There were two words of English that they spoke perfectly and it went for uniforms, beds, food and in fact everything in general about the army and that was those never forgettable two words: "NO GOOD." Everything was "no good," especially the food. It was pitiful, too, with the little fellows so far from home, most of them mere boys and in their teens, but splendid musicians. . . . I don't know what their great expectations were in coming to New York, the great city of their dreams, to play in Jim Europe's big Concert Band, but I do know their minds could not possibly have pictured the first appearance they actually made, and that was the parade that they made from the Harlem Casino to the foot of One Hundred and Twenty-fifth Street and Hudson River where the Regiment entrained for Peekskill.

According to Sissle, the "Porto Ricans" were so astonished by the sight of Harlem residents "poking their half awakened selves out of windows" at seven o'clock on a Sunday morning to see the sixty-five-piece band and of crying relatives walking alongside the marching soldiers that they forgot to march and play their instruments. Other descriptions indicate Sissle's own lack of familiarity with the musical culture of Puerto Rico. As saxophones were found on the island from the mid-nineteenth century, it is unlikely that the musicians had never seen them before. Nevertheless, Sissle commented that "the Porto Ricans wanted the most expensive instruments and the saxaphones [sic], the likes of which they had never seen before, were immediately pronounced 'NO GOOD,' yet, they had none of their own. Jim did not want to hurt their feelings, but their childish enthusiasm was very aggravating in the brief space we had to get ready for the next day's departure." [18]

While the adjustments between the Puerto Ricans and the black American musicians were significant, looming ahead were the far greater challenges of performing and fighting a war as members of a racially segregated division. Even after the difficulties of forming the regiment were resolved, Colonel Hayward struggled to equip it and to keep it going. The men in training were given the Harlem Casino, a nightclub, in which to practice maneuvers. The dance hall burst at the seams with the would-be soldiers from Brooklyn, Birmingham, and Borinquén, and a number of the squads took to the streets with their nightly drills. The residents of Harlem watched with disbelief as the men trained with broom handles, for the Army was reluctant to issue them real weapons. The regiment was even denied permission to participate in a march with the rest of the New York National Guard before leaving the state. Although the Twenty-seventh Division was known as the "Rainbow Division," Colonel Hayward was informed that "black was not one of the colors of the rainbow." [19]

After many difficulties in getting a place to practice, the Fifteenth was finally assigned to a camp in Spartanburg, South Carolina. Immediately, a group of irate white citizens warned that "the most tragic consequences would follow the introduction of the New York Negro with his Northern ideas into the community life of Spartanburg." [20] While the regiment's white officers exhorted members to keep their head even under strong provocation, they employed the bands of the regiment in an active public-relations effort.

Simultaneously, the Puerto Ricans had to learn the importance of the distinctions the Spartanburg whites made between northern and southern blacks and to actively participate in peacemaking through music. Jim Europe's outfit took part in semiweekly open-air concerts and was subsequently invited to play at a dance at a white country club. Nevertheless, after a series of tense confrontations with hostile townspeople, the black soldiers were hastily removed from the camp with orders to go to the front. Drum Major Noble Sissle was one of the soldiers publicly humiliated and provoked by an aggressive white town resident. He later wrote bitterly that his regiment was "denied the right to train in camps in our own country" and "literally 'kicked to France.'" [21] On New Year's Day of 1918, the Fifteenth became the first black regiment to arrive in France. Its troops had had a scant three weeks' training for their war efforts.

Noble Sissle recounts a moving interaction with one of the Puerto Ricans toward the end of the tense period in Spartanburg. As Sissle angrily reflected on "our boys volunteering to fight a war for Democracy and then having to stand for your own country to kick you about like any dog and not allowed to strike back," his unhappiness was observed by one of the new recruits. "I was called to task by one of the Porto Ricans in broken English," Sissle remembered. "[He said] 'Sgt. Sissle, what make you look mad; there no German here, yet?'" Somehow, the minority-within-a-minority status of this unnamed "Porto Rican" seems to have brought a new perspective to Sissle, who remarked that "the sound of the voice of one who was so far away from home and a descendant of such a wronged people, caused me to brush away my personal feelings."[22]

How did the Puerto Ricans themselves make sense of all these racial and regional clashes? How must they have felt, observing that all their officers were white, that as black soldiers they spent their first weeks in France unloading ships and laying railroad tracks, while many white regiments went directly into combat? While the musicians certainly had some celebrity status within their regiment and later throughout France, their nonmusical work was decidedly unglamorous. Rafael Hernández and several of his *compatriotas* spent much of their time as part of the Ambulance Corps, "running from trench to trench offering help to the wounded more than playing music."[23] In a rare comment on his war experience, Rafael Hernández remarked in 1962 that he was relieved when he got his sergeant's stripes because it enabled him to get away from doing cleaning and other menial tasks.[24] As musicians he and the other band members were warmly received by the French, but as soldiers they were exposed to racial epithets, poor camp conditions and equipment, and restrictive army rules that were not applied to white soldiers.

On the musical level as well the Puerto Rican recruits must have learned a great deal, for carefully selected, eclectic programs were the hallmark of the regimental band's experience in the United States, on the ship, and throughout France. While their work in the Cine Tres Banderas and at dances in the San Juan area had undoubtedly given most of the Puerto Rican recruits some familiarity with North American popular music, here they were exposed to a greater variety of U.S. regional, primarily African-American forms embedded in an entirely new context. In parades they played English-language standards such as "Onward Christian Soldiers" and "Auld Lang Syne," as well as "Over There," a new George M. Cohan song composed especially for this war. Church services on deck included traditional African- and Anglo-American hymns and ensemble singing by the regiment's own quartet.

This intertwined musical and social reeducation for the Puerto Rican musicians continued in France as well. In between bouts of manual labor and months of trench warfare, Jim Europe's outfit toured France playing open-air and formal concerts, operas and vaudeville. As the band traveled, its members were told by their commanders "that they were upon a mission of great importance; that they were not merely musicians and soldiers of the American Army but that they were representatives of the American nation."[25] Top officials begged them not to do anything that might inspire racial prejudice in the still-pristine minds of the French people.

The band clearly worked hard to please its diverse audiences. Jim Europe challenged the ensemble by accepting requests from civilians, working from sheets of favorite folk songs or handwritten compositions timidly proffered to him. From all reports, the group gave remarkable concerts featuring a wide variety of music. In one such program, played before an entirely French audience, the band started with a French march and a series of well-known overtures. The tone changed as they followed this with a Sousa march and an arrangement of "Plantation Melodies." When the band began to play a jazzy version of W. C. Handy's "Memphis Blues," the crowd went wild with dancing and laughter. All over France the band enchanted audiences, and local musicians begged the Hellfighters to teach them ragtime. The joke was on the French, who did not realize that this music was almost as new to some of the band members as it was to them.

Yet along with the different social experiences and musical repertoires of these African-American and Puerto Rican musicians, there were some similarities and crossovers that promoted exchanges between the two groups during the war and later. Both African-American and Puerto Rican music were based largely on the interactions between the members of a forced African diaspora and a European colonizer. Ongoing infusions of African, Latin American, Caribbean, and European migrants added to the musical melange, as did internal migrations within each country. The resemblance between the musical development of New Orleans, the birthplace of much of the most innovative African-American music, and that of the islands of the French and Spanish Caribbean was particularly striking.[26]

Musically speaking, therefore, James Reese Europe and Rafael Hernández perhaps had more in common than at first met the eye. As composers and performers, they had worked within somewhat analogous musical forms. Hernández, who had begun to write songs when he was fourteen, had already composed several *danzones,* a Cuban form with more than a passing similarity to ragtime. Both were syncopated descendants of various strains of rather marchlike nineteenth-century European dance music. They were instrumental, multisectioned musics, featuring a series of self-enclosed musical themes that often incorporated motifs from other popular, folk, and classical songs. And what was most significant socially, both were the products of reading musicians of color who aspired to make both their music and themselves middle-class and respectable.[27]

There were musical crossovers as well as affinities between the musicians' two groups. The *danzón* and ragtime had influenced each other as a result of close commercial ties between the ports of Havana and New Orleans. James Reese Europe was himself involved in the spread throughout the United States of the *tango,* already popular in Puerto Rico. Europe's collaboration with dance trendsetters Vernon and Irene Castle brought the *tango* as well as African-American based dances such as the fox-trot before a national audience for the first time. While the people of Harlem went "tango mad" in 1914, Puerto Ricans were beginning to hear fox-trots as accompaniments to silent films and to dance to them in *casinos.*[28]

In many ways, then, the World War I interaction between African-American and Puerto Rican musicians made sense. It is not surprising that it continued after the war. In New York, such collaborations were reinforced by demographic and social factors that often grouped North American blacks and Puerto Ricans together. The parallel oppressions and musical developments of the past combined with close quarters in the present to promote ongoing musical exchanges.

MUSIC STAND MUSICIANS

After the armistice in November 1918, the members of the 369th U.S. Infantry went home heroes both for their bravery in prolonged combat and for their music, to which "France had sung and danced and cried."[29] The entire 369th was awarded the croix de guerre. On February 17, 1919, the regiment finally had its triumphal parade up Fifth Avenue in New York City. Warmly greeted by a spectrum of the city's population, they were even more fervently cheered when they reached Harlem.

James Europe's 369th U.S. Infantry Band went on a postwar tour of the United States and began recording for the Pathé label. The Hernández brothers, Rafael Duchesne, and the other Puerto Rican band mem-

bers were almost certainly involved in Europe's recording of early ragtime, jazz, and blues classics, including "Indianola," "Clarinet Marma-
lade," and "Memphis Blues." They might have continued in a successful
mainstream recording career if not for a bizarre and tragic incident. In
May 1919 James Reese Europe was fatally stabbed in a quarrel with his
drummer, and the band abruptly dissolved.

The honeymoon was over in more ways than one. The public's enthusiastic reception of the regimental bands and the many African-
American veterans with impeccable war records had led numerous black
leaders to believe that racial barriers were being erased through both
patriotism and good music. But the war's end heightened white racial
anxieties that had been exacerbated by significant demographic changes.

During the war, xenophobic fears of "hyphenated Americans" had
led government leaders to accept, albeit reluctantly, the recruitment of
black and Puerto Rican troops. In the context of the anti-German hyste-
ria these people of color were thought to be more loyal than many white
immigrants and their scions. In turn, thousands of African-Americans
and Puerto Ricans welcomed the opportunity to prove their loyalty to
the United States. By showing that they were good Americans, many
blacks hoped to achieve basic social and economic rights within the
United States. Similarly, leaders in Puerto Rico felt that this demonstra-
tion of loyalty would win them more economic and political autonomy
for their island.

But during and after the war, as Congress sharply curtailed migration
from Europe and Asia, a tremendous exodus of African-Americans from
the South began to change the racial contours of northern cities. In New
York, this situation was compounded by the in-migration of thousands
of Puerto Ricans whose economic situation on the island was deteriorating rather than improving. Once again, there were parallels between the
Puerto Rican and the African-American experience: members of both
groups left behind the constant struggles of farming under increasingly
difficult conditions or the disappearing crafts that had sustained them
in urban areas to look for factory jobs in the North. Although the particularities of their cultural and economic backgrounds were quite different, Puerto Ricans and African-Americans were both swept up in the
tensions surrounding this adjustment between blacks and whites in the
urban North. In the period during and immediately after the war there
were race riots, and a revived Ku Klux Klan spread throughout many
states. In New York City the two groups faced increasing segregation in
housing and discrimination in jobs and unions. Within both their daily

lives and their artistic careers, Puerto Rican musicians within a rigidly biracial North American society were caught up in "Negro" problems. Thus, their musical development in New York City must be understood within the context of opportunities for black artists.

Typically, the world of African-American popular music not only reflected these social tensions but had its own dynamic. The postwar period demonstrates the ever-shifting fortunes of black musicians in New York City, dependent on a fickle, white-dominated music industry and audience that placed them in and out of fashion. The fate of black performers often depended both on the achievements of individual African-American personalities and on a variable American racial climate rather than on a systematic and progressive acceptance by white America. Moreover, the perennial stereotypes plaguing black musicians before and during the war continued to haunt them afterwards.

While the goodwill spread by the Hellfighters and other wartime bands did not eradicate existing or growing social tensions, it did create some new opportunities for black musicians. On the heels of their success during World War I, black bands became almost fixtures on Broadway during the 1920s. Indeed, James Reese Europe's work before, during, and after the war had left behind an enduring legacy: "hundreds of Clef Club and 369th Infantry Regiment musicians were now the leavening of any musical effort."[30] The efforts of black musicians before and during the war combined with a surge of Prohibition era entertainment activity to produce a new black theater. While this entertainment was generally backed and produced by whites, who received most of the financial benefits, it gave black performers an opportunity to do significant work both in Harlem cabarets and on Broadway.

The pioneers in this renaissance of black theater were Eubie Blake and Noble Sissle, alumni of the Clef Club and Hellfighters and in a sense Jim Europe's heirs. Their musical extravaganza *Shuffle Along* opened in May of 1921 at the Sixty-third Street Theater and became an instant hit. Legions of other black writers, as well as ambitious white producers, continued the trend, creating new opportunities for black actors and musicians.

Not surprisingly, some of the Puerto Rican musicians who had triumphantly marched with Jim Europe's band down Fifth Avenue in 1919 became a part of these new musical ventures, as did other recently arrived *boricuas*. Because of the lack of written records and living sources and the apparent penchant for some of those musicians to Anglicize their names under xenophobic pressure, we will probably never know just how many Puerto Rican musicians joined U.S. orchestras in the period prior to World War II. We do know, however, that a number of musicians who became well-known jazz players, particularly on brass and woodwind instruments, came from Cuba and Puerto Rico, as well as Panama, Mexico, and other parts of Latin America. Ray Coen, whose stepfather, Augusto, was a trumpeter who benefited from the receptive climate toward Puerto Rican musicians within this world, explains why they were welcomed:

> The musicians who went there were what are called music stand musicians. They know how to read music, they know how to play different types of music. They were zarzuela musicians. So when [Augusto Coen] went to New York the American orchestras, the black American orchestras, were very good musicians, but they didn't have the training that the Puerto Rican musicians had. At that time there were shows. . . . Noble Sissle, they had the *Blackbirds* of 1921, 1922 on Broadway. The black American orchestras used Puerto Ricans a lot to read the parts of the Broadway shows. So there were Moncho Usera, Ismael Morales, [Rafael] Escudero, who played bass.[31]

Scant historical records confirm this participation, suggesting that many more Puerto Rican and Latino musicians formed part of these pit bands and jazz orchestras.[32] A salary list for the 1922 *Shuffle Along* company indicates that such shows could provide a good, if ephemeral, living for Puerto Rican performers. One Francisco Tizol, undoubtedly from the famous San Juan municipal bandleader's family, was listed as a musician making seventy dollars per week, more than twice as much as the show's not yet famous chorus girl Josephine Baker.[33] Other sources show Ralph [Rafael] Escudero, from Manati, in the orchestra of the *Chocolate Dandies* in 1928. Another Puerto Rican, Ramón "Moncho" Usera, played in Lew Leslie's *Blackbirds* orchestra in the same time period. The Cuban flutist Alberto Socarrás also performed in many of these shows.[34]

The surge of white exposure to black theater, combined with a 1920s dance explosion, brought about a new general popularity for black cabaret and ballroom ensembles as well. With the advent of Prohibition, white and black entrepreneurs and organized-crime figures developed Harlem into a paradise of forbidden nocturnal pleasures for whites on slumming expeditions. In turn, the black bandleaders hired for these nightspots incorporated Puerto Rican and other Latino musicians into their groups with relative frequency. Latinos' work with black bandleaders continued even after the black shows that were a staple of Broadway during the heyday of the Harlem Renaissance had gone out of style for the second time in the still-young twentieth century. Noble Sissle must have been well pleased with the performances he saw during World War I and the black theater renaissance, because his orchestra became a veritable incubator of such musicians. Moncho Usera spent years as an important clarinetist and arranger for the group, going to France with them and starting his own jazz orchestra in Europe.[35] Oscar Madera, a violinist from a famous Puerto Rican municipal band family, recorded with Sissle from at least 1934. In turn, such musicians formed a network that helped other Latinos to get jobs. Arriving in New York in 1930, within a couple of years Cuban clarinetist and trumpeter Mario Bauzá had integrated himself into this scene: "I joined Sissle after they broke up with *Shuffle Along*. Sissle opened with his orchestra in the Park Central Hotel. And they got two Puerto Rican people there, the one that got me into there—Ramón Usera, Moncho—and the other was Duchesne, Raf[ael]."[36]

Puerto Rican involvement in this postwar African-American entertainment scene did not come about so automatically, but within the complexities of a multiethnic world in which they formed an ambiguous part. In the postwar period Puerto Ricans were still a nearly invisible minority among New York's ethnic populations. While an estimated 35,000 Puerto Ricans lived in New York by the war's end, the African-American population there had reached about 150,000.[37] Black American musical groups received the support of both their own sizable communities and the white audiences with whom they were currently popular. Meanwhile, the *tango* craze had cooled, and other types of "Latin" music had not yet reached the ears of white America. There were few Latino ensembles in New York City during the 1920s, and Puerto Ricans of color were barred from participation in white orchestras. Thus Puerto Rican and Latino participation in African-American ensembles was conditioned in part by their prior experiences and in part by the range of options they saw around them. At the same time, Puerto Rican instrumentalists usually did not operate exclusively within a black field. Like other musicians, they took the opportunities they could and carved some out for themselves.

When Jim Europe's band broke up, for example, ex-sergeant Rafael Hernández took off for Cuba, where he spent five years as the director of a cinema orchestra in Havana. Returning to New York in 1925, he formed his own ensemble of Puerto Rican musicians, which had a triumphant debut in the prestigious Palace theater. Hernández spent several months touring the United States with the band of Charles Luckeyth

"Lucky" Roberts, one of the finest black stride pianists of his time, and soon after formed his own *trío*. Hernández, and undoubtedly other Puerto Ricans as well, sandwiched musical jobs with African-American groups between performances in Latino musical ensembles.[38]

Puerto Rican experiences in African-American orchestras were also conditioned by the needs and desires of black musicians, who were constantly battling pernicious stereotypes. Jim Europe's polished society bands before World War I and Sissle and Blake's Broadway performances afterwards sought to bring dignity to African-American music and theater. In *Shuffle Along* Sissle and Blake set out to create the first black show to feature "honest, unburlesqued, romantic love."[39] It was one of the first to eliminate the standard black and blackface minstrelsy—burnt cork, old overalls, thick dialect—and to allow black people to express universal human emotions.

Dignity was important to these musicians, who had spent years performing in impeccable dress before New York's elite, top U.S. military brass, and respectful European audiences. But the stereotype of African-Americans as instinctive musicians continued to plague them and to determine their performance strategies. Pianist Eubie Blake vividly describes constraints upon black pit musicians. The band of "*Shuffle Along* and the bands of ensuing productions had to commit entire scores to memory. " 'We did that because it was expected of us,' remembers Eubie. 'People didn't believe that black people could read music—they wanted to think that our ability was natural talent.' "[40]

Puerto Rican musicians had to adapt to both white racist expectations and African-American strategies to subvert stereotypes. Just as the white world believed that blacks were natural musicians, it tended to categorize all their music as "hot" or "jazz." In fact, jazz historians have often distinguished the New York African-American jazz and popular music scene of the early twentieth century from its counterparts in New Orleans and other areas by the formal and elaborate arrangements and sophisticated musicianship demanded by its audiences and practiced by its performers.[41] New York–based musicians such as Ellington, Fletcher Henderson, and Don Redman were careful orchestrators and arrangers who resented being categorized as "hot" jazz musicians. Their enthusiasm for Puerto Rican musicians probably represented their desire to combat prevalent stereotypes by producing a smooth, refined sound. In an atmosphere where training often counted more than improvisational ability, Puerto Ricans and other Latinos from a municipal band background were prized figures. In addition to their reading abilities, other attributes of these musicians made them desirable for black show and cabaret bands. Duke Ellington describes being taken with a group he saw in Washington, D. C., in 1920: "Around this time I met Juan Tizol, the trombonist who came to the Howard Theater with a band from Puerto Rico led by Marie Lucas. This group impressed us very much, because all the musicians doubled on different instruments, something that was extraordinary in those days."[42]

Ellington was so impressed that several years later he invited Tizol, the nephew of San Juan's municipal bandleader, to join his orchestra in New York, starting a musical association that would last many years. In the meantime, Ellington had a chance to see another Puerto Rican performer up close when he and Ralph Escudero came up to New York together in 1922 in clarinetist Wilbur Sweatman's band. Puerto Rican musicians were thus incorporated into the defensive planning of African-American musical leaders.

Other indignities and problems were chronic for black musical groups and, in turn, for their Puerto Rican members. Tuba player Ralph Escudero and Ponce trombonist Fernando Arbello both played with Fletcher Henderson, the most popular black orchestra leader in New York for much of the 1920s, for several years. When Henderson was contracted in 1924 to play in the Roseland Ballroom opposite a white band, the white musicians objected. A few months later they quit in protest.[43] Underpayment, lack of union protection, and tremendous difficulties in making sleeping and eating arrangements when on tour (usually in segregated theaters) were standard in the lives of black musicians of the period. While black shows were popular on Broadway during the 1920s, they operated on shoestring budgets, which all but evaporated during the Depression era. Only a small number of black performers made it to the big-time vaudeville theaters, and they were taboo in most of the elegant downtown hotels and nightspots. And the Harlem nightclubs where they could perform were often barred to black patrons. John Hammond, a record producer who did much to promote black musicians from the 1930s onward, was partly inspired by witnessing their struggles in this period: "The fact that the best jazz players barely made a living, were barred from all well-paying jobs in radio and in most nightclubs, enraged me."[44] Hammond remembers a rampant segregation, persisting well into the 1930s, in which mixed bands were banned in public and black and white musicians rarely knew each other. Even recording studio work with mixed personnel was risky for an ambitious white artist until near the close of the decade. In any case, white musi-

cians and their contractors virtually monopolized studio work, just as
they reaped most of the fame and money in the swing band era. The
conspicuousness of a few black bands only helped to mask these conditions. As Hammond wrote in 1936, "The spectacular colored bands,
such as Ellington, Calloway, Lunceford, with their gleaming tympani
and flashy uniforms, have given the impression that Negro musicians are
on the top of the economic ladder. Little does the public know of the
tremendous odds even the greatest of colored musicians must constantly
battle: racketeering managers, Jim Crow unions, outright discrimination."[45] Indeed, even among the most famous black performers salaries
varied greatly. Jack Schiffman, the son of the Apollo Theater owner,
noted that "there wasn't any rhyme or reason to band salaries in the
thirties." While Duke Ellington and Cab Calloway's bands earned several thousand dollars a week in 1932, Fletcher Henderson and his musicians got only $950. Other performers, such as comedian Pigmeat
Markham, received less than a hundred dollars weekly.[46]

COMMUNITY CONTEXT

The Puerto Rican musicians who participated in African-American
bands were caught up in their struggles to earn a living under decent
conditions with as much dignity as possible. When they were performing or on tour, they had to play the same music and face the same
humiliations and dangers as American blacks. When they returned
home, however, their identities might undergo a change.

Puerto Rican musicians generally lived among their nonmusical *compatriotas* in working-class neighborhoods. While the demographic accident that had brought Puerto Ricans and African-Americans to New
York City at the same time resulted in a proximity that meant opportunities for cultural and occupational mingling for those who were musicians, it created competition for most members of both groups, who
fought for jobs and housing in an era of increasing occupational and
residential restrictions for people of color. Within New York, newly arrived as well as established African-Americans and Puerto Ricans and
other "West Indians" jostled each other for the few jobs that would
accept them and apartments in the few neighborhoods not off-limits
to them.

The day-to-day tensions between African-Americans and Puerto Ricans were undoubtedly exacerbated by the struggles of nonwhite *boricuas* to come to terms with the monolithic "Negro" identity imposed

upon them from the outside by a racist North American society. In case they forgot, the signs on many New York City apartment buildings that read "No Dogs, No Negroes, and No Spanish" reminded Puerto Ricans and other Latinos that many whites put them in the same inferior category as they did black Americans.[47]

While Puerto Ricans had the experience of being perceived by whites as black or as ethnic undesirables akin to African-Americans, they often maintained an internal cultural sense that was both positive and defensive. Contemporary accounts suggest that Puerto Ricans of color resisted identification with the African-American community, an attitude that did not endear them to these neighbors and coworkers. Their first- or secondhand view of the treatment of black Americans usually made them less than anxious to accept the crossover thrust upon them and could have a strong effect upon their actions.[48] In the experience of a contemporary sociologist, "the darker the person from the West Indies is, the more intense is his desire to speak only Spanish, and to do so in a louder voice." He found that Puerto Ricans tried to avoid moving into houses whose inhabitants were all African-Americans and would not send their children to summer camps sponsored by social agencies if it meant that they would attend with Negro children. This same commentator observed that Puerto Ricans were much more prone to settle in pockets with their lighter *compatriotas* than to accept external definitions of themselves and move into the black American sections of Harlem. Nevertheless, racial schisms and tensions developed among Puerto Ricans in New York, partly as a result of prior island attitudes but largely because of the enduring strength of the biracial North American classification scheme.

Some Puerto Ricans, fearful of the stigma of an African heritage, went so far as to deny their nationality.[49] Within such an atmosphere of mutual distrust, how Puerto Ricans identified themselves and even where they lived could be important, if not linked, issues. Bernardo Vega remembers that when black Puerto Rican bibliophile and collector Arturo Schomburg moved from a Puerto Rican community to an African-American neighborhood in Manhattan, he was criticized by some *boricuas* for "trying to deny his distant homeland." Vega defended Schomburg's move, affirming that "he always had a deep love for Puerto Rico. But his interest in the history of the Negro, their African origins and contributions to American society, led him to identify closely with black people in the United States."[50]

Unfortunately, the geographically and culturally divided nature of

Schomburg's adopted society forced the issue of ethnic loyalty and identification in racial terms. Such extremes were also apparent in a rigidly
segregated music industry that separated American black musicians
from their white peers. African-American musicians might be discrimi-
nated against, but they could at least maintain a subcultural integrity
and creative ferment among themselves. For Puerto Ricans, who
spanned both American race categories, it meant complex intra-ethnic
divisions and confusing choices.

Puerto Rican artists' struggle to earn a living in New York almost
inevitably involved some measure of crossover to the North American
mainstream popular music scene. But that scene presented very different
choices to musicians of darker and lighter complexions. The bluntly bipolar racial situation, manifested so strongly in music as well as in daily
life, did a great deal to bifurcate the career paths of Puerto Rican musicians. Unlike the relatively isolated North American black and white
musicians, a spectrum of Puerto Ricans might know each other intimately through Puerto Rican and New York community ties, shared
professional experience on the island or mainland, or *compadrazgo*
(godparenthood) or even family connections. One extreme example,
given by Mario Bauzá, was of Rafael Duchesne, a relative of the World
War I Hellfighters clarinetist of the same name, and his brother Miguel:

> There were two [Duchesnes], Miguel and Raf.... When the Radio City
> opened, Miguel was in the pit orchestra with the Figueroa brothers [members
> of another famous Puerto Rican family of primarily classical musicians], and
> Raf Duchesne was a jazz player with the Noble Sissle orchestra. You know
> what happened with the two brothers? They had nothing in common. The
> one at Radio City used to cut his hair with a machine so they didn't see it,
> and tried to pass for something like half Jew. The other one had better hair,
> but [was] a little darker.[51]

The emotional costs of passing versus not passing must have been
especially great within families such as the Duchesnes, who had such a
longstanding and proud tradition of music making on the island. We
can only speculate about the heavy costs dark Puerto Rican musicians
faced in adjusting to the identity of the African-American in the years
following World War I.

Bauzá's own history gives us some idea of one black Latino's volun-
tary construction of an African-American musical and social identity
and the tensions among New York's Latinos that it both reflected and
caused. Raised by white godparents in Cuba, Mario Bauzá was forced
early on to confront issues of racial identity in a country that he claims

was more racist than the United States. And yet musically speaking, this child prodigy had training and experience paralleling that of many Puerto Rican musicians of the same era. Schooled by private teachers and in public bands, while still a boy Bauzá was playing operas, ballets, zarzuelas, and other classical works in the Havana Symphonic Orchestra. Nevertheless, Bauzá's first glimpse of Harlem in 1929, while he was recording in Victor's New York office studios with a Cuban group, fascinated him: "Here a big black race, they had everything, they had shows, they had good orchestras, good artists." Upon his return to Cuba, when his *padrino* (godfather) inquired about his future plans, he replied, "I only got one plan. I want to be with the people like me, [to] know what it is to be a black man in a black country. My roots have got to be there." Despite linguistic and cultural differences, not to mention the potentially greater prestige of playing in a symphonic orchestra in his native country, Bauzá chose to throw in his lot with African-Americans playing popular music. He spent the next ten years with the orchestras of Noble Sissle, Don Redman, Cab Calloway, Chick Webb, and others. Feeling betrayed by the racism of lighter-skinned Latinos, he lived in a black section of Harlem. According to Bauzá, this horrified many Latino acquaintances, who, if they could not live downtown, were going to maintain themselves as a group apart from the unenviable North American black population: "All these Puerto Rican families wanted me to move to their house. I was a single man. 'Mario, why don't you live with us?' 'No, no, I'm working with these people and you know, I want to be with them. . . . I'm making my living with them.' 'Well, all right, but you know these black people . . .' 'But I'm black too. What are you talking about?'"[52]

Not every case was as dramatic as the Duchesnes' or Bauzá's, but it was clear that white or light-skinned Latinos with talent and ambition found success, if they were lucky, in ways that were not open to even the finest Afro-Latin musicians. Such divergent career models for people so intimately connected must have caused great community tensions. Within the jazz world, for example, Louis "King" García, a trumpeter who moved to the United States in the early 1920s after working in the San Juan Municipal Band, was cited by Bauzá as "looking like a German."[53] A good player, his complexion gave him access to the Dorsey Brothers' and Benny Goodman's bands. Miguel Angel Duchesne, a cousin of the brothers cited above, spent years as orchestra leader Paul Whiteman's "hot Spanish trumpet."[54]

Since the segregation was to a certain extent one-way, however, light-skinned musicians might have multiracial career options. Juan Tizol, who was white, spent years shuttling between the orchestras of Duke Ellington and Harry James. Moncho Usera played with Xavier Cugat and arranged for him and a number of white bands as well as for Noble Sissle and black Latin ensembles.

LATIN BANDS

With the onset of the Depression and the scarcity of jobs, white swing bands crowded most black ensembles out of the musical scene. The band business during these years became increasingly expensive, elaborate, and centralized, and blacks were often shut out of the national tour circuits and network radio, which had become necessary for an ensemble's commercial success. Not surprisingly, the racism affecting the development of the North American popular bands in which Puerto Ricans played also had its effects on the Latin music scene coming into prominence in the late 1920s and 1930s. The difficulties experienced by most African-American bands undoubtedly led to severe unemployment and underemployment for the Latino members. It is likely that the circumstances pushed many Puerto Rican and Latino musicians who had dreamed for years of creating Latin orchestras to strike out on their own.

But when Puerto Rican and other Latinos decided for commercial or personal reasons to "go back" to Latin music, the choices for darker- and lighter-skinned musicians were again geographically and racially separated. The downtown Latin "relief" bands, which alternated with featured orchestras in elegant hotels and clubs, were usually made up of whites only. While the rules may have been made by the ballrooms and hotels, the bandleaders rarely challenged them. Mario Bauzá remembers a number of them: "Well, there was a few big bands. Enrique Madriguera was one, Eddie LeBaron, the band in the Martinique, there was a band in the Stork Club, there was in the Morocco, all the swanky places."[55] Puerto Rican Juanito Sanabria was playing at the Havana-Madrid, and Cuban Anselmo Sacassas at La Conga. Although Xavier Cugat employed a number of Puerto Ricans in his stint at the Waldorf Astoria, he never hired those with dark skins. Singer Bobby Capó remembered that even in the 1940s, when restrictions were looser, Cugat regretfully refused his services saying, "What a pity you are so dark," because he feared a violent response in his southern tours to Capó's slightly more than olive hue. Capó also recalled that Aguadillan pianist and bandleader Noro Morales, who spent years playing at the Stork Club, had a similar policy.[56]

As in their jazz band careers, interpersonal connections among the artists made such situations ironic as well as unfair. Rafael and Victoria Hernández's family had *compadrazgo* ties with the Morales family. But whereas Noro and his brother Ismael, who played flute with Cugat's orchestra, had successful downtown careers performing for North American audiences, Rafael had played with the great but mostly unrecognized and unrewarded Luckey Roberts. Pedro Ortíz Dávila, known as "Davilita," became an important vocalist with uptown Latin bands and small groups, but unlike his compatriot and fellow singer Johnny Rodríguez, he never made it to the wealthy white cabaret audiences.

To a certain extent the irony worked both ways, at least for the really successful musicians. Hernández may have been restricted to uptown live-performance sites in New York, but he became internationally famous partly as a result of racism. Seeking countries where he could be a respected orchestra leader, composer, and radio personality, Hernández and his compositions traveled to Cuba, Mexico, and finally back to Puerto Rico. Conversely, the light-complexioned Latin relief bands that were fixtures in downtown ballrooms during the 1930s had a high social status in a society that equated white skin and plush surroundings with success. At the same time, their very categorization as relief bands was a ruse that allowed club owners to pay them less than union wages for work under grueling conditions. Bauzá, however, who willingly lived and worked among African-Americans, got his most lucrative jobs in their musical circles. "In Harlem I was a big shot. I was one of the best-dressed musicians in Harlem. They [the other Latino musicians] were making thirty, forty dollars a week and I was making four, five hundred recording. All the black musicians, they look for me for jobs."[57] Bauzá was making much more money in the African-American ensembles than his ostensibly higher-status compatriots were making in the relief bands. He also claims that the musicianship in his groups was far superior. According to Bauzá, light-skinned Latin relief bandleaders' pandering to the racism of white club owners not only hurt them musically but socially and economically divided the Latino artistic community. Much of the tension between Afro-Latin artists and members of this light-skinned relief band workforce came out in a meeting that turned into a confrontation between Bauzá and such musicians in the late 1930s:

> One day, I just arrived from the road with Chick Webb [paraphrases from letter he received]: "Dear Brother Mario Bauzá, we want to get together such and such a day in the Toreador Night Club because we feel discriminated

[against] here because the Latin bands is being classified as a relief band."
Naturally they're relief band because they go there and play [sings] "Oyeme
Cachita, ticky ticky ticky" and the other band was a white band play show
and everything else. So they didn't want that title no more. They grow up
already. So I went to the reunion. I wonder what the "brothers" got to say.[58]

Bauzá, who was the only black person in the gathering, felt that he
was being used because of his prestige and connections gathered from
his experience with famous African-American bands. He quickly got up
and made a few criticisms, which he claims ended the whole meeting:

> I'm working American bands, I don't work with them. They don't use nobody
> like me in those nightclubs, Rainbow Room, Morocco. And I say, the reason
> why you people been classified like that [is] the musical standard you people
> don't have. You people know where I am. But all the people in New York
> that look like me, they don't have no chance because you don't use them,
> so how the hell you going to call me to go and demand something to the
> local 802?[59]

Accommodating the racism of the society they found themselves in,
the bandleaders had failed to organize themselves along cultural lines.
The net result, according to Bauzá, was a weakening of both their musical and their economic bargaining positions. Among Latino musicians
in New York there was no equivalent to Jim Europe's Clef Club to bind
them together as an entity or to provide an alternative to racist or inadequate performers' institutions such as the American Federation of Musicians' local.

In the meantime, musicians such as Bauzá and legions of other dark-
skinned Latinos were channeling their apparent liability toward the formation of an exciting uptown Latin music scene. This scene was largely
made up of veterans of the African-American popular orchestras. To a
certain extent these artists were going back to their musical roots, thus
belying the stereotyped picture of ethnics on a slow and steady road
toward assimilation into "American" culture. At the same time, they
were following a particular musical path shaped by their racial circumstances. Moreover, the whole concept of going back was tempered by
the inevitable influence of their years in one particular kind of North
American ensemble. These musicians returned to El Barrio to play Latin
music before Hispanic audiences; the music itself was greatly influenced
by African-American jazz. A look at the career of Augusto Coen, the
first Puerto Rican to head a prominent uptown Latin orchestra, shows
one black artist's journey through several musical worlds.

AUGUSTO COEN: A PROFILE

Augusto Coen (1895–1970) was born in Ponce, the child of a Jewish father from the mainland United States and an Afro–Puerto Rican mother. High-school educated, Coen was a passionate baseball player whose pitching skills made him famous throughout Puerto Rico. At the same time, he was adept at guitar, trumpet, and other band instruments, having received music lessons from an early age from Domingo Cruz, or "Cocolia," the well-known leader of the Ponce Municipal Band. Coen played the trumpet in both the Ponce High School band and the Municipal Band. Although Coen was a lieutenant in the United States Army during World War I, it is not clear whether he served overseas or in one of the black regimental bands. He did, however, move to New York, according to his stepson Ray, in the immediate postwar era, "when all the Puerto Ricans ran there [corrían pa'llá]." [60] Coen studied and worked in the post office and began to find jobs in music. A Puerto Rican newspaper article looked back on this triumphant native son as follows: "Coen arrives in New York with the intention of studying law at Columbia University; he meets some friends who let him know of the scarcity of musicians and how much money the few there are are earning; Augusto forgets the University, leaves pencils and paper to the side and taking up his cornet, begins to walk down the path of triumph in a foreign land." [61]

His stepson remarks that in this period, the early 1920s, Latin music barely existed in New York, and so Coen found work with African-American popular orchestras. Coen's first job was in Harlem's Audubon Ballroom. Soon he was a pit musician in African-American shows, including some of the *Blackbirds* productions and *Rhapsody in Black,* working with leaders such as Duke Ellington, Noble Sissle, and Fletcher Henderson. Ray Coen tells us: "My father did that work, and he left his job in the post office and began to work exclusively in music. And he was playing with a lot of orchestras, with Duke Ellington, when they needed a first trumpet to play in those Broadway shows, with Eubie Blake. So he performed with what were called pit musicians." [62] Coen apparently never recorded with these outfits, and thus his impact on them would be invisible were it not for family oral histories and newspaper interviews with Coen himself.

Traveling with these black bands and shows in the 1920s, Coen began to compose his own songs in Spanish, later recording them when he formed his own group. His vision of heading his own Latin orchestra dates from at least that period, according to Ray Coen and Petra Coen, his widow. Another intermediary musical experience brought him one step closer to this goal.

By the early 1930s Coen had entered the orchestra of Afro-Cuban flutist Alberto Socarrás. Like Coen, Socarrás had played with black revues, and he had already begun an extensive recording career with Clarence Williams, Benny Carter, and other African-American bandleaders. At the same time, Socarrás led his own uptown Latin orchestra, which for years was the house ensemble at the Campoamor Theater, one of the few entertainment sites for Harlem Spanish speakers. Socarrás and his orchestra broadcast live from the Campoamor. They also performed at neighborhood clubs and at special community events. According to Ray Coen, "Socarrás was a classically trained musician, a first-class flutist and arranger and conductor. But [Coen] didn't see eye to eye too much with Socarrás. He had his own ideas, his own compositions." [63] In taking steps to fulfill his goal of organizing his own group, Coen had learned a great deal from his days as an African-American band musician. As with Socarrás and later with Bauzá, who was instrumental in the formation of Machito's Afro-Cubans in 1940, playing with the "Americans" became a means "back" to the desired goal of setting up a Latin band. In effect the American bands, rather than being a seductive course of no return, provided a sort of apprenticeship; it gave Coen and others who were developing as leaders and performers musical and organizational ideas, financial resources, and invaluable contacts. Moreover, the successive stages of this "reverse journey" make it all the more intriguing, moving, as it did, from African-American to Cuban to Puerto Rican, and taking elements from each heritage and each leader's way of working. There was room for genuine creative fusion between the musical forms Coen had been exposed to. Coen, as well trained as many of his compatriots, was what his son called a "complete musician"; that is, he was capable of composing, conducting, playing, and creating his own arrangements. He chose to do the first three, selecting for arrangers *compatriotas* such as "Pin" Madera and Moncho Usera. These men and several other musicians in his group, Augusto Coen y Sus Boricuas, had also spent years mediating between African-American and Latino popular music, commercial demands and personal visions. The inclusion of so many veterans of this experience suggests that there were many musicians looking for a Latin nucleus to organize themselves around and helps us to understand why jazz would be an ongoing and tremendous influence in their groups.

Coen, Usera, and others continued to work as arrangers and songwriters for North American ensembles, especially when the Latin craze reached its peak among whites in the 1940s, while remaining involved in their own uptown projects. Coen's stepson and others represent him as a man who had musical integrity but did not eschew commercialism. When Ray Coen was asked whether his stepfather would have refused to play for the non-Latino audiences at the Waldorf Astoria if such opportunities had not been off-limits to him, his reply was emphatic: "No no no no no. My father was strictly commercial. If he would have had the opportunity, because he had been there before [i.e., downtown, when he played Broadway shows]. His experience had led him to believe that all he had to do was just play good music."[64]

We must take into account the entire context of Coen's and his personnel's careers and attitudes toward music making when we look at the formation of his uptown Latin band. Contrary to some historians' accounts, Coen, Socarrás, and others were not creating a principled, purist, uptown sound but were working within the circumstances in which they found themselves and drawing upon a host of influences. Thus, when Coen formed Augusto Coen y Sus Boricuas in about 1934, he was among the first to apply the Big Band concept to Latin music, as Ray notes:

> The Big Band formula is pure American. The municipal bands [of Puerto Rico] were bands, different from the orchestras. . . . Bands in the classical sense, with clarinets, no strings. Because that type of orchestra with saxophones and trumpets was an American invention. That didn't exist here [Puerto Rico], nor in Cuba. Fletcher Henderson was the father of that combination—of saxophones, and trumpets and trombones with the rhythm section; drums, bass, and piano, and arrangements made for that combination.[65]

Much like Socarrás, Coen fronted a small orchestra that typically consisted of two or more each of trumpets and saxophones, piano, string bass, trap drums, maracas, and at times flute and violin. Conversely, although a variety of Latin American, particularly Cuban, genres were featured by the orchestra, Latin percussion was downplayed. This is ironic in the face of scholars' claims that downtown leaders were playing "commercially watered-down Latin tunes to please anglo ears."[66] In fact, North American crowd-pleasers such as Xavier Cugat and don Azpiazú used more Latin American instruments than leaders such as Coen and Socarrás. The latter, on the other hand, played Latin tunes with the sounds of a smooth, refined, highly arranged orchestra, which closely resembled the style of Duke Ellington or Cab Calloway.

In many respects, Coen's uptown Latin career paralleled that of Socarrás. Coen's orchestra was indispensable as accompaniment to shows in the burgeoning uptown Latin variety theaters and for dances at community clubs and large ballrooms such as the Park Palace. Up until at least the World War II period Coen recorded with Columbia, Victor, and Decca and was much in demand as an arranger who could impart Latin flavor to American pop tunes. Like Socarrás, he spent years dividing his time between jazz and Latin orchestras, as well as creating fusions between the two.

The repertoires of both bandleaders had differences as well as similarities that reflected their common training and their different national loyalties. Like Socarrás, Coen played specifically Afro-Cuban works. In addition to doing the standard *boleros, guarachas,* and *sones,* however, Coen incorporated Puerto Rican genres such as the *danza* and the *plena.* In both spheres, the influence of African-American orchestras is apparent. In his *danzas,* for example, Coen used a saxophone as part of the rhythm section in place of the more traditional, tuba-like *bombardino.* Coen's *plena* "El Ratón" (The Mouse), recorded in 1938, combines Afro–Puerto Rican rhythms and *panderetas*[67] with a full jazz orchestration and a bluesy trumpet and singing style reminiscent of songs such as Calloway's "Minnie the Moocher."[68] Another work, the "Plena de Sociedad" (Society *Plena*), also contains this hybrid instrumentation. Its words, however, express particular pride in Puerto Rican and Cuban genres and instruments, citing them as a way to cross ethnic barriers. The lyrics proudly state that the narrators will be able to get the Germans and the Japanese to dance and play *son* and *plena* and presumably forget their differences with the Allies. Recorded during the rumblings of World War II, the song had the ebullient faith in the power of music found in bands such as Jim Europe's during World War I.

"Ño Colá," recorded in 1938 and listed by the Victor Company as an "Afro Cubano," has the "folkloric" self-consciousness of the Ellington who explained that "during one period at the Cotton Club, much attention was paid to acts with an African setting, and to accompany these we developed what was termed 'jungle style' jazz."[69] It is likely that Coen had Ellington's "jungle" experiments in mind when he developed his occasional Afro-Cuban novelties, just as the *afro cubano* style he used was probably influenced by the self-conscious *afrocubanismo* movement pervading the arts in 1930s Cuba.[70] The song was played in a rhythm scheme popular among Latino dancers of the era, employing a *bolero* at the beginning of the song and a fast *son* at the end. It used heavy drumbeats with an exaggerated accent at the end of the measure.

The singer and melodic instruments performed within a pentatonic (five-note) scale, a code commonly used to denote stereotyped "exotic" music to Western ears.

It is clear that despite the basically similar eclectic origins of groups like Coen's and Socarrás's or their affinities with African-American styles, the national backgrounds of these bandleaders had an importance for audiences that went beyond the content of the music. Barrio promoters, ever careful to package shows attuned to the ethnic pride of the various Latino groups in New York City, exploited these music-transcending loyalties. Max Salazar gives an example:

> During the last half of the 1934 [sic], Hispanic New Yorkers were treated nightly to live Afro-Cuban music of flutist-bandleader Alberto Socarrás over radio station WMCA from "el Kubanacan" night club located on the corner of 114th Street and Lenox Avenue. The following year Fernando Luis, a dance promoter, used a gimmick which made him a bundle of money and strained the relationship between Cubans and Puerto Ricans. He convinced Cuban bandleader Alberto Socarrás and Puerto Rican bandleader Augusto Coen to play a dance which would be promoted as a musical war between two Caribbean countries. The following day each time the movie ended at a local theater, messages flashed against the screen in bold black letters against a white screen read: FLASH! FLASH! FLASH! then WAR! WAR! WAR! ... BE-TWEEN CUBA AND PUERTO RICO ... AT THE PARK PALACE LOCATED AT 110th STREET AND 5th AVENUE ... BETWEEN ALBERTO SOCARRAS OF CUBA AND AUGUSTO COEN OF PUERTO RICO. The dance was a monetary success and paved the way from musical battles between Cuban and Puerto Rican musicians. Ethnic pride urged dancers to support their countrymen. The enthusiasm resulted in the first fights, and the gimmick was abandoned.[71]

Audience response made it clear that musicians were not just providers of entertainment but also important symbols of national culture. Yet the music of Coen, like that of his Cuban counterpart Socarrás, was shaped by the simultaneously commercial and creative, restricted and ranging circumstances within which an adopted African-American found himself in the entertainment world. At the same time, such music was also formed by the complexities of a "return" journey, with many steps and influences along the way. Coen's career and his music were the product of a number of ascribed identities that took on lives of their own. He was viewed by the white North American world as an African-American and by his own *compatriotas* as a Puerto Rican playing in El Barrio who was, by extension, playing Puerto Rican music.

CHAPTER THREE

Pipe Wrenches and Valve Trombones

Puerto Rican Worker-Musicians

In the 1920s and 1930s, *tríos, cuartetos,* and *orquestas* were a growing part of New York's cultural landscape. While North American jazz and Argentine *tango* captivated the popular imagination in Puerto Rico, New York became the virtual headquarters for an evolving Caribbean sound largely produced by Puerto Rican migrants.

The municipal bands and popular orchestras of Puerto Rico were the incubators of many of these New York performers of the 1920s and 1930s. There was a new type of musician on the rise as well. Aided by the very mechanisms of the growing commercial music industry, non-reading, untrained composers, singers, and instrumentalists became increasingly prominent in the "Latin" music scene in New York as well as back on the island.

The diverse backgrounds and aspirations that had shaped musicians' experiences in Puerto Rico helped determine their goals for the mainland. Within a framework of particular historical possibilities and imperatives, Puerto Rican musicians had personal and sometimes non-musical reasons for coming to New York. There were different paths leading to musical careers, and not even the road of the old-fashioned reading musician was straight and narrow. Paquito López Cruz, for example, who had had musical training and performing experience by the time he left Puerto Rico in 1927, came to the United States primarily to study. But he needed to earn a living because "the economic situation in Puerto Rico was disastrous. There, in the United States, it was the era of the Depression. And when there's a depression there, here there's a depression and a half! I didn't go to the United States with a musical profession in mind. I went to continue studying and to get a bachelor's in education."[1] López Cruz got his degree, but he found himself involved in a full-time musical career. Twelve years later Bobby Capó came to the United States with the idea of studying law but lacked the money to follow through with his plans. It was comparatively much easier for him to get work as a vocalist and pursue a career in music.

Still others came to New York precisely because they had heard it was a hotbed of "Latin" music both for North American audiences and for displaced Latinos from a spectrum of countries. The Puerto Ricans who returned to their island from playing and fighting in World War I undoubtedly brought back tales of musical activity, as did those who migrated in the postwar years. A Puerto Rican had to go only as far as the local cinema, however, particularly after the advent of sound, to absorb tantalizing images of a rollicking musical world centered in a mythologized Broadway.

The words of the anonymous man who had learned trumpet in a Santurce orphanage reveal both the sacrifices performers had to make in Puerto Rico in order to pursue a musical career and the way coming to New York became a desired goal:

> My relatives were poor people. I couldn't even start playing in an orchestra because I didn't have an instrument. Decided to take a messenger's job at the West Indian Gasoline Co. for $3.50 a week. Saving my pennies little by little at the end of six months I could afford to buy a trumpet. Soon after I found a job with a group of young musicians and started what is known today as the Borinquen Serenaders. Two years after this happened I was leading the orchestra and also composing popular music. At this time my income was about $20 per week and I had saved enough money to come to New York, where the melodies of the tropical music had started to be a real hit.[2]

Arriving in New York City in 1930, when movies and music with a Latin American flavor had begun to entice the Yankees, the trumpeter had no problems getting a job, as he told a Works Progress Administration (WPA) interviewer at the end of the decade: "At this time, as in the present, there was a constant demand for what natives call here 'Cuban musicians' and it wasn't difficult for me to find a job in an orchestra playing in one of the Spanish Harlem cabarets."[3]

In many ways these cases were exceptional. For most Puerto Rican musicians it was not so easy to make a living in music in New York. In their migration to that city musicians were pushed and pulled to a new but at the same time familiar world. In New York, as back on the island, they found themselves juggling an assortment of musical and non-musical jobs and synthesizing and performing many types of songs. Now, however, musicians faced other problems in addition to their struggle to earn a living and audiences' attempts to articulate class and racial affiliations through music. Cast into a multi-Latino and generally multiethnic environment, Puerto Ricans had to contend with a range of new cultural, social, political, and economic contexts. In their work, home, and recreational lives Puerto Ricans combined, splintered, and measured themselves against each other and other ethnic groups to formulate overlapping and ever-evolving identities.

TRIOS, CUARTETOS, AND THE GOLDEN AGE

Whether they were displaced from municipal bands or cinema orchestras on the island, catapulted to the mainland through their participation in World War I, or simply among the thousands upon thousands of compatriots who came looking for work, many Puerto Rican performers sought their fortune in a powerful music industry. New York City was the world's center for recording, sheet music, piano rolls, and radio. It represented the possibility of performing for North American, African-American, and other ethnic American audiences. The increasing numbers of homesick *compatriotas* in Manhattan and Brooklyn also boded well for migrating musicians. As New York gradually became the economic capital of Puerto Rico, it became the hub of Puerto Rican cultural production as well. *Boricuas* came to the Iron Babel hoping to make records or to play club dates, much as they would go to seek work in the city's factories, hotels, and restaurants. The difference was that their work in the music industry had far-reaching symbolic effects as well as immediate material benefits. In the interplay between these material and symbolic spheres, pan-Latino and Puerto Rican music was created for diverse New York audiences.

In New York City during the Depression, Puerto Rican musicians filled out the "Cuban" ensembles that were becoming the rage among a middle-and upper-class white populace. Indeed, in the era of Prohibition many North Americans of the upper classes had become acquainted with Havana, "the Paris of the Caribbean," where the liquor still flowed freely and music exotic to their ears could be found in most tourist spots. It is not surprising that members of such audiences, many of whom had frequented African-American Harlem during the 1920s, would spend the following decade looking for fresh excitement, a new "primitive" thrill, or that they would find it in Latino music. What *is* astonishing is that it was also in this period—in New York City—that music played by small ensembles, composed by and for Puerto Ricans, entered a golden age. The sojourn of many Puerto Rican musicians in New York between the world wars actually produced many of the enduring classics that are still enjoyed by *boricuas* on both sides of the ocean.

Throughout the 1920s and 1930s a constellation of Puerto Rican *tríos* and *cuartetos* formed and re-formed in New York City. Rafael Hernández, the child from Aguadilla who had resisted becoming a musician, the man who fought in World War I and played in its most famous African-American regimental band, was the universally acknowledged leader of this trend. Back from several years of conducting a cinema orchestra in Cuba, leading his own ensemble in New York's Palace theater, and touring with black stride pianist Lucky Roberts, Hernández decided to form his own *trío*.

Hernández founded Trío Borinquen in New York City in 1926 and Cuarteto Victoria six years later. Both the *trío* and the *cuarteto* were showcases for the music of their prolific leader. Hernández, a well-trained musician who would later graduate from a musical conservatory in Mexico, created songs with complexly weaving vocal patterns, minor-to-major shifts, and highly poetic sentiments. Like most of his contemporaries in these all-male groups, he wrote numbers praising women or complaining about their betrayal. Hernández also composed many patriotic or praise songs to Puerto Rico and still others more explicitly protesting the island's poor economic condition and colonial status. Hernández was like "a magician pulling pigeons out of a hat," often producing several songs a day.[4] Some people even claim that he composed more than two thousand songs before he died at the age of seventy-two.

Rafael Hernández possessed an infectious energy, an unpretentiousness, and a mischievous sense of humor that endeared him to many. As a bandleader, however, he was a perfectionist who demanded a great deal from his musicians, as his recorded songs, with their meticulous arrangements, confirm. "If they didn't read music, he didn't use them," remembered his sister, Victoria Hernández. Rafael's philosophy of music making did not allow for improvisation, an attitude probably reinforced by his role in African-American bands fighting the stereotypes of blacks as spontaneous musicians. Victoria remembers one time when her brother was rehearsing with some pickup musicians for a performance and the pianist began to embellish upon some of Hernández's sheet music. "Either you clean up that passage or you leave," Hernández told his musician.[5]

Most Puerto Rican *tríos* and *cuartetos* followed the stylistic lead set by Trío Borinquen and by the highly influential Cuban Trío Matamoros, which had formed one year prior to Hernández's group. Typically, these ensembles were vehicles for the music of their leaders and featured a tenor first voice with a bass or baritone doing harmonies. The style of their vocals had more to do with the lyric opera popular in Cuba and Puerto Rico since the previous century than with the gravelly or closed-throat tones associated with the *plena* or *música jíbara*. In live performances most groups stayed with simple instrumentation. In the recording studio, however, piano, brass, flute, bass, and additional percussion were sometimes added to the basic guitars, *güiros*, and *maracas*. The advent of electrical recording and broadcasting during the mid-1920s, however, made it possible for even small groups to produce a big sound. It is surely no coincidence that Cuban and Puerto Rican *tríos* and *cuartetos* became popular precisely at this technological juncture.

Despite the common formula, there were important variations that gave each group its distinctive personality. The new mechanical media that proved so propitious for small ensembles also widely disseminated the music of nonreading popular musicians. Pedro Flores (1894–1979) was one of these. Born in Naguabo, on Puerto Rico's eastern coast, Flores worked on the island as an English teacher. Upon arriving in New York in 1926, Flores was reportedly goaded by the musical accomplishments of Rafael Hernández, with whom he had a lifelong love/hate relationship. In 1928, thirty-four years old and utterly innocent of musical training, he decided to follow the Aguadillan's lead and establish his own small group.[6] "The idea occurred to him to start another musical group that would play more upbeat music *[música movida]* so that people could dance in their get-togethers. Rafael's group was basically for romantic themes."[7] Commercially successful ensemble leaders in the Puerto Rico of Flores's and Hernández's childhood were almost by definition "complete" musicians. Within the increasingly specialized world of popular music, however, the technically limited Flores could depend upon the transcribing and arranging abilities of more skilled *boricuas* such as Moncho Usera. A change of repertoire within this new industrial and commercialized musical setting also helped nonreading musicians. Recording and club musicians had to master dance forms, not the folk, classical, and semiclassical forms on which reading musicians on the island had honed their skills.

Like Hernández, Flores was known for his nostalgic, romantic, and patriotic *boleros*. He was more famous, however, for *sones, guarachas,* and *rumbas* that humorously depicted ordinary people in everyday situations. One music historian has even suggested that Flores's down-to-earth songs made him a favorite of the working classes, whereas Hernández's lyrical and composing ability gave his numbers a more universal appeal.[8] Even Flores's *boleros* did not have the sophisticated harmonic structure, vocal style, and meticulously planned arrangements characteristic of Hernández's work. In fact, many of Flores's records exhibit the strong influence of not only percussion-heavy Cuban popular instrumentation but also Cuban-style improvisational riffs.

Groups such as Hernández's and Flores's served as incubators of talent, not only producing music but also spawning new ensembles, which often took their own direction. Performing for a relatively small population and working within a recording and club industry that saw its ethnic wing as a marginal sideline, these groups competed against each other and looked for new ways to please audiences. Group leaders might be not only untrained but relatively unmusical, basing their success on their ability to sell record companies and audiences a novel approach to small ensemble music. Thus, more folkloric or more exotic approaches were linked to the necessities of a commercial market, and the small ensemble style lent itself to enterprising businesspeople as well as to great composers in the making. Manuel "Canario" Jiménez, for example, originally the lead voice of Trío Borinquen, left to form his own group by 1927, featuring a popularized version of the *plena*. Comparing him with Rafael Hernández, the standard against whom everyone was measured, *cuarteto* veteran Paquito López Cruz remembered that "Canario was a group mainly of *plenas* and *guarachas*. Grupo Victoria was more sophisticated, romantic, beautiful songs. You had to be a better musician to be in Cuarteto Victoria than with Canario."[9] Like Pedro Flores, Canario was untrained, but he rarely wrote his own music, preferring to beg, borrow, or steal it from Hernández, Flores, and other composers.

In an era when little copyright protection existed for ethnic compositions, group leaders could freely borrow each other's work in a sometimes friendly, sometimes litigious atmosphere. Pedro "Piquito" Marcano, another singer and group leader who served his apprenticeship in

Flores's group, utilized the music of his mentor and other Puerto Rican composers when he formed his Cuarteto Marcano in 1936. Others who rarely or never performed with organized groups in New York lent their talents to those who did. The itinerant guitarist Alberto "Titi" Amadeo drifted in and out of groups and sporadically formed his own, but he was best known as a composer. He and the musically unlettered Felipe "don Felo" Goyco, who never left Puerto Rico, are emblematic of Puerto Rican musicians whose songs, if not their live musical skills, formed an integral part of the developing New York scene.

Even in New York's Cuban *cuartetos*, Puerto Ricans had a strong presence. Cuarteto Machín and Cuarteto Caney, two 1930s groups led by Cubans, both had Puerto Rican members.[10] Machín's lead trumpeter, Plácido Acevedo (1903–74), like Hernández and many other musicians, was a native of Aguadilla, the town "where even the stones sing."[11] His father, a bandleader, had trained him in *solfeo* and on the flute. After playing trumpet with various Cuban and Puerto Rican ensembles, Acevedo formed one of the most celebrated Puerto Rican small groups, Cuarteto Mayarí, in 1937. An insomniac, solitary wanderer as brimming with music as his *compueblano* Rafael Hernández, Acevedo was an important *bolero* composer and instrumentalist whom López Cruz remembered for "a style solely his own . . . because the unique arpeggio of the guitar and the adornments with which the trumpet embroiders the melodies of his songs lend that flavor so characteristic of that popular *conjunto* [Mayarí]."[12] The leaders and members of these groups composed and performed some of the tunes that are now standard in the repertoire of Puerto Rican popular music. "El Buen Borincano" (The Good Puerto Rican) and "Perfume de Gardenias" by Rafael Hernández, "Mi Adorada Ilusión" (My Adored Illusion) by Titi Amadeo, and "Sin Bandera" (Without a Flag) and "Amor Perdido" (Lost Love) by Pedro Flores were among these treasures. Indeed in New York "the popular Puerto Rican song became more Puerto Rican than it has ever been before or since." Puerto Rico had the dubious honor of being "the only Latin American country whose popular music was created mainly on foreign soil."[13] At the same time, such music was anything but traditional folk songs preserved in an unspoiled community setting.

Historians have described Puerto Rican *tríos* and *cuartetos* as groups that were "strictly local" to El Barrio and produced "traditional Puerto Rican music," but the situation was much more complex.[14] These small ensembles were local in that they were generally headquartered in East Harlem, swapped personnel and songs, and lived with, fought with, and challenged each other. The patriotic words and the quoted musical phrases of many of their compositions strongly identified them as Puerto Ricans. Pedro Flores and Rafael Hernández, for example, had a some-times friendly, sometimes antagonistic musical rivalry in which each tried to outdo the other in composing the best nostalgic or political an-thems to Puerto Rico. On the other hand, the music to which these East Harlem musicians wrote their intensely nationalistic lyrics bore un-mistakable international and popular influences.

In New York informal and usually little-recognized groups playing the *música típica* of the Puerto Rican countryside and its more urban-ized coastal areas did exist, but the music and groups of this "golden age" of Puerto Rican song were somewhat different. While the more traditional groups might limit themselves to handmade instruments and older folk or popular genres, these *tríos* and *cuartetos* became increas-ingly involved with newer forms of dance music, such as the *bolero*, the *rumba*, the *guaracha*, and the *son*, internationalized by way of Cuba, as well as with American, European, or other Latin American dance genres.

Pedro Flores's *cuarteto*, which was often a *sexteto* or even an *or-questa*, frequently used the Cuban *tres*, *bongó*, *marímbula*, and trum-pet, playing *sones* and *guarachas* as well as up-tempo *boleros*.[15] Rafael Hernández's groups also played and recorded Cuban dance genres and forms from various Latin American countries. In fact, Trío Borinquen's output included many Dominican songs. While recording lists may not always closely reflect live-performance repertoires, and while these songs were probably intended for export rather than local consumption, such evidence indicates that these small ensembles had to be well versed in a variety of musical styles.

The recording industry had given many of these artists a fame *that* extended far beyond El Barrio, into the Caribbean and Latin America. Whether or not they were internationally renowned, however, such per-formers usually were not humble "folk" musicians who had never left El Barrio but polished performers who had toured with their ensembles and who had often served their time playing with North American white, black, and Asian ethnic bands or with more "sophisticated" Latin ensembles. Nor were Puerto Ricans the only members of the small groups. Canario's successor in Trío Borinquen was Antonio Mesa, a Dominican, and numerous Cubans integrated the Puerto Rican ensem-bles, just as Puerto Ricans were often found in Cuban groups.

It is true that within a highly commercialized music industry, ethnic

musicians often had to make both their authenticity and their unique-
ness a selling point with club managers and record companies. At the
same time, it is important not to reduce the prolific Puerto Rican music
making of this era to a crass marketing strategy. That Puerto Rican audiences took these songs to their hearts and made them enduring classics
says a great deal about their own needs and longings, about their personal relationships to the musicians and their output. The production
of Puerto Rican music in New York was inextricably bound up with
boricuas' desire to maintain cultural boundaries where social and political ones were ambiguous. Like North American bluegrass, a music that
became more fiercely rural in its instrumentation and images as its practitioners moved cityward to find jobs, Puerto Rican music came into its
own in the context of the migration experience. While musical eclecticism and social boundaries existed in Puerto Rico, they were different
in New York, where Puerto Ricans were just one of many ethnic groups.
Music that Puerto Rican migrants could identify as their own gave them
an enduring heritage and, like bluegrass, immortalized a way of life back
home that was fast disappearing. These sounds also had a great deal to
do with Puerto Ricans' current lives and struggles.

Music historians often write about performers in snapshot fashion,
solely in terms of their musical accomplishments, and generally ignore
the history of the daily struggles of both famous and little-known artists
to achieve artistic, financial, and other goals.[16] In fact, most musicians
were not rich or famous but laborers both within and outside of music
who generally lived in the same communities as their audiences. It is
only in terms of their whole lives and their relationship to their fellow
migrants that we can understand their musical responses. To a large extent, it was the performers' nonmusical jobs and communities that conditioned their musical production.

LABORERS AND ARTISTS

An anonymous commentator in the 1929 *Directorio hispano,* a guide
to Latino-owned businesses in New York City, noted: "Today this country is full of artists, adventurers and merchants of our nationalities,
while in our lands Yankee oilmen and opportunists abound. It's a practical interchange . . . [but they] have the advantage, because they leave for
us the most difficult part, to reach the skies by force of talent or muscle."[17] The divisions between talent and muscle, however, were not necessarily so clear-cut. When fledgling artists such as Rafael Hernández,

Pedro Flores, and Pedro Marcano stepped off the boat in New York between the late teens and the late thirties, they may have expected to concentrate on the former, but circumstances often pushed them toward the latter. In general, Puerto Rican musicians not only lived but also worked with nonmusical *compatriotas* and members of other ethnic groups.

During World War I and in the 1920s, Puerto Ricans, drawn to New York by positions formerly occupied by newly arrived European immigrants, "became entrenched in garment manufacturing and light factory work, hotel and restaurant business, cigar-making, domestic service and laundries within a short time."[18] While it was relatively easy to get a job before the Depression, the typical Puerto Rican worker found low wages, poor working conditions, employer and union discrimination, unstable employment, and jobs in which the skills he brought with him were useless or outmoded. During the Depression this situation became more acute, as recent Puerto Rican migrants competed with members of other ethnic groups for scarce unskilled jobs.

Musicians were no exception to this general trend. As in Puerto Rico, they faced discrimination and de-skilling in their "practical" fields and lack of opportunity in their creative one. According to Victoria Hernández, in the period following World War I there were few opportunities for most Puerto Rican musicians. Consequently, after their triumphant postwar tour as part of James Reese Europe's orchestra, Rafael and his companions found themselves working in a factory. "In that era," she explains, "Latin music wasn't well known here. So [Rafael] had to go work in a bedspring factory—he and my brother [Jesús "Pocholo" Hernández] and all the musicians who came here from France. But since he didn't have experience in that, [his thumb] got caught in the machine."[19] Hernández's unfortunate experience cost him part of a thumb. Such accidents are evidence of not only the dangerous conditions under which Puerto Rican laborers often worked but how such conditions could be directly hazardous to a musician's career. Musicians were laborers like their nonmusical peers, but their supplemental skills made for some basic differences. Musicians had an additional source of livelihood to protect and played an important role in the community as cultural figures. Industrial accidents and other consequences of routine jobs could therefore be especially ominous for them.

Nevertheless, musicians found themselves by necessity in a variety of jobs while they waited for a big musical break, a wait that for most would last a lifetime. Pedro Flores wielded pick and shovel in the construction of the new Eighth Avenue subway line and later supported himself as a housepainter. Flores and most musicians did not drop these pursuits when they began their artistic career—they simply could not afford to—and their nonmusical jobs continued to affect their musical career. Canario's career as a merchant marine, for example, frequently interrupted his performing and recording activities; it was cited by Rafael Hernández as the reason he discontinued using the singer in Trío Borinquen.[20]

In the struggle to survive, some musicians were astonishingly eclectic in their pursuits. Titi Amadeo was a jack-of-all-trades. His son remembers, "He used to do almost everything. If you asked him about pipes, he was a plumber; meat, he was a butcher."[21] Instrumentalists and composers also tried to support themselves in music-related fields where possible. Amadeo built classical guitars, Rafael Hernández perforated pianola rolls, and others worked as arrangers for Latin or American bands.

For most, music remained in the category of a welcome supplement to working-class jobs, a secondary occupation more than a primary concern. Clarinetist Catalino Rolón commented, "The musicians worked in factories, or they couldn't live here. They paid ten dollars per week or twelve dollars on a power press. If you gained four, five dollars [in music], you were a king."[22]

Puerto Ricans' residential life in New York City also tempered and influenced their musical creations. From earliest times, Puerto Rican cultural expression took place within the context of daily contact with European- and African-Americans, as well as other Latinos.

PUERTO RICAN SETTLEMENT IN MULTIETHNIC NEW YORK CITY

Although Puerto Ricans had been arriving on the mainland since the mid-nineteenth century, it was not until they were granted U.S. citizenship, in 1917, that people began migrating from the island in substantial numbers. As U.S. citizens, Puerto Ricans were not included in census population counts of the foreign-born; therefore there is some controversy over their numbers, with estimates ranging between 45,000 and 100,000 by 1930.[23]

Members of this post–World War I migration settled in five distinct neighborhoods of Brooklyn and Manhattan, clustered near waterfront, factory, and cigar workshop jobs. Within these areas, Puerto Ricans found themselves living in scattered pockets among a constellation of ethnic groups. The population of these neighborhoods was not only variable but constantly shifting, as were the Puerto Ricans' residential, work, political, and social relationships with their multiethnic associates. Cigar maker Bernard Vega's first impressions of what would later be called Spanish Harlem were of a neighborhood with distinct class and ethnic divisions:

> When I took up residence in New York in 1916 the apartment buildings and stores in what came to be known as El Barrio, "our" barrio, or the Barrio Latino, all belonged to Jews. Seventh, St. Nicholas, and Manhattan Avenues, and the streets in between, were all inhabited by Jewish people of means, if not great wealth. . . . The ghetto of poor Jews extended along Park Avenue between 110th and 117th and on the streets east of Madison. It was in this lower class Jewish neighborhood that some Puerto Rican and Cuban families, up to about fifty of them, were living at that time. Here, too, was where a good many Puerto Rican cigarworkers, bachelors for the most part, occupied the many furnished rooms in the blocks between Madison and Park.[24]

Such class stratifications within ethnic groups, true for Irish, Germans, African-Americans, and Italians as well, meant that working-class ethnics of different backgrounds lived together in pockets with affordable housing, as close as possible to their workplaces. Puerto Ricans carried on daily interethnic negotiations with these people among whom they worked and lived, often within the intimacy of boarding arrangements. Likewise, in the waterfront area of downtown Brooklyn, where the Puerto Rican ranks were somewhat smaller, there were "numerous Italians, and a few Irish . . . Brazilians, Syrians and Egyptians." Even by the late thirties, the Puerto Ricans were "comparatively newcomers, and constitute one of the smaller racial groups."[25]

With competition for housing, jobs, political positions, and business ventures rampant within a continuously evolving community, intergroup conflicts were an inevitable part of the history of Harlem. Catalino Rolón, who came with his family from Puerto Rico in 1926, remembers a complex ethnic geography within a relatively small area:

> The blacks were over in the area of 125th Street. . . . In those times they didn't come below Lenox Avenue. Lenox Avenue was completely Jewish. . . . They had their sections around 125th and Eighth, Sixth and Fifth, and they didn't want blacks around there then. . . . The Italian neighborhood of that time [extended] . . . from 120th and Madison and Fifth till Second and Third Avenue. The Latino neighborhood was from 100th and 102d till 96th. Past 96th they didn't want Hispanics there. Around 90th and Park Avenue it was Jewish. . . . When the Latinos came it happened that once we had a fight, Lat-

inos fighting with Italians because the Italians were then between First and Second Avenue. . . . Between 108th and 100th . . . they were all Italians.[26]

A number of musicians mentioned especially strong turf battles with Italians. "If I crossed Third Avenue by mistake, I barely escaped getting killed," commented Johnny Rodríguez about relations with Italians in Harlem, where he came to live in the mid-1930s.[27]

Within this atmosphere of turnover and turmoil, the different groups tried to separate themselves and mark off distinct boundaries, particularly in the cultural realm. Puerto Ricans found that they could identify with each other on a national basis or make common cause with a variety of other Spanish-speaking groups also living in New York City.

BASES FOR CONTACT BETWEEN
SPANISH SPEAKERS IN NEW YORK

From the late nineteenth century, when the first small groups of Puerto Rican merchants, artisans, and cigar makers settled in New York City, occupational and revolutionary activities brought Cubans, Puerto Ricans, and even some Spaniards and Sephardic Jews together. A large percentage of the thousands of small cigar workshops in the city were owned by Spaniards and other Latinos and employed many Cubans and Puerto Ricans.[28] At the same time, mutual aid, cultural, and political organizations flourished among these workers. In many cases Puerto Ricans and Cubans worked closely together both to defend themselves as workers in New York and to plan for the overthrow of Spanish rule over their respective islands. Additionally, numerous publications, literary societies, and other organizations with greater or lesser degrees of political involvement brought diverse Spanish speakers together, and by the turn of the century boarding houses in which these groups mingled. For years before World War I, New York's Puerto Ricans could identify themselves within political, national, or somewhat more pan-Latin circles.

In the first decades of the twentieth century New York was still host to a growing and diverse Hispanic population, of which Puerto Ricans formed just a small part. Even as late as 1930, the census year in which Puerto Ricans became numerically dominant among Latinos, a New York Welfare Council report based on the census suggested that out of some 100,000 Spanish speakers in the city, only about 40 percent were Puerto Ricans. The count, which included first- and second-generation settlers but possibly omitted people of color, showed 22,509 Spaniards, 18,741 Central and South Americans, 7,893 Cubans, and 3,405 Mexicans.[29] This population was scattered throughout the five boroughs, the largest concentrations living in a few sections of Brooklyn and Manhattan. These groups both mingled and developed their own settlement patterns. In Manhattan, for example, Mexicans, Puerto Ricans, Cubans, and South and Central Americans were overwhelmingly concentrated in Harlem, though not necessarily in the same proportions in the same areas. Large numbers of Spaniards were to be found in Harlem as well, though their greatest concentrations were in areas of lower Manhattan.

As with the non-Spanish Europeans and African-Americans with whom Puerto Ricans also shared work environments, communities, and sometimes houses, the numbers and configurations of these populations were constantly shifting, and therefore their relationships to one another were changing as well. In the early part of the century, for example, most of New York's Spanish-speaking population were Spaniards. In 1910 there were about 3,759 Spanish-born residents in New York City, compared with about 500 Puerto Ricans.[30] The Federal Writers' Project reported that about 15,000 Spaniards came to New York between 1914 and 1919, settling mainly in the South Ferry, Chelsea, and Greenwich Village areas. Many settled in New Jersey as well. Mostly working-class, these immigrants were seamen, dock workers, and laborers in heavy industry, many of whom were attracted by a boom in shipping during and immediately after World War I.[31]

While these were not the first neighborhoods in New York to have Spanish-speaking residents, they frequently became the hubs of future multi-Hispanic settlement, as businesses, boarding houses, and social and cultural institutions geared to Spanish speakers developed in them. Thus, neighborhood development among Spanish speakers was a dynamic process without a fixed geographical center. The East Harlem Barrio was by no means the first or only center of cultural activity, but rather one of many, which might be separate from where many of their patrons actually lived. This diversity would influence Puerto Rican musicians and audiences alike.

The already far from unadulterated Puerto Rican customs were not preserved in consensus nor in isolation, but with constant reference to both the changing divisions among Puerto Ricans and to the people of varied backgrounds who surrounded them in their residential, work, and cultural lives. Puerto Rican musicians formed their musical groups within this complex new environment. These groups, their compositions, and the settings within which they performed were simultaneously recreational, practical, a celebration of cultural expressions brought from the island, and a defensive affirmation of culturally based national boundaries.

In the days when the Puerto Rican community was still small the celebrations at which musicians played tended to be modest. Bernardo Vega, who came to the Iron Babel on the eve of World War I, recalled a small community of *boricuas* engaging in energetic cultural activities. While in the early days "entertainment for Puerto Ricans in New York was confined to the apartments they lived in," those apartments hosted birthdays and weddings, Christmas and New Year's parties, celebrated with friends and neighbors to the accompaniment of small musical groups.[32] The singer Pedro Ortíz Dávila, better known as Davilita, came to New York City from Bayamón in 1926, when he was fourteen years old. He lived in East Harlem with his mother. "This neighborhood," he remembered, "like anywhere Puerto Ricans lived together, was very happy and fun." In El Barrio of the 1920s, "wherever you looked there were parties to celebrate any little thing." Because it was the time of Prohibition, some migrants clandestinely "distill[ed] rum in stills and ferment[ed] barley, from which they'd get a beer called 'Home Brew.'" In Davilita's experience, "two glasses of that beer were enough to fight with Jack Dempsey or with Gene Tunney, or with both at the same time."[33]

Migrants remember that such festive gatherings with music not only created entertainment but also served practical functions. Apartment parties raised rent for the host family through admission fees and through sales of homemade liquor and Puerto Rican food. Esperanza Delgado, who came to live in El Barrio in 1927, vividly recalls these parties in connection with the particular circumstances of the 1930s:

> Do you know, the people were so needy of money, because we had Depression here. You say to me, "Esperanza, this month I'm going to make a party." They used to charge twenty-five cents to go in, and the moonshine, twenty-five cents for a drink. "King Kong," "Arráncame La Vida," all those names they used to call it because it was terrible to drink. . . .
> The *trío* used to come to the house and play for the drinks and for the dinner. They didn't get paid. So whatever money I get, I get to pay my rent. Those years the rent was fifteen dollars, twenty dollars, twenty-three dollars, fifty dollars, that was a castle. . . .
> I do it this week, you do it next week. [There] was no welfare. Welfare came when Roosevelt.[34]

These frequent apartment parties may have raised rent for the resident families and given audiences a chance to listen to both older and newer musical forms from home, but they were clearly not very lucrative for the musicians themselves. Nevertheless, according to Mike Amadeo, all the Puerto Rican small-ensemble musicians used to make the apartment party rounds: "Most of these people used to do that, not for the money really: they used to get together with their friends and try to show off the music." [35]

As Bernardo Vega reminds us, Puerto Ricans' celebrations did not take place in isolation, but with constant reference to the ethnic groups that lived around them. Not only were such festivities defensive cultural bulwarks but "boisterous Puerto Rican parties would often disturb neighbors of other nationalities, which led to some serious conflicts and unpleasant quarrels." [36] The protective ethnic cocoon portrayed in so many stories of early Puerto Rican settlement was violated by thin walls, cramped apartments with too many people in them, hot summer nights with the windows open, along with the demographic realities of Puerto Ricans of different backgrounds possibly mixing together for the first time in New York, as well as the close presence of people from other cultures who had no appreciation of loud revelry in a language they could not understand.

Sometimes the close living conditions of such poor neighborhoods proved a boon to budding musicians, who quickly got to know one another. The beginning of singer Daniel Santos's (1911?–92) career is a good example. Santos and his parents, who moved to New York when he was ten years old, were so poor that during the Depression he moved into a little room of his own and supported himself by shining shoes, selling ice and coal, and doing whatever other odd jobs came his way. His situation would improve when he joined the Civilian Conservation Corps (CCC). Meanwhile,

> The room in which I lived before the CCC took me was rather uncomfortable, since at that time the bathroom wasn't inside but out in the hall, adjoining the other rooms. This inconvenience helped me to become a professional singer, because one day, while I was bathing, I began to sing the only two songs I knew, and at once my first contract arrived. I remember I was singing a *guaracha* that said, "Sola va, sola va la mariposa llorando," by Rafael Hernández. . . .
>
> I was in the middle of my profoundest inspiration when all of a sudden I heard a knock on the door, and upon opening, I faced one of the members of the Trío Lírico, a musical group that played at dances, baptisms, and other activities of the exiled Latino community. He told me that I sang very well and that when I came out he wanted to talk to me. I finished bathing, and then I got together with him and the other members of the Trío. They listened

to me sing, liked it, and invited me to participate in a party at which they were singing the following Saturday. That's how I became a professional singer.[37]

Usually, the contacts musicians made were more modest and less dramatic. Just as they would with other co-ethnics, Puerto Ricans frequently took their newly arrived and struggling musical *compatriotas* under their wings. Being a musician gave these migrants a special community status, or at least an immediately useful skill. Paquito López Cruz remembered that when he first came to El Barrio in the late 1920s,

> I had a lot of help from friends from my town, Naranjito. I have to say that I found myself with true friends in New York. And that's a lot to say, because New York is a city where when one doesn't have, it's difficult to get. But I never had to go to bed without eating. Maybe because of the music as well, right? But I was overwhelmed with invitations. "Come one day to eat at the house." "When are you coming to the house?" I arrived with my guitar, and I also entertained with it. I haven't forgotten that helping attitude those people from Naranjito had toward me.[38]

López Cruz was initially poor because of his vocational choice, but he surmised that he was also popular because of it. The guitarist became one of the lucky few who earned a living from music, and in turn he helped others in the community through his trade. As a result, he viewed music not only as a creative means of survival for himself but as a way to aid others, even, and especially, during the Depression: "I had luck because of music. On top of that, I helped many who couldn't get jobs. They weren't musicians! Well, they could work in a factory, but there weren't jobs there either. I didn't help one, I helped many. Not only Puerto Ricans, but I helped two from Uruguay also, and a Venezuelan. Why? Because of the music! The music saved me."[39]

Often it was the members of the "neighborhood" *tríos* and *cuartetos* who would take care of younger musicians fresh from Puerto Rico. Having established even a tentative place for their groups within clubs and recording studios, they assisted a second wave of artists, giving them places to live and contacts with other musicians and music industry personnel. *Cuarteto* leader Piquito Marcano is remembered with particular fondness by many younger musicians. When Johnny Rodríguez arrived in New York in the late 1930s to fulfill a contract for RCA Victor, he remembers, "as I was a young boy, I moved to a room in the house of someone who was then a star [in New York], Piquito Marcano. And with Piquito Marcano I got to know Claudio Ferrer [a guitarist, singer, and composer who also worked with *tríos* and *cuartetos*]."[40]

The musicians who were veterans of the New York experience sometimes incorporated these new arrivals into their groups, and they were
able to steer some to other musical jobs. For those who wanted to earn
even a few dollars in music, it was necessary to get beyond rent parties
and family celebrations and explore other options within and beyond
the neighborhood. One source of sporadic income for many musicians
was the ethnic club.

The ongoing arrival of Puerto Ricans and other Spanish speakers to
New York had spawned a variety of recreational, cultural, and political
associations. Puerto Rican clubs and entertainment developed simultaneously with ethnic clubs among Spanish speakers from Europe, the Caribbean, and Central and South America. Within these centers, Latinos
asserted separate or overlapping cultural identities according to the circumstances. Clubs and activities, like ethnic identity in general, might
be formed by Spanish speakers against a non-Hispanic world, by members of particular regional, racial, political, class, or special-interest
groups. Music and other cultural entertainment within these settings
followed their own eclectic paths.

The Spanish organizations that had flourished in lower Manhattan
since the late nineteenth century, for example, continued to proliferate
until the postwar period. These associations often followed distinct patterns of regionally based Spanish settlement and displayed varying degrees of receptivity toward people from other parts of Spain and from
Latin America. These organizations were thus simultaneously emblems
of community cohesion and of community division. Cherry Street,
which had a large Basque population, had the Centro Vasco Americano,
a benevolent organization with sickness benefits, literary club, and a
folk dance group. Founded in 1913, it owned a five-story building with
a cafe, a billiard room, and a jai alai court. A Federal Writers' Project
investigator surveying such clubs commented that this one pointedly did
not serve the Galicians, Andalusians, and Valencians in the area. The
Centro Asturiano, another benevolent society, was located on Fourteenth Street. It was started in 1923 to serve Asturians and was later
opened to include all Spanish speakers, provided they were white. The
Centro Andaluz, a recreational club in downtown Brooklyn, was opened
in the same year to cater to the regional population clustered there. Galicians, Catalans, and Valencians were among other regional groups who
had their own centers, some of which were disbanded during the Depression. Organizations such as the venerable Unión Española de Bene-
ficencia on Fourteenth Street, which was established in 1912, existed

presumably to serve Spanish nationals but actually included large numbers of Latin Americans and Puerto Ricans from all over the city.[41]

In the years between 1910 and 1930 Spanish organizations, restaurants, and cultural activities were especially visible in New York City. During the 1920s there arose a number of other regional Spanish clubs, as well as Ecuadoran, Mexican, Cuban, Chilean, Honduran, Argentine, and Venezuelan organizations. The wide variety of events sponsored by these organizations almost always included dances with live bands. Such festivities were combined with literary readings, zarzuelas or other dramatic works, variety shows including dancers, singers, and comics, or boxing exhibitions. Some were regularly scheduled weekend night happenings. Others were celebrations of special events, such as a nation's independence or a religious holiday. Still others were benefits for visiting Latino artists, the victims of a hurricane in Puerto Rico or an earthquake in Costa Rica, or the opening of a Hispanic hospital facility in New York City.

From earliest times, diverse Latino populations mingled at many cultural events, both public and private. A *velada,* or soiree, in a private house in 1919, for example, was made up of a mix of Costa Ricans, Cubans, and Dominicans celebrating a recent marriage.[42] Francisco López Cruz, who played in many of the small nationally organized clubs, stressed that there was no hostility between groups of Hispanics but that there *were* cultural divisions between them. "Generally, if there was a party in, let's say, the Colombian Club, well, they were there by themselves. But there was no antagonism with the Puerto Ricans. If some Puerto Rican was a friend of one of them, he was also welcome."[43]

By the early 1920s, New York City had a number of officially pan-Latino clubs. Although such alliances were fragile and often short-lived, they were constantly forming and reforming in the period between the wars, often in response to social crises shared by the city's Spanish speakers. Whatever their origins, they almost always sponsored entertainment. By 1922 there were monthly festivities in the Club Latino Americano and regular dances sponsored by the Asociación Hispano Americana. Given this sometimes regional, sometimes national, sometimes pan-Latin configuration of clubs and audiences, the question of individual and group Latin identity becomes very complicated.

Not only did pan-Latino and even nationally and regionally identified clubs often have mixed audiences but they frequently had mixed musical repertoires as well. A dance sponsored by the Sociedad Hispano Americana in May 1924 at the Casino Ibero, in downtown Brooklyn, had both

North Americans and Latin Americans from different countries in attendance. In the intermission between dances the entertainment featured
"aires españoles," including the famous and "deliriously applauded"
Mexican song "Cielito Lindo," a speech by the president of the Club
Portorriqueño [sic], American songs performed in honor of the American families present, and a *tango* exhibition, reported to be "exception-
ally attractive to the young people."[44]

The younger generation from all Latino ethnic groups wanted to hear
the latest music from Latin America, regardless of its country of origin.
They were also enthusiastic consumers of the reigning North American
popular sounds. Contrary to what one might expect from reading the
typical ethnic-to-American profile, these clubs did not offer a choice
only between American popular music and the folk music of the particular Latino ethnic group catered to by a club. The ethnic clubs of Brooklyn and various parts of Manhattan offered a much broader range of
choices. Latinos might come to dance to small combos made up of community members or to an American jazz band. Puerto Ricans played for
Colombians, Argentines for Venezuelans, and a mixed Hispanic audience was often in attendance. Most ads and articles about dances
stressed that the orchestras that would be playing the latest North American and Latin American dance music. The programs for these events
usually included one or several American popular songs, the latest Latin
American popular music, and whatever were considered the traditional
dances of the country of the sponsoring club, which usually meant the
popular dances of the older generations.[45] The dance program at the
Club Social Venezolano, for example, might include Charlestons, *tangos,* and *joropos;* there might be a dance contest based on the American
popular dance, the Argentine popular dance, or the Venezuelan "traditional" dance. A description of a dance sponsored by the Centro Asturiano de la Habana Delegación en Nueva York, already a testimony to
several migrations and cultures, shows the variety of audiences and of-
ferings likely to be found at such an event: "Getting together in the
116th Street ballroom was a sizable Spanish colony, along with represen-
tatives of several other colonies, among them the Chilean, the Cuban,
the Peruvian, which with the opening chords of Caras's orchestra, which
was unbeatable, they danced [everything] from the old *pasodoble, vals,*
and *danzón* to the black bottom and other modern dances." Aiming to
dance, these audiences, musicians, and reporters seemed to find nothing
inconsistent about offering "danceable Yankee and Hispanic numbers."[46] The Centro Andaluz even sponsored an old-fashioned American

barn dance in 1927![47] Judging from newspaper reports, Spanish speakers were often wide-ranging in their tastes, mixing multinational folk, popular, and even art music in the same program, and simultaneously pan-Latino, nationalistic, and North American in their self-identities.

This fluidity of ethnic identity, however, included some harshly divisive realities. An advertisement for a 1932 dance illuminates this point. The Club Azteca, a Mexican group that followed the apparent tradition of crossing ethnic boundaries while maintaining a distinct identity, celebrated Columbus Day in 1932, donating the proceeds to the victims of the most recent hurricane in Puerto Rico. But not only was the dance, held at the elite Hotel Pennsylvania, too expensive for the average working person but it was "para raza blanca," that is, for whites only. Events held at the downtown hotels were automatically off-limits to Latinos of color and without economic means.

Indeed, emotionally charged holidays such as Columbus Day forced issues of boundary construction and identity formulation along both class and ethnic lines. A Federal Writers' Project description of a day symbolically significant to many ethnic groups highlights some of these issues:

> Dia de la Raza, (the Day of the Spanish Race) Columbus Day, on Oct. 12 . . . is cause for celebration among all the Spanish speaking groups in New York City. A parade is held on this day from the Plaza Hotel to the Statue of Columbus in Central Park . . . by the Spanish sculptor, Sonol (a replica of the original in Madrid). The Spanish speaking groups do not want to have this statue confused with the Italian monument at Columbus Circle. The mayor and Governor send representatives to the festivities. The honor of addressing the assembly is rotated among the consuls of the various countries participating in the celebration. The speechmaking is usually followed by a lavish banquet for the wealthy few and picnics in the park for the others.[48]

Columbus Day was celebrated by all Hispanics in a bloc that was emphatically not Italian. After the statue ceremony, however, the Spanish speakers disappeared into their different or unpredictably mixed ethnic clubs, and an international Hispanic elite convened at elegant hotel banquet tables. The holiday was a reaffirmation of a collective Latino identity, distancing even those outsiders who commemorated the same event, and a day that provoked telling national and class divisions among the celebrants themselves.

Puerto Rican clubs in the post–World War I era developed in this multi-Latino ambiance and followed similar formats. Like the apartment parties, their events usually had both cultural and practical functions. In 1923 there was already a constellation of Puerto Rican clubs cooperating to put on a *velada* in honor of the anniversary of the death of patriot José de Diego, and in the same year the "entusiastas asociados" (enthusiastic members) of the recently formed Club Cívico Puertorriqueño celebrated a "gran fiesta" in their new club on West 125th Street. The club's own house band played a combination of American dances and Puerto Rican *danzas* for a mixed audience. In the following year an inaugural dance for the Puerto Rican Brotherhood of America took place in the Park Palace, a Harlem dance hall available for rental.

During these years the other Spanish-speaking societies, the Spanish foremost among them, continued to outstrip the Puerto Rican groups in visible cultural activities. But the proliferation of community groups in the wake of a 1926 conflict between Puerto Ricans and Jews in East Harlem led to the rise of more specifically Puerto Rican events. As often happened in those years, a social conflict spawned some positive cultural consequences.

Like the other Hispanic societies, the Puerto Rican groups presented programs of mixed genres and nationalities for mixed audiences either in their own halls, generally in Harlem or downtown Brooklyn, or in rented quarters. Once again, the emphasis in these semipublic places was on Latino and American *popular* music. As López Cruz pointed out, during those years Puerto Ricans, strongly influenced by the cinema, "mainly listened to artists who came from South America and Mexico."[49] In the clubs and associations, apparently community-based orchestras with such names as Tropical Serenaders and Original Broadway Serenaders played the combinations of music required. Indeed, performances of Puerto Rican folkloric music such as that of the *jíbaro* tradition seem to have been rather a novelty. *Cuatro* player Efraín Ronda's 1926 performance at the Club Democrático Portorriqueño [*sic*] was reported as the "first-time presentation in Brooklyn of the typical and original *cuatro* of native Puerto Rican music, directed by Mr. Efraín Ronda with his accompanist on guitar." It was sandwiched in between a typically eclectic offering, including a poetry recital, the Charleston Kids Orchestra, and *tango* and Charleston exhibitions by veterans of the American vaudeville stage.[50]

As time went on, however, many of the Puerto Rican associations tried to employ more of their musical co-ethnics within their varied entertainment programs. Mother's Day, for example, an important holiday all over Latin America, in the late 1920s and early 1930s meant elaborate festivities at Harlem's Wadleigh High School. Organized by the Liga

Puertorriqueña e Hispana (Puerto Rican and Hispanic League), these free festivities included speeches, piano and poetry recitals, and performances by community members. While Peruvian trios, Mexican singers, Dominican poets, and Hawaiian and classical music were all fair game for these programs, the biggest attractions were some of the finest Puerto Rican folk, classical, and popular musicians of the time. Heriberto Torres, "King of the Puerto Rican Cuatro," would be on hand with his *trío* to play his "repertorio criollo." The operatic-style tenor Virgilio Rabén performed songs dedicated to "madres hispanas" written by Rafael Hernández, who was present with an *orquesta* or a small *conjunto*. Canario, at his peak as an inventor and performer of *plenas,* sang a variety of popular songs.[51]

Such events reveal both the community's appreciation of the musicians and the availability of these performers, some of whom were already famous, for relatively humble activities. Even within a constantly changing and growing Latino community, however, jobs playing for local ethnic clubs were sporadic and paid next to nothing. Moreover, local Puerto Rican musicians often had to compete with other Latino and North American bands from both New York and other areas.

Musicians who attempted to earn even a partial living playing for the small local clubs were faced with other difficulties as well. Since Puerto Rican clubs constituted only a small portion of the many neighborhood associations organized by Spanish-speaking groups, musicians frequently crossed over to the clubs of other Spanish-speaking nationals. A musician attempting to capitalize on their varied musical events needed to be well versed in their particular national styles, as well as the constantly changing internationally popular dance genres. Often the differences between musics were subtle and challenging, as Victoria Hernández, herself a pianist, explained: "[Venezuelan] music is not our music. Let's take the waltzes of Peru. They're not our waltzes, nor are they the American waltzes. All are 3/4 [meter], but the rhythm is different. The Peruvian waltz is syncopated. The Central Americans, the South Americans, don't have the same rhythm as we do."[52]

Playing in these small clubs was also a logistical challenge for musicians, as Francisco López Cruz remembered. These modest enterprises were virtually invisible to the American Federation of Musicians, but even so, López Cruz, a union member, had to be careful when playing these nonunion jobs, which undoubtedly paid well below scale: "In order for me to play for those dances, I had to do it clandestinely. [The union] didn't know. Because it was prohibited to play without taking a contract to the Federation. But since for them El Barrio was nothing, little Barrio dances, they ignored it."[53]

López Cruz's comment conveys well the plight of the "ethnic" musician who worked within a small ensemble and tried to cater to an economically struggling community. At the same time, his words indicate the lack of respect with which Puerto Rican musicians and their places of work were treated by organizations ostensibly meant to help them. This situation was exacerbated by the difficulties of the Depression and of technological changes within the entertainment world. Just as Puerto Rican movie theater musicians had been forced out of work by the new sound films of the late 1920s, for example, so had their colleagues in New York. Puerto Rican musicians' migration to the mainland to offset such losses unfortunately created more competition for fewer jobs.

In many cases, the struggling ethnic community itself formed the alternative networks and competition. In the process, this community developed a unique relationship with its musicians. Similarly marginalized African-American performers and composers had coped with the racism of the American Federation of Musicians and of the entertainment world in general by forming alternative unions and societies such as the Clef Club and the Tempo Club, as well as founding a few record companies and sheet music publishers. Puerto Rican musicians apparently relied on informal networks of family members, friends, and colleagues and the support of a relatively well-developed merchant class.

PUERTO RICAN MUSICIANS AND THE COMMUNITY

In more or less altruistic ways, community and mercantile networks available to musicians helped sustain them through hard times and gave them connections to musical work. Although there is not yet enough information on the important roles female friends and relatives of the mostly male musicians may have played in supporting their careers, the activities of Victoria Hernández provide an instructive clue. The participation of this multitalented woman in her brother's milieu suggests that women, as well as merchants, may have served as caretakers for these musicians in their day-to-day life though not entirely in traditional ways.

Victoria Hernández came with other family members to live in New York in July 1919, several months after her brother Rafael was discharged from the army. After sewing in a factory and giving piano lessons on the side, in 1927 Hernández opened what was probably the first Puerto Rican–owned music store in New York City. The store and her

ongoing piano lessons earned her enough money to support Rafael and
other relatives, and it gave the composer a quiet back room with a piano,
in which he spent hours writing music. Victoria's business also gave Rafael Hernández a certain community status, although he had little to do
with it and was, according to his sister, a "bohemio" with no head for
money at all:

> He was a musician, a composer. He didn't want to know when the light, the
> gas were paid. Opening the business cleared a path for him [se abrió el cam-
> ino]. He was like one among the many, but when the business was opened
> that said Casa Hernández, well, now he wasn't just Rafael Hernández the
> composer, he was Rafael like the biggest business, [even though] the business
> was mine.[54]

Victoria Hernández was herself a trained musician, but she claims that
she never thought of becoming a professional. Observing that a musician had to be both an "inspirado" and an "enamorado,"[55] she felt that
neither her talent nor the demands of her business allowed her to devote
herself to music. Fitting squarely into the tradition of the classically
trained Puerto Rican female musician, Victoria Hernández "never
wanted to exploit music" by having a popular career.[56]

The contradiction between Victoria Hernández's words and actions
is notable, however, and probably a result of both community-mandated
gender roles and the relative status of different professions. Within the
Barrio community of that time, being a merchant was clearly more respectable than being a musician. However, in numerous ways, both
humbler and more prosperous merchants could have a powerful influence on musicians' careers. Victoria Hernández is a case in point. While
she never became a popular musician, she was involved with popular
music in every way short of playing it herself.

Victoria Hernández's business acumen not only gave her brother the
time he needed to concentrate on his musical groups and compositions
and the wherewithal to avoid more gruesome industrial experiences, but
she was also indispensable as an organizer of his musical projects and
became official manager for his *cuarteto,* which was named Victoria in
her honor. Victoria organized tours and record dates and made sure that
her brother and the other *bohemios* in his group fulfilled their contracts.
In fact she did everything possible to combat the image of the musician
as *bohemio,* down to making sure its members wore suits and ties rather
than the stereotypical ruffle-sleeved rumba shirts. Impeccably dressed
on and off stage no matter what their fortunes, the Cuarteto Victoria

was dubbed by other Barrio musicians "El Cuarteto Rico" (The Rich Quartet).[57]

Victoria Hernández's activities as a booking agent and liaison with record companies served not only Rafael but also many other Puerto Rican musicians: "I was the one who helped them. And do you know what the musicians called me? 'La Madrina' [The Godmother]. They were poor; some of them didn't have shoes."[58] Victoria's motives were not entirely altruistic, however. She would serve as an intermediary with record companies such as Columbia and Victor, advancing pay for recording sessions to the usually hand-to-mouth musicians, in exchange for a cut of the fee. Members of the Cuarteto Victoria complained of being shortchanged in their salaries, especially when Victoria and the group went on tour. Artists advertised Victoria's business tactics with still another, less flattering nickname for Victoria, "La Judía" (The Jew).

Victoria Hernández's business activities and the musicians' attitudes toward them reflect the important concrete roles merchants could play in musicians' careers, as well as the mixed feelings they evoked. Within a multiethnic residential and business community, intergroup relationships became an important frame of reference for characterizing the behavior of even a Puerto Rican. Dramatic occurrences such as the Harlem Riots of 1926, in which thugs apparently hired by Jewish merchants tried to intimidate the increasing numbers of Hispanic shopkeepers in the neighborhood, produced reactions within the Puerto Rican community. So did the more gradual changes such an event reflected. As with many ethnic groups, specific types of businesses owned by Puerto Ricans developed early on in areas of heavy Puerto Rican settlement, the initial boardinghouses and barbershops being followed by groceries, restaurants, and music stores. Larger professional and commercial concerns developed as well. These enterprises coexisted with those owned by others, most notably Jews and non–Puerto Rican Latinos, holdovers of earlier neighborhood settlement patterns and/or ongoing hierarchical economic relationships between groups. Galicians and other Spaniards were among the most prominent entrepreneurs in these districts, just as they had been in Cuba and Puerto Rico. Businesses owned by Jews and other Europeans also continued to proliferate even as their respective populations fled areas such as East Harlem. Victoria Hernández's store, for example, at Madison Avenue and 114th Street, was located among a number of cigar, fur, trimmings, and other garment-related businesses owned by Jews, Italians, and Armenians.[59]

At the same time, the growing range of Puerto Rican businesses were developing a multifaceted relationship to specialized ethnic products, including music. John Bukowczyk has described the Polish-American business community as comprising two classes: small proprietors, who were just a stone's throw away from "slipping back into anonymous blue-collar jobs," and successful immigrant entrepreneurs, who were often among the cultural pillars of the community.[60] Puerto Rican businesses could also fall into either of these categories, but both humble and more prosperous merchants were involved in the founding of ethnic associations and services and the organizing of community-based cultural events. As F. Arturo Rosales has observed in relation to another group of Latino immigrants, in the Southwest, their merchants were most successful when they provided services ethnic outsiders could not supply; these included businesses in food, publishing, and entertainment.[61]

Among Puerto Ricans as well, both economically marginal businesses and thriving merchants looked to music and other cultural activities as means to enlarge their incomes. Within this context, "Latin music expressed the development of the *colonia* on two levels: The cultural, as an expression of Puerto Rican heritage and creativity; and the physical, as an example of Latin entrepreneurship."[62] As in the case of Victoria Hernández, Puerto Rican merchants helped community musicians with their careers and simultaneously supplemented their own incomes. Not only Hernández provided services for musicians: her competition, the other Latino-oriented music stores beginning to emerge, mainly in El Barrio, did so as well. Santurce-born Gabriel Oller, who opened the Spanish Music Center in the early 1930s, told Max Salazar that it quickly turned into a musicians' headquarters. Located near some of the major theaters in the community, the corner on which Oller's store stood became a hangout for Latino musicians. If a bandleader was looking for a particular type of group or instrumentalist, he called the store, knowing that Oller just had to step outside to recruit somebody.[63]

Even nonmusical merchants might provide connections. Barbershops, pharmacies, and other enterprises sold records and probably served as recruiting stations for record companies. Non–Puerto Rican neighborhood businesspeople were among such unofficial liaisons, as Efraín Vaz, a drummer from Aguadilla, described:

> Whatever musician you'd want to get, there was a pool hall on 103d and Madison where the musicians also hung out a lot. And there one got jobs. And in that pool hall there were five, six tables, and there was a blackboard

on which was written "Open, I'm open for the weekends." [The owner] was
a Spaniard, a good man. They called him El Gallego [the Galician]. You
could leave your instruments there safe and no one would touch them.[64]

Probably receiving a fee from the musicians or their seekers, "El Gallego" kept a list of possible jobs on the blackboard.

The more prosperous community merchants were able to promote
musicians in more elaborate ways. Representative of this group was Julio
Roqué. The son of a wealthy white family from Aguadilla, Roqué had a
thriving Harlem dental practice by the early 1920s and quickly established himself as "the Gertrude Stein" of the Puerto Rican and Latino
musical community in New York City.[65] Roqué's radio show, *Revista
Roqué* (Roqué's Revue), begun in 1924, was probably the earliest
Spanish-language radio program in New York City. The program aired
"the exotic melodies of Spanish America," performed by local and visiting artists, and featured Roqué's own orchestra and many of his compositions.[66] In between selections there were advertisements of Roqué-
brand antiseptic and toothpaste. The program simultaneously promoted
local artists, furthered the dentist's creative ventures, and aided his professional practice.

For years, Roqué was involved in a variety of music-related activities
in New York. According to one admirer, the Argentine orchestra leader
Terig Tucci, "He was in love with music, and he actively practiced it as
a pianist, violinist, composer, arranger, lyricist, and orchestra director;
in recordings, radio performances, and in the theater. This agreeable bohemian was the very personification of a hobo. . . . His odontological
consultation office appeared to be a theatrical agency. Any artist who
came to the city with difficulty neglected to visit him."[67] Roqué fixed
the musicians' teeth for free and turned his office and his home into
informal gathering places for them. As a recording artist with Victor, he
helped secure contracts for others, and he featured new vocalists with
his orchestra. He found performance spaces for more than one visiting
or recently immigrated Hispanic popular or classical artist. While
Roqué was clearly a remarkable figure, his wealth and professional status undoubtedly contributed greatly to his many artistic and promotional achievements. Roqué was El Barrio's version of the professional
patron of the arts, and such indigenous support may help explain why
Latin music flourished uptown at a time when the Depression destroyed
the fragile underpinnings of the African-American Harlem Renaissance,
on the wane just a few blocks away.[68]

THE PROFESSIONALIZATION OF
LATINO ENTERTAINMENT

The late 1920s and early 1930s brought the rise of theater, film, and variety shows organized by professional promoters. A weekly Hispanic activity organized at the Apollo Theater from at least 1926 symbolized the transition from community-club-sponsored dances, plays, and variety shows to their professionally organized counterparts in commercial theaters. In a sense, the Sunday variety shows at the Apollo Theater were a dress rehearsal for what would come later. They were a semiprofessional entertainment that both drew from older forms and served as the pilot for a new era.

The Apollo Theater to which Hispanic patrons flocked was not the institution that later gained international attention but "a small but elegant 900-seat theater with a huge stage," located about a block away on 125th Street.[69] Showcasing mostly burlesque acts, the theater was located above the Harlem Opera House, which featured stage comedies and musicals starring artists such as Al Jolson and the Marx Brothers.

The beginning of the Spanish-language shows at the "old Apollo" theater—the show moved to the present-day Apollo for a brief time around 1930—is another example of an entertainment form unfolding not in isolation but in a multiethnic setting, and in a period of profound transition. The Spanish-language shows started at a time when the major movie and stage show theaters of Harlem were owned by a handful of white, mostly Jewish men who were battling for dominance of the local entertainment scene.[70] During this period, when Broadway theater owners were able to lure white performers downtown with increasingly large fees, the uptown operators began to cultivate African-American artists, who were less upwardly mobile and could be hired for far less money. These entrepreneurs began to cater to the growing black audience, staging shows affordable to working-class people. Whereas 125th Street had been a white, primarily Irish strip, and the heart of black entertainment had been further north, by the late 1920s and early 1930s increasing numbers of black artists and audiences were to be found on 125th Street. Conversely, white ethnics were gradually leaving the neighborhood.

The Puerto Ricans and other Hispanics, who generally lived east and south of the Apollo area, were probably part of this new trend. The organizing and the content of the shows both reflected current general conditions and models and were out of step with them. The rise of the

Apollo shows and subsequent Spanish-language stage shows in the neighborhood, for example, took place at a time when their English-language equivalents were declining due to radio, talking pictures, and the general effects of the Depression. While Hispanic programming was certainly affected by such factors, in general the decade of the 1930s was a renaissance period for Spanish-language theaters and cabarets. These shows were often sponsored by local Latino merchants, especially the ubiquitous Roqué, contracting with the white theater owners for these Sunday performances.

The Apollo shows continued the Hispanic neighborhood clubs' traditions of elaborate zarzuelas, comedies, and dramas, whose equivalents were not to be found in the typical North American stage show lineup. Within its first few months, the Spanish theater was joined by a comic revue, which often dealt with life in New York or in Latin America. A June 1926 performance had both a Spanish version of *The Barber of Seville* and a revue, *Cuando Nueva York Duerme* (While New York Sleeps), featuring a range of Hispanic vocalists and dancers, some of whom had performed in North American vaudeville.

The combination of forms in these programs reflected the beginnings of a change in Latino tastes and in the character of the Barrio audience. At first the Apollo was an important stop for the local Spanish repertory companies, which for years had made the rounds of Spanish-speaking audiences in New York and New Jersey. By the late 1920s and early 1930s the multinational character of the city's Latino population was on the decline. Hard times compelled many Spaniards and Latin Americans to return to their countries. Ironically, the same Depression brought a variety of Latino artists, particularly Mexicans, to New York as they fled from folding clubs and theaters in the Southwest. Nevertheless, through both the decline in other groups and their own large in-migration, Puerto Ricans became the dominant Latino group.[71] The theatrical forms best known to the primarily working-class members of these groups were not the zarzuela or the Spanish drama but the *bufos cubanos.* The Apollo revues built around the *bufos* formula increasingly became the most important part of the show. While they sometimes featured companies visiting from Cuba, the *bufos* also incorporated a variety of Latino artists, including dancers, acrobats, magicians, *conjuntos, orquestas,* and a surprising number of operatic singers. In the Apollo and subsequent theaters, the *bufos* used local talent, drew upon older forms familiar to at least Caribbean Hispanics, and provided an opportunity for New York's Spanish-speaking population both to unite physi-

cally and to humorously comment upon the divisions and power relations between them. A February 1930 performance, "De Cuba a Puerto
Rico" (From Cuba to Puerto Rico), dealt with a company of Cuban
actors, contracted by a Catalan, who go to Puerto Rico to perform. The
comedy results from cultural differences, such as the Cubans' ignorance
of the Puerto Rican names of the fruits that they encounter.[72] In March
of the same year, a Park Palace performance of "Llegó el Lechero" (The
Milkman Arrived) depicted an argument between Caribbean Hispanics
in Harlem and Spaniards living in the Cherry Street area. The comedy
was acted, sung, and danced by an international cast, and Cuban and
Puerto Rican orchestras closed the evening with everything from Puerto
Rican *plena* and Cuban *danzón* and *son* to Spanish *pasodoble* and
North American fox-trots.[73]

The era of the Apollo-type show was over by 1930; it was replaced
by a series of theaters presenting Spanish-language entertainment on a
daily basis. In trying to cater to the tastes of a multinational population,
show-business entrepreneurs delicately navigated between the eclectic
tastes of their clientele and their sense of ethnic pride. Like the neighborhood clubs, they maintained a balance between the multi- and the
monoethnic, the Latino and the North American. Señor Del Pozo, a
Mexican who opened the Teatro Hispano in 1937 in the old Campoamor, was careful to stage revues featuring Latin themes and artists
of various nationalities, sometimes within a single week. *La Prensa* reported on a Monday in June 1938: "Friday was Argentinian day, Saturday the Puerto Rican, and yesterday, Sunday, the Spanish. Today is the
Mexican day."[74] To a certain extent, then, Del Pozo was geographically
and temporally telescoping the functions of the many noncommercial
Latino organizations. Ironically, his different-nationality days were a
great deal more purist in their collections of performers than were most
ethnic club functions.

It is likely that entrepreneurs such as Del Pozo and the Cuban-born
Fernando Luis saw that there was money to be made by offering special
entertainment to a growing Hispanic community, once the Apollo had
proved such a successful pilot that the show was moved to a bigger theater. But there were important differences. The opening of the Teatro
San José on Fifth Avenue and 110th Street and its later incarnations
both in the same location and on 116th Street made Spanish-language
films, rather than plays, the center of their shows. While they featured a
constellation of Latino artists and revues tailored to the Spanish speakers of New York, they added North American innovations such as lines

of chorus girls and held international dance contests, which had often characterized the nonprofessional ethnic clubs. Occasionally, they employed non-Latino performers. A November 1932 performance at the San José was called "Los Escándolos de Nueva York" (The Scandals of New York), undoubtedly inspired by the Broadway shows of the kind made by Flo Ziegfield, Lew Leslie, and George White.[75] It featured Los Cuatro Lavanderos Trovadores, who were actually a North American washboard band.[76] Other shows used Chinese magicians or international vaudeville stars. Thus, these theaters simultaneously gave important breaks to Latino artists, provided the first commercial Spanish-language vaudeville and variety shows, and allowed American formats to shape their programming. Once again, a give-and-take between numerous ethnic and American formulas was more the rule than a linear development from one to the other.

Impresarios such as Fernando Luis and Señor Del Pozo were acutely conscious of both the commonalities and the divisions between different groups of Latinos. On the one hand, they realized that an artist's popularity did not necessarily correspond to the number of his *compatriotas* to be found in New York City. A 1934 Campoamor premiere of the film *Cuesta Abajo* (Downhill) starring Argentine *tango* king Carlos Gardel, featured not only a live performance by Gardel but also *bufos,* the immensely popular Cuban Trío Matamoros and Alberto Socarrás with his orchestra, and an appearance by Harlem Congressman James Lanzetta. The show drew a crowd of over ten thousand people. The clamor of the disappointed who could not get into the fifteen-hundred-seat theater was so great that manager Fernando Luis had to arrange for speakers to broadcast the film's soundtrack to the crowd outside.[77] On the other hand, the impresario was also aware that Gardel's enormous popularity among Puerto Ricans did not dispel their desire to hear performers from their own ranks. *La Prensa* reported in early 1934 that "Fernando Luis, realizing that it's been some time since he presented something genuinely Puerto Rican, brings us Grupo Canario. . . . And of course the repertory is the most extensive that has been seen in *sones* and songs from beautiful Borinquén."[78] Although at this point in their career they were performing primarily Cuban music, Canario's group was made up entirely of Puerto Ricans and therefore had a special meaning for the migrants living in New York City. Other Puerto Rican performers got occasional jobs on a similar basis in the uptown theaters.

Nevertheless, even these professional venues hardly made it possible for performers to earn a decent living, even after the Latin music scene

had become rather firmly entrenched in New York City. In the late
1930s, for example, Rafael Hernández discovered Myrta Silva, who became one of the first Puerto Rican female singers of popular music.
When Hernández saw her, she was barely into her teens, a former dish-
washer and chambermaid who was performing twenty-one shows
weekly at the Teatro Hispano for twenty-five dollars. Even the elegant
uptown cabarets paid little. Victoria Hernández remembers bringing
Trío Matamoros from Cuba in the 1930s to play a show at the Toreador,
a club geared toward wealthy white audiences, for one hundred dollars.
The rates for lesser-known local groups were undoubtedly much lower.

Under such circumstances, Puerto Rican merchant and community
networks were but a small part of the apparatus of the music industry,
not creators of permanent internal means of sustaining performers and
composers. Professional performers had to piece together a living within
an interethnic musical network. Puerto Rican *trío, cuarteto,* and *orquesta* musicians traveled between different musical worlds that often
existed in a hierarchical relationship to one another. Their professional
lives involved crossing national, class, and geographical boundaries,
even frontiers of good taste, as they self-consciously catered to ethnic
stereotypes both downtown and uptown. In the process, they brought
new sounds back to local audiences. Thus, their interests and experiences both overlapped and diverged with those of their nonmusical *compatriotas.* Adapting to these conditions, Puerto Rican musicians gained
a reputation for being "strong in the hybridizing wing"[79] and indeed
often prided themselves on being the ethnic group that could play "any
kind of music."[80]

The experiences of many of the musicians who migrated from Puerto
Rico bear this out. Well-trained reading musicians were especially likely
to be involved in a range of ensembles. Manuel Peña, for example, the
municipal bandleader's son from Humacao, came to New York in 1929.
After a brief career as a boxer, he joined a Filipino orchestra.[81] Pepito
Arvelo, who came from Lares in 1935, "the year Carlos Gardel died,"
was playing guitar with a Hawaiian group by the following year.[82] On a
less formal level as well, Puerto Rican musicians mingled with members
of other ethnic groups, frequently transcending the ongoing antago-
nisms between people of different backgrounds. Efraín Vaz, who by day
might play with Tommy Dorsey, remembered after-hours jam sessions
with black groups in Harlem. López Cruz complained bitterly about
hostile relations between Jews and Puerto Ricans in El Barrio as well as
about the virtual monopoly he felt Jews had on show business. In the

next breath, however, he glowingly described Sunday afternoons spent with a Jewish woman friend who was an accomplished pianist and a lover of Puerto Rican music.[83] Francisco López Vidal, who came to the United States for the first time in 1933, became friends with Guy Lombardo's saxophonist and exchanged Latin rhythm lessons for instruction in saxophone technique.[84]

On the business level as well, Puerto Rican musicians were constantly in touch with a multiethnic world. While the uptown theaters were turning increasingly to Hispanic programming by the end of the 1920s, their ownership generally remained white. The same was true of the large neighborhood dance halls, such as the Park Palace and Laurel Gardens. Throughout New York City, Italian and Jewish mobsters controlled many of the clubs and cabarets of the Prohibition era, and the ethnic pattern, if not the criminality, continued even after the repeal of the Volstead Act. Indeed, reminiscing about the beginning of his career in the early 1940s, pianist Charlie Palmieri could still remark that "Most clubs were owned by whites. The managers were Latin."[85] Even when clubs were owned or managed by Latinos, they were rarely Puerto Ricans. Puerto Ricans constituted an increasing majority of New York's Spanish-speaking residents and Latin orchestra personnel, but most Latino business leaders were from other ethnic groups.[86]

This intra-Latino hierarchy also extended to most *orquestas,* especially during the 1920s and early 1930s, and was very much determined by dominant popular styles. While Spanish, Argentine, and Mexican music had enjoyed simultaneous or successive bursts of popularity in the early part of the century, by the late 1920s Cuban music was centerstage for many Latinos and non-Hispanics alike. Although some chroniclers attribute the rise of Cuban music to the sudden popularity of "El Manisero" (The Peanut Vendor), played on Broadway in 1930 by don Azpiazú's Havana Casino Orchestra, Cuban musical influences and group leaders had been around a good deal longer than that, both uptown and downtown.[87] Close economic ties between Cuba and the United States, helped by the onset of Prohibition, made Havana an important city for North American business and tourist traffic, a favorite spot for drinking, gambling, and music. Moreover, just as jazz had become popular in Cuba, Cuban music had filtered into the United States for years through ports such as New Orleans and New York City. When North American publishers began to "discover" Cuban music in the late 1920s, they found an audience receptive to the music their salesmen brought back. The explosion of Cuban dance forms in the United States in the late 1920s and throughout the 1930s fixed this category of Latin musician in the popular imagination and had an effect on the careers of Puerto Rican artists.

Cuban dance genres were, of course, prevalent in Puerto Rico as well, and they became staples of the repertoires of the New York–based *tríos* and *cuartetos,* some of which comprised members of both nationalities. When Cuban music became popular in New York City among non-Latino and Latino audiences alike, there were Puerto Rican musicians in virtually all of these "Cuban" groups. While there were some Puerto Rican *orquestas* in El Barrio, the first prominent large ensembles were Cuban-led. Ten- or twelve-piece groups headed by Cubans such as pianist Nilo Meléndez, trumpeters Pedro Vía and Vicente Sigler, and flutist Alberto Socarrás played at the large weekend dances and variety shows held in Harlem halls and theaters, with their playing and singing contests, amateur nights, theme balls, and live radio broadcasts. At times the neighborhood-spawned *tríos* and *cuartetos* would perform in these varied programs. More often, their personnel would moonlight with the larger groups. Vocalists were especially versatile in this regard. Davilita is best remembered as the classic lead voice of Cuarteto Victoria, but he also sang with the *orquestas* of both Alberto Socarrás and Puerto Rican trumpeter Augusto Coen. Johnny Rodríguez, who had his own *trío,* also sang at the Teatro Campoamor with Socarrás for several weeks in 1935, before going on to a career downtown. Other Puerto Rican musicians played in these *orquestas* before forming their own.

During the 1930s, club and theater managers looking for profits exploited the popularity of Cuban music among North Americans. They worked overtime trying to make El Barrio and Latino musical forms in general seem exotic. Although sociologist Lawrence Chenault, observing El Barrio in the late 1930s, claimed that "few people other than the residents seem to come into the area at night, as New Yorkers who frequent Harlem in 'late parties' usually go further uptown," by this time black Harlem nightlife of the type catering to whites was largely in decline.[88] One of the new vogues attracting this white clientele looking for exotica in its own backyard was "Spanish Harlem," adjacent to and somewhat interwoven with this African-American area. Writers surveying the uptown neighborhood in the late 1930s ignored its poverty as well as its North American cinemas and eclectic dance repertoires and celebrated its ostensibly Spanish flavor:

Spanish atmosphere is most readily sensed in the colony running north from One Hundred and Tenth to One Hundred and Sixteenth Streets between Third and Fifth Avenues, although this is largely a Cuban and Puerto Rican neighborhood. For its front yard this colony has Central Park; for its Main Street, Fifth Avenue. The Teatro Cervantes and the Teatro de Variedades, both exclusively Spanish vaudeville and motion picture houses, are separated by little more than the distance covered in a tango, and within that distance soft language, gay music and exotic patterns of living characterize, at least for visitors, the essence of Old Spain.[89]

The language barrier would have discouraged non-Hispanic visitors to these vaudeville houses or the small clubs catering to those who spoke Spanish, preventing the sort of white invasion of nightspots typical of African-American Harlem. Excitement-seekers did, however, have El Toreador, on 110th Street facing Central Park, whose prices were "high for the working man, but there is real Spanish dancing and music."[90] Paquito López Cruz, who played there, remembers the components of what the Federal Writers' Project reporters described as its "gay, sparkling Spanish American revue," served twice nightly along with a house orchestra and Mexican food.

That club filled up with people at night, especially Fridays and Saturdays. It was elegant, but it wasn't a very big place. And there the combination was Juan Hernández, who had studied with me in high school in Bayamón. Hernández played the guitar, I played the *cuatro*, a Cuban, Carpentier, played the piano, and another Cuban, Varona, played the violin. A curious combination, piano, violin, *cuatro*, guitar, and rhythm. We accompanied the show. There was a singer, and a pair of Mexican dancers, for example, dancing about three months there. We made a [radio] program on Thursday afternoons, and that program was what attracted so many people.[91]

These uptown nightspots and the elegant midtown and downtown clubs and cabarets take on an entirely different aspect when viewed through the eyes of Puerto Rican musicians. In general, the primarily working-class Puerto Rican audiences living in El Barrio and downtown Brooklyn were limited by class, race, and budget to the Harlem clubs, whereas artists such as Johnny Rodríguez were casting their eyes downtown in the hopes of expanding their careers and earning more money. While Barrio audiences were by all accounts wildly receptive to visiting Latino artists and flocked to see, for example, the movies of Carlos Gardel, those around the famous *tango* singer felt that extensive performing in El Barrio might hurt his career. Fernando Luis offered Gardel a contract for a weekly salary of six thousand dollars plus fifty percent of box office receipts, an incredible offer at that time. Nevertheless, the Argentine's manager felt that a performance before a general audience on Broadway would serve his client's ambitions much better.[92]

Performers had their own ideas about the appropriateness of working within certain types of music and performance halls, which they used as touchstones against which to measure their own careers. Johnny Rodríguez, for example, defined himself and his ambitions in relation to those among whom he had lived and played during his early days in New York, the *trío* and *cuarteto* musicians in El Barrio: "I left that bunch. They always worked for the Latins. [They were] too Latino for the East Side, very Puerto Rican in the musical sense. They were already a good deal older, first. Second, they didn't have the personality that I had. And third, they left here [Puerto Rico] directly to continue their rhythm [in New York]. And I went to record with RCA Victor."[93]

Rodríguez appreciated the support and caring of both the elder musicians and the uptown audiences, but they and their neighborhood represented to him an unchanging and old-fashioned environment. After his initiation into New York life uptown, Rodríguez moved downtown in both his residence and his musical career: "Frankly, I didn't like El Barrio too much because, musically speaking, it had no atmosphere. I played fourteen, fifteen weeks in the Teatro Hispano, singing for the Puerto Ricans [with] lines three rows deep. But [those] people were stagnant. And I wanted to see the world."[94]

The uptown venues were scarce and offered sporadic work opportunities to only a relatively few musicians. Fernando Luis's spectacular offers to international stars notwithstanding, most musicians got a good deal more money and work in the downtown clubs geared to American audiences. In spite of the financial incentives, however, the choice to play in American-oriented clubs was not necessarily a simple or a natural one. Many factors went into making such a decision, and it was by no means a one-way, irrevocable, or unambivalent one. In fact, musicians' attitudes toward uptown versus downtown revealed how varied they were in their experiences, attitudes, and ambitions. While Johnny Rodríguez saw his decision as primarily an artistic one, Charlie Palmieri stressed the financial lure of full-time work: "It had nothing to do with type of audience. It was strictly work-wise. The Latin musicians would work whatever work was available. It was not that the musicians downtown did not want to play uptown (they would have loved to) but once you started playing downtown you had no time to play uptown."[95]

LATIN RELIEF

If we take into account Harlem clubs like the Toreador, the categories "uptown" and "downtown" become more symbolic than geographical. Most of the clubs catering to whites and affluent Latinos, however, were located well outside El Barrio, as well as beyond the pocketbooks of its residents. El Chico, which existed from at least 1927, was located in Greenwich Village. Run by a Spaniard and his Puerto Rican wife, it offered a Spanish meal, cooked by a Spanish chef, for $2.00 and an American meal, cooked by an American chef, for $1.25. At a time when a working-class Puerto Rican's weekly salary might be $25 or less, these were hefty prices. El Chico also offered nightly dances and variety acts, while apparently catering to a crowd that included many Americans, as López Cruz remembered: "[El Chico] was so famous that you could go any night and see Hollywood artists there. It was famous for having a Spanish atmosphere. The times that we went to play there with Canario's group, well, besides us, there was always a pair of Spaniards dancing with castanets."[96]

Terig Tucci frequently went to El Chico with his affluent and artistic friends. He recalls one memorable occasion:

> El Chico [was] the most aristocratic Hispanic cabaret in New York. . . . Señor Collada and his charming wife, Rosita Ríos, made time to make us welcome. Upon entering the spacious vestibule, we left New York behind, to enter into a Sevillian manor. As we descended the circular staircase leading to the basement where the cabaret was, the Iberian impression heightened.
>
> The establishment appeared more museum than cabaret. Gorgeously decorated in Spanish motifs, the hall exhibited a collection of ceramic, majolica ware and glazed tiles imported from Spain, which presented scenes from the different regions of the Peninsula, famous passages from Quixote, miraculously illuminated pictures by Sorolla, iron railings with flowery vines embracing them, balconies adorned with pots of red carnations. And up high, in a corner of the hall, an enormous parrot, prisoner in an immense cage hung from the ceiling, seemed to stand guard.

Bullfight posters hung on the wall of the hall, which had room for about a hundred people at spacious tables. Tucci and his entourage, including the immensely popular Carlos Gardel, watched a show that included Spanish and Venezuelan singers, the ubiquitous pair of dancers, a flamenco guitarist, and a Mexican mariachi trio. The show was organized by an Argentine music director and master of ceremonies conducting a Spanish house orchestra.[97]

El Chico's success inspired the proliferation of legions of similar establishments in the Greenwich Village area. Ironically, this "Spanish atmosphere" came about at a time when the Spanish population was itself on the decline. Nevertheless, the demand for such clubs increased, putting pressure on locations with a non-Latin atmosphere. Marta's Spanish Gardens, for example, at 23 West 8th Street, was "once Italian but now gone Spanish in response to the public demand."[98] Probably as a result of stiff competition, Hollywood films with ever-expanding Latin American locales, and the proclivities of their owners, the clubs became increasingly specialized, at least according to their ad campaigns. As time went on and styles changed, advertisements boasted authentic Cuban, Mexican, Argentine, and Spanish atmospheres. For all, however, entertainment meant variety shows featuring performers from different countries and stressing the usually one dominant Latin music style of the moment. A glance at El Chico's advertisements shows that Collada was constantly changing his show to adapt to the times. The *tangos* and *pasodobles* performed by the house band and the guitar ensembles of the late 1920s gave way to "authentic" Argentine, Mexican, and many Cuban entertainers, sometimes overshadowing the ever-present Spanish artists who gave the place its reputation.[99]

A club undoubtedly inspired by El Chico, El Don Julio, on West 10th Street, advertised itself in 1935 as "the only Mexican cabaret in the City of New York."[100] Don Julio himself was a radio and cabaret star who had opened his own nightspot, quickly making it, according to Tucci, one of the most amusing places in the city. "The show begins with a sparkling Spanish number, a *pasodoble* sung and danced by the chorus girls. A pair of comedians follow. The chorus girls, attired now in the typical dress of the Peruvian Indians, dance with the naive grace of the Huaino. . . . At once, a group of Cuban musicians, bringing a festive note to the program, amuse us with a lively and frolicsome *guaracha* entitled 'El Botellero.'" The floor show of this "authentically Mexican" cabaret finally included a Mexican dancer and closed with the owner himself, an enormous man with an equally large mustache, dressed in *charro* style. Entering the stage with boots and spurs, guitar on his back, and brandishing pistols, he fired into the air and let loose a long barrage of insults against the ostensibly tightwad *gringos* in the audience, who loved every minute of it.[101]

By the late 1930s a number of elegant nightspots had opened in the midtown district as well. With names like Havana-Madrid, Club Yumuri, La Conga, and Casa Cubana, it was clear that they were trying to capitalize on the current craze for the *rumba* and other Cuban dance forms. The demand for Latin music among a general New York audience was by this era so widespread that even clubs and hotel ballrooms without an explicitly Latino orientation were compelled to hire Cuban-style relief bands to alternate sets with their swing bands.

Latino musicians in relief bands played between the sets of big-name American ensembles such as those of Tommy Dorsey or Guy Lombardo, thus giving audiences continuous entertainment. While their members were often from many cultures, Puerto Ricans were virtually always present. Since most of these clubs were off-limits to people of color, only light-skinned or white Puerto Ricans played in such groups.

Xavier Cugat, a Catalan who spent much of his childhood in Cuba, was probably the most famous of the downtown Latin bandleaders. A thwarted classical violinist, in the mid-twenties he formed a popular group that used instruments ranging from *marimbas* to *congas* and played an equally wide variety of Latin American numbers for North American audiences. While chroniclers of Latin music have generally dismissed such large downtown orchestras as watered-down imitations of a genuine uptown Latin music, it is important to look at these ensembles in the context of the musicians' lives and their communities. Pepito Arvelo and Manuel Peña, both of whom worked with Cugat briefly, spoke of him in admiring terms. While they described Cugat as "commercially minded," they praised the quality of his ensemble, noting that he attracted the best musicians because of his ability to pay.[102] Indeed, Cugat and his many Puerto Rican musicians benefited mutually from their work together. The bandleader needed performers who were proficient on their instruments and able to read music. For the musicians, such positions brought steady though not especially well-paying work. Catalino Rolón earned forty dollars per week playing for Cugat in the mid-thirties. He had a grueling seven-day-per-week schedule, playing for an afternoon hotel buffet and then relieving the featured band in the evenings.

There were economic as well as physical hardships associated with such a life, and musicians developed their own creative coping mechanisms. Cuban-born Desi Arnaz, the famous bandleader, television star, and producer, began his career as a singer for Cugat. In the band at the same time as Rolón, he had replaced the Puerto Rican vocalist Pedro Berríos. In his memoirs he notes:

> I had been featured at the Waldorf; I had been the closing act in his theater show; but I was still getting only thirty-five dollars a week. To live on thirty-five dollars a week in New York, even in those days, was very difficult. . . .

Having to go through the Waldorf kitchen to get to the bandstand helped. I
lifted all the celery, olives, carrots, pieces of bread, buns and butter and whatever else I could stash into my rumba shirt every time we came back through
the kitchen for our ten-minute rest. Those wide, full sleeves with all the big
ruffles were very useful.[103]

Although these clubs were beyond the financial means of the majority
of the Hispanic residents of New York City, they were integral to the
lives of members of the working-class Puerto Rican and Latino communities. Not only did they employ musicians from these communities but
they had a parallel and sometimes overlapping relationship to the many
clubs and theaters catering to the Latino working class in New York
City. Variety formats, trends in popular Latin and American dance music, and even artists were shared by ostensibly different types of performance spaces. A cursory inspection of lists of performers for the Apollo
Theater, for example, indicates that some of them worked simultaneously in American vaudeville, in legitimate theater, and at the fancier
clubs. Thus the same act might play before audiences of varying ethnici-
ties and classes, and better-known performers might rub elbows with
up-and-coming or humbler ones.

The prestige accruing from membership in a band such as Cugat's
was also an important benefit not only for Puerto Rican musicians but
also for their neighbors. The performers who went downtown may have
had little time to play for their *compatriotas,* but their mainstream success had a special meaning for those who had housed, fed, and inspired
them. Rather than opposing these jobs on the grounds of an abstract
musical purity, Barrio Puerto Ricans celebrated the achievements of
their musical friends and family members, a triumph in both symbolic
and material terms. Puerto Ricans, who along with other Latinos were
routinely portrayed in the mainstream press as criminals or dissolute
and lazy figures, appreciated the good publicity their famous musicians
brought them. On a more concrete level, successful musicians also
brought money to their families and communities.

Nor were the musicians who played for Cugat and other downtown
Latin and North American groups irrevocably fixed on a path leading
toward musical homogenization. Some musicians traveled uptown after
hours to play the rest of the night in Barrio clubs and small ensembles.
Music and arrangers also floated between the two spheres, making their
differences, as John Storm Roberts suggests, less than "watertight."[104]

In fact, the careers of most musicians involved a good deal of traveling back and forth between the two spheres and multiple types of music,

all in the interest of earning a living. The New York career of Francisco López Cruz illustrates this point and shows the range of prospects for a literate, versatile, light-skinned Puerto Rican musician in the 1920s and 1930s. Early in his career he performed for gangsters in the Gallant Fox, a midtown speakeasy with a Puerto Rican *trío* playing both American and Latino dance music. He worked with Cuban trumpeter Pedro Vía on a radio program aired on NBC and freelanced as a guitarist for Latino groups doing recording. He played at various Hispanic-nationality ethnic clubs and at going-away parties for Puerto Ricans returning to the island. toward the end of the 1920s and in the early 1930s he played in the small ensembles of Pedro Flores, Canario, and Rafael Hernández.

López Cruz's career breaks down many stereotypes and misconceptions regarding ethnic musicians. He played Latin music for Americans and American music for Latinos. His abilities and repertoire spanned the spectrum of Puerto Rican music and incorporated many other sounds. He played for humble ethnic clubs and NBC. His career and those of many other artists reveal their often economically induced versatility. At the same time, they suggest that musicians were able to travel "backward" from work within Americanized settings to closer identification with Puerto Rican or Latin American sounds. López Cruz's New York career began downtown and ended with the *cuarteto* sound.

PERFORMANCE STRATEGIES

Although the musicians made choices that were logical for them and were often supported by their uptown *compatriotas,* there is no doubt that their pieced-together work lives had some effects on both their Puerto Rican and their non-Latino audiences. As mock Cubans or simulated Mexicans in a North American entertainment world anxious to see and hear their ideas of what a "Latin" was like, Puerto Ricans were involved in self-conscious self-stereotyping that was at times relatively benign, at times blatantly denigrating to their ethnic community's image. Some of this stereotyping was accepted and incorporated within a community that still maintained a high level of ethnic pride, and all of it was fraught with ambiguity and irony.

Puerto Rican music and musicians were important visible and auditory symbols for an ethnic group fighting against the onslaught of constant negative images presented in the mainstream press, cinema, and other media. At the same time, Puerto Ricans sometimes had roles in the very movies that helped to create these stereotypes of a generic Latin.

López Cruz, for example, was drafted along with his brother into Mexican films made in an uptown studio:

> In upper Manhattan, around 125th Street in Harlem, there was a studio that prepared Hispanic shorts and sold them to Hollywood. The musicians who played were Mexicans. And they recruited me and my brother. They paid us fifty dollars an hour. In that era fifty dollars was a big sum. They gave us two dollars for lunch. No one ate two dollars' worth in that era. We ate with fifty cents, sixty cents, the most that we could.[105]

Playing roles that were probably typically "Mexican" or "Argentine" was, in the context of the times, extremely lucrative for musicians. Efraín Vaz was explicit about this incentive: "I did everything. The thing was to earn myself cash *[chavo]*, to the point where one time I made a Mexican film. They came to the union: 'I need men with mustaches and everything.' I held a big *guitarrón* and faked playing it *[haciéndolo a guaje]*."[106] Such morally questionable projects not only earned money for the musicians but helped their communities in direct and indirect ways. Were it not for the enormous sums mentioned above, for example, López Cruz could not have provided financial assistance to so many struggling Latinos. Additionally, such work sustained him in New York and thus enabled him to make many fine contributions to Cuarteto Victoria and other groups producing a more "patriotic" sound.

In live performance, musicians also catered to North American perceptions of Latinos, which reveals some interesting dimensions of the performers themselves. Johnny Rodríguez, for example, expressed himself in no uncertain terms about the correctness of his choice to work downtown. At the same time, he maintained a cynical attitude about American entertainers. He was convinced that Americans were superficial in their appetites, more taken with visual spectacles than with good music. "As I was a little boy *[muchachito]* who had personality, I entertained more than I sang. I learned that from the Americans. The Americans who sing are always good entertainers."[107] Performers such as Rodríguez were acutely aware of what they had to do to evoke the appropriate images for middle-and upper-class North American audiences. In the more Americanized Latin clubs, such as the Toreador, El Chico, and numerous venues in the midtown area, Puerto Rican musicians were required to play different types of Latin, American, and Americanized Latin music for Latino and non-Latino audiences. In turn, the Americans and others who frequented such places formed images of Hispanic artists, music, and dance from the shows they saw there as well as from the popular Latin songs or movies of the moment.

Rodríguez used visual clichés probably drawn from Latin American–flavored movies to entrance his audience at the Stork Club, for whom he prepared a new Latin show. After his female vocalist sang "Quiéreme Mucho" (Love Me Madly), "I put on a *guayabera* with beautiful colors, a Cuban *guayabera,* and that was very new there. I went by the tables dancing. I danced with a glass [of water] on my head, and that was a sensation."[108]

Musicians would sometimes use the very stereotypes of Spanish speakers held by North American audiences to trick them and show off their own inventiveness. López Cruz liked to hoodwink his audience with his own versions of "authentic" Latin songs. Doing so, he managed to please audiences while still rebelling in a personally creative manner: "Sometimes we musicians took advantage of the dancers. A person who we knew was an ignoramus would come and say: 'Play something Spanish and upbeat,' and I would say, 'Oh sure, of course.' Then I'd invent something and my brother accompanied me, and the güiro as well, and they [the audience] would dance to it, and they'd applaud a lot. All musicians do that."[109] López Cruz punctuated his point with a hummed rendition of a "typical" Spanish tune, along the lines of a *pasodoble,* the type of song an American or even a Latino would associate with a bullfight scene in a "Spanish" movie. To an extent, musicians had to be aware of and utilize these stereotypes in catering to their audiences. Their repertoires were full of riffs that were ethnic clichés embodied in music but nevertheless had powerful connotations for their listeners.

Puerto Rican and Latino audiences sometimes accepted and perpetuated these sorts of stereotypes. Puerto Ricans and other Latinos in New York were able to celebrate the achievements of their artistic compatriotas outside of the ethnic community and to adapt North American–produced materials to their own needs. They welcomed their compatriots when they returned from their multiethnic odysseys, accepting the new musical ideas and fusions they brought with them. Just as the distinctions between uptown and downtown were not watertight in terms of personnel, nor were they in terms of repertoire. For example, Latino audiences were prone to ask for the same stereotyped Latin songs that took American audiences by storm. López Cruz remarked that even for such audiences, "you had to play what they asked for. . . . They always asked for what was in style. When 'El Manisero' arrived, that's what everyone asked for."[110] It got to the point where López Cruz and his group could predict when someone approaching the bandstand was going to ask for that well-worn number (in the first half of the 1930s this usually meant every request), which was even performed by the supposedly more "folkloric" groups, such as Canario's.

Stereotypes could be perpetuated in more subtle ways as well. When López Cruz worked in the Gallant Fox, for example, he played American songs, but without vocals. As vocalist Bobby Capó has pointed out, unlike heavily accented French performers such as Maurice Chevalier, Latin American performers singing in English with a heavy accent have never impressed American audiences as charming.[111] In American-oriented venues, performers cut the songs shorter than they would for Latinos and concentrated on the types of danceable Latin numbers known to North Americans, for which the lyrics were not so important.

In this way, Americans could continue to stereotype Latin Americans as naturally rhythmic people whose music was all dance-oriented. North Americans knew "El Manisero" but missed out on Rafael Hernández's "Lamento Borincano" and other fervent political and romantic songs that were often the staple of large and small Puerto Rican and Latino ensembles. Such songs were as classic to Puerto Ricans in their time as those of Cole Porter and Duke Ellington were to their North American contemporaries. While New York's Puerto Rican audiences and musicians were familiar with Porter and Ellington, however, names like Rafael Hernández and Plácido Acevedo meant nothing to North Americans. It was left to Puerto Rican working-class audiences to listen and dance to the fiercely patriotic and nostalgic numbers their *compatriotas* composed for them.

ORDEN DE BAILE

PRIMERA PARTE

Vals: **Lágrimas Borinqueñas** .... Con...............

Danzón: **Qué me haré** .... Con...............

Foz Trot: .... Con...............

Danzón: **Pocho las lágrimas se
me salen** .... Con...............

Fox Trot .... Con...............

Danza: **Flor de Canela** .... Con...............

SEGUNDA PARTE

Vals: **Son tus Ojos** .... Con...............

Danza: **El Bouquet** .... Con...............

Fox Trot .... Con...............

Danzón: **Lo sé todo** .... Con...............

Danza: **Laura y Georgina** .... Con...............

Fox Trot .... Con...............

Danzón: **Caramelo Santo** .... Con...............

Rumba Final .... Con...............

Orquesta *"Los Hijos de la Noche"*

Dirigida por *Yeyo y Pocholo-*

Conserve éste y úselo en la noche del baile

(Keep this and use it the night of the ball)

1. Dance card *(carnet)*, 1923. Although this dance program is from a dance sponsored by the "Porto Rican" Worker's Alliance in New York City, it gives an idea of the format of the *carnet* and the order and mixtures of dances. Courtesy of the Jesús Colón Papers, Benigno Giboyeaux, for the Estate of Jesús Colón and the Communist Party of the United States of America, Centro de Estudios Puertorriqueños, Hunter College, New York.

2. Aguadilla school band at the turn of the century. Bandleader José Ruellán Lequerica is in the front row, at left. Rafael Hernández is in the front row, third from right. Courtesy of the Instituto de Cultura Puertorriqueña, San Juan, and of Héctor Campos Parsi, Cayey, Puerto Rico.

3. Orquesta Happy Hills, San Germán, Puerto Rico, early 1930s. Pepita Nazario, center, pianist and musical director of the group, may have been the first female member and leader of a popular ensemble in Puerto Rico. Courtesy of Pedro Malavet Vega, Ponce, Puerto Rico.

4. Rafael and Jesús "Pocholo" Hernández as soldiers during World War I. Courtesy of Donald Thompson, Río Piedras, Puerto Rico.

5. Francisco "El Paisa" Quiñones, Puerto Rican singer and sugar mill mechanic, shown as a soldier in World War I. Courtesy of Ovidio Dávila, Vega Alta, Puerto Rico, and La Casa Alonso, Vega Baja, Puerto Rico.

6. James Reese Europe and his band en route to France, December 1917. Courtesy of the National Archives, Washington, D.C., and of Donald Thompson, Río Piedras, Puerto Rico.

7. Augusto Coen and his Golden Casino Orchestra, New York, 1930s. Singer Davilita (Pedro Ortíz Dávila) is seated at the far right, and Augusto Coen stands next to
him. Courtesy of the Jesús Colón Papers, Benigno Giboyeaux, for the Estate of Jesús
Colón and the Communist Party of the United States of America, Centro de Estudios
Puertorriqueños, Hunter College, New York.

GRAN BAILE

ORGANIZADO POR EL

CLUB AZTECA

PARA CELEBRAR LA

FIESTA DE LÀ RAZA

a beneficio de los damnificados de

PUERTO RICO

EN EL BALL ROOM DEL HOTEL PENNSYLVANIA

CALLE 33 Y SEPTIMA AVENIDA

Sabado 15 de Octubre de 1932

A LAS 9 P. M.

2 - ORQUESTAS - 2

ADMISION:

Caballeros: adelantado $1.00 . . . . Damàs $1.00
"   en la Taquilla . . . $1.50

Con autorizacion del Puerto Rico Hurricane Relief Committee.

No es requisito traje de etiqueta.   Para raza blanca.

Tickets de venta en: Libreria Cervantes - 62 Lenox Avenue; Fotografía Torres - 224 West 116th Street;
Restaurant El Rancho - 57 Lenox Avenue; Constance Hand Laundry 104 W. 111th Street y en los princi-
pales establecimientos de Manhattan, Brooklyn, Queens, Bronx y Richmond.

Triangle Printing Company, 9 West 19th St., New York.

8.   Flyer for Columbus Day dance, 1932. Note the words "Para raza blanca" (Whites only) in the lower right-hand corner. Courtesy of the Jesús Colón Papers, Benigno Giboyeaux, for the Estate of Jesús Colón and the Communist Party of the United States of America, Centro de Estudios Puertorriqueños, Hunter College, New York.

9. El Chico offered pan-Latino entertainment to affluent audiences. The performers pictured here include a Guatemalan bass player, a Mexican *maracas* player, and Spanish dancers. The Puerto Rican guitarist, José Armengol Díaz (standing with guitar, second from right), also played with Rafael Hernández, Pedro Flores, and Canario. Courtesy of José Armengol Díaz, Passaic, New Jersey.

10. Mother's Day celebration in Brooklyn at a Puerto Rican branch of the International Workers' Order, 1937. Courtesy of the Jesús Colón Papers, Benigno Giboyeaux, for the Estate of Jesús Colón and the Communist Party of the United States of America, Centro de Estudios Puertorriqueños, Hunter College, New York.

11. Puerto Rican and Hispanic League, Brooklyn section, ca. 1920s. Courtesy of the Jesús Colón Papers, Benigno Giboyeaux, for the Estate of Jesús Colón and the Communist Party of the United States of America, Centro de Estudios Puertorriqueños, Hunter College, New York.

12. Lower East Side Hispanic Drum and Bugle Corps, New York City, 1937. Courtesy of the Jesús Colón Papers, Benigno Giboyeaux, for the Estate of Jesús Colón and the Communist Party of the United States of America, Centro de Estudios Puertorriqueños, Hunter College, New York.

13. Julio Roqué, the musical dentist. Courtesy of Rafael Portela, Río Piedras, Puerto Rico.

14.   Trío Marcano, in the *rumba* shirts many Latino performers wore during
the 1930s. From left: Piquito Marcano, Pepito Arvelo, and Claudio Ferrer.
Courtesy of Ovidio Dávila, Vega Alta, Puerto Rico, and La Casa Alonso,
Vega Baja, Puerto Rico.

15.   Cuarteto Machín, 1926. Plácido Acevedo, the group's Puerto Rican trumpet player, is at the left. The other members of the group were Cubans: from left, Daniel Sánchez, Antonio Machín, and Cándido Vicenti. Courtesy of Ovidio Dávila, Vega Alta, Puerto Rico, and La Casa Alonso, Vega Baja, Puerto Rico.

16.   Nathaniel Shilkret with the Victor Studio Orchestra, which played behind many ethnic musicians during recording sessions. Courtesy of the Harold D. Smith Collection, National Library of Canada, Ottawa.

17. A young Davilita, just a few years after his first recording, "Lamento Borincano." Courtesy of Ovidio Dávila, Vega Alta, Puerto Rico.

18. Rafael Hernández in his New York *bohemio* days. Courtesy of Rafael Portela, Río Piedras, Puerto Rico.

19.   Cuarteto Victoria. From left to right, Davilita, Rafael Rodríguez, Francisco "Paquito" López Cruz, and Rafael Hernández. Courtesy of Ovidio Dávila, Vega Alta, Puerto Rico, and La Casa Alonso, Vega Baja, Puerto Rico.

20.   Canario y Su Grupo in one of its numerous incarnations, 1931. From left
to right, in white shirts: Peyín Serrano, Pedro Marcano, Francisco "Paquito"
López Cruz, José Armengol Díaz, Ramón Quirós. Manuel "Canario" Jiménez
is in suit and tie. Courtesy of Pedro Malavet Vega, Ponce, Puerto Rico.

CHAPTER FOUR

"Vénte Tú"

Puerto Rican Musicians
and the Recording Industry

"If they had to give up eating, they gave up eating in order to buy records," declared Francisco López Cruz, remembering his *compatriotas* living in New York City in the 1920s and 1930s. "It was more important to be happy in one's heart than to have one's stomach full. That's the way the Puerto Rican is."[1]

The records made by Puerto Rican musicians took their place among a variety of popular sounds as an indispensable part of the cultural world of their co-ethnics. Many Puerto Ricans eagerly bought the dozens of new *boleros, rumbas, sones, danzas,* and *guarachas* that were regularly offered by the record stores of New York's Spanish-speaking neighborhoods. Some hired musicians or prevailed upon friends to play, but often as not, the Victrola was the sole source of musical entertainment for working-class Puerto Ricans. For a relatively small investment, these migrants could liven up the atmosphere of the humblest private celebrations. Puerto Rican records, often made by their neighbors, provided a backdrop for romance, expressed nostalgia about the island or complaints about life in New York, and translated political discontent into a more acceptable cultural format.

The intensity such music had for its composers, performers, and audiences, however, was tempered by the commercial circumstances of its creation. While guitarist López Cruz perceptively commented on the passion with which his neighbors embraced these mechanically reproduced sounds, such music had one meaning for its ardent consumers and another for its creators. During the era between the world wars, making records was not an end in itself for Puerto Rican musicians but a source of at least occasional income and a crucial promotional tool for artists. Semiprofessional and professional Puerto Rican popular musicians might move in different circles and each piece together his or her own patchwork of a career, but virtually all of them had one thing in common, namely, the time spent in the recording studio. Making records was especially important for *tríos, cuartetos,* and *plena* ensembles. If New York City gave birth to a golden age of Puerto Rican small-ensemble music, the record industry was its midwife.

The North American record industry had its own relationship to this unique musical ferment among migrant Puerto Ricans. Record production, especially ethnic record production, was as much a sideline for North American companies as it was for musicians, though for different reasons. Whereas artists used records to promote their live performances, companies utilized them to promote their phonographs. The net result of this confluence of motives was the almost incidental preservation, with substantial commercial and mechanical mediation, of a primarily working-class ethnic American music.

A complex business involving production, promotion, distribution, and consumption, the recording industry required the collaboration of many people. The ethnic audiences who eagerly sought tangible proof of their continuing culture, as well as the musicians and their merchant, promoter, and club owner collaborators, who wanted to earn a living, all worked in conjunction with the more formal mechanisms of the recording industry. Artists and other entertainment figures struggled with a balance between versatility and authenticity, marketability and aesthetic virtue, as did the recording executives they came into contact with, though not always in entirely compatible or parallel ways. Their complex interactions would, in turn, have cultural consequences for the consuming audiences they spent so much energy trying to please.

RECORDING IN LATIN AMERICA

The foreign activities of the Victor Talking Machine Company, the Columbia Phonograph Company, the Edison National Phonograph Company, and other firms were an important precedent their ethnic recording efforts in the United States.[2] In their overseas work the U.S. companies developed attitudes and selection and marketing practices that would carry over to their work with North American ethnics. From the early twentieth century they influenced the musical tastes and expectations of foreign musicians and audiences, Spanish speakers being prominent among them. In turn, this would have an effect on musical culture in Latin America. Both recording ethnic musicians in their native countries and making sounds from the United States available to them, Victor, Columbia, Edison, and other companies made sure that Puerto Rico and its neighbors acquired a mixed musical legacy. The early activities of the recording industry in Latin America provided exposure to a variety of musics for both musicians and audiences migrating from the region. Latin American expectations of mechanical musical production and consumption were tempered by a commercial connection dating to the late nineteenth century.

By the 1890s the phonograph was a commercially viable, if crude, machine and the first record players and discs were manufactured by several North American companies and their European subsidiaries and competitors. Despite the popularity of records by a few early artists, such as Italian tenor Enrico Caruso and North American bandleader John Philip Sousa, selling phonographs was the central and most lucrative business of Columbia, Victor, Edison, and their contemporaries. The domestic market was quickly flooded with these "talking machines," forcing companies to look further afield for their customers.

Years before Rafael Hernández, Pedro Marcano, Plácido Acevedo, and their contemporaries immortalized their small-ensemble sound on disc, North American record companies had captured a worldwide market. By the first decade of the twentieth century, Columbia, for example, was selling and recording in central Africa as well as in central Europe. Russia, Poland, China, Japan, and Australia were among other countries that felt the effects of this expanding musical empire. Latin America, so close geographically to the United States, so politically and economically intertwined with its business interests, figured prominently in this early trade. Columbia was making records in Mexico City as early as 1904, and Victor, by 1905.[3] Before the decade was over, they would also be active in Havana, Buenos Aires, and San Juan, Puerto Rico.[4] By 1915 virtually all of Latin America had been penetrated by North American phonograph companies.

In many ways, the powerful North American phonograph and record industry possessed striking parallels to other neocolonial, capitalist business arrangements developing in Latin America at the same time. There was a pattern here: extraction of natural resources, which were then refined, processed abroad, and resold to the people in the country of origin. The music industry recruited its raw material, live talent, from virtually all parts of the region and recorded those artists in makeshift studios in their home countries. The companies pressed the records in the United States and then marketed them to the populations of the countries from which the music had come. Victor, Columbia, and their contemporaries enticed Puerto Rican and other Latin American merchants with exclusive dealerships for their phonographs and records and in turn employed these merchants as scouts for native talent. In Puerto Rico, for example, these companies—like the sugar and tobacco industries—were enriched by the efforts of their island intermediaries. At the same time, the invasion of external technological and economic agents stymied the development of indigenous industries. In the case of music, this would create cultural as well as economic repercussions.

AQUATIC AGENTS AND FLOATING STUDIOS

Like the European monarchs four centuries before them, Victor, Columbia, and their ilk employed professional explorers who spent years continent-hopping by boat. These modern conquistadores, however, went in search of new phonograph consumers and "native" talent. They were not so much experts in Latin American music as functionaries who transferred successful selling formulas and ideas about music selection from one place to another. Indeed, many company agents who worked in Latin America had begun in a completely different part of the world.

Newspaper articles and surviving recording ledgers provide a fascinating glimpse into the lives of these agents. Commercial expeditions to Puerto Rico began at least as early as June 1909. The visitor that summer was William Friedberg, a Columbia recording-lab expert who had previously collected music in China and Japan. He was assisted by Columbia distributor González Padín Hermanos. This department store subsequently carried the records, which were also listed in export catalogs to be sent all over Latin America. A *Talking Machine World* report on the expedition is typical of trade magazines' misunderstanding of and contempt for the music their constituents were collecting for their profit. It also illustrates the incredible Yankee ignorance of Puerto Rican sounds in particular:

> In the course of the next three or four months there will be let loose on the blasé American public an assortment of canned music that will be calculated to put life into even the most bored. Love songs in the original Porto Rican language, whatever that may be, will be heard floating from every apartment house window on quiet summer nights, vieing [sic] with the industrious mos-

quito in making sleep a longed-for and unachievable goal. Porto Rican folk dances will assault the ear from every source, while no public place will be completed [sic] without a phonograph, including a record imprinted with the Porto Rican equivalent of "We Won't Go Home Until Morning.". . .

The expedition which is to corral these harmonic efforts of the guileless Porto Rican aborigine will leave to-morrow morning.[5]

With the help of its commercial representative, the department store of Luis Sánchez Morales, Victor kicked off its own 1917 Latin American and Caribbean tour with forty-eight selections recorded in Puerto Rico.[6] Scouts and recording engineers had an extensive, hectic itinerary, only a tiny portion of it in Puerto Rico. Just a few days on the island in early January were followed by about two weeks in various regions of Venezuela. After a brief return to New York, the crew continued to Barbados, Uruguay, Argentina, Chile, Bolivia, Peru, Ecuador, Panama, and Colombia, docking for just a few hours in some cities. In their eleven-month tour the group braved many disasters—drunk musicians, one-legged singers who missed their recording dates, squabbles between rival ensembles, shipments of broken records, town fires.[7] The crew adapted the performers' sounds to the technical capacity of their equipment, starting a process of subtle modification. A note from their sojourn in Venezuela, for example, mentions that a crew member had taken the seeds out of an artist's *maracas* and replaced them with ball bearings, which were easier to capture on records.[8] Undoubtedly this crew, which learned only the basics of Spanish and of Latino music as they went from country to country, changed a great deal more as well.

Company scouts and recording engineers who traveled to Latin America inevitably had preconceived ideas of what was appropriately commercial music and how to get at it. A balance had to be struck between the selection processes they had used in other countries and the local circumstances in which they found themselves. For example, though the genres recorded depended upon the country and what was popular, decisions were based on the ideas of an elite merchant class and the tastes of those who could afford phonographs. Local merchants were often both the intermediaries who found the artists and the providers of hastily improvised recording studios. They received an exclusive dealership from one of the North American record companies and in turn brought hopeful talent in from the hinterlands. In Havana, for example, the agent was La Casa Humara. A hardware store founded in 1854, it had both contacts and clients throughout the island and "a solid prestige, something Victor needed in order to introduce such novelties as windup Victrolas and records." As store personnel sold phonographs all over Cuba, they kept their eyes out for local talent. Victor executives would periodically visit the island to make final selections and sign the contracts before recording got under way.[9] After the recording, the master disks were sent by boat to New York or New Jersey for processing, and then they were prepared for reexport to Latin America. The company would issue a few thousand records, and the artist would tour the island with the store's promotional agent, who was often the very same Victrola salesman and talent scout.

In Puerto Rico a similar structure meant that formal orchestras and bands, operatic singers, and concert instrumentalists were immortalized on discs. Despite the tiny size of the island, neither Victor nor Sánchez Morales seems to have made an effort to recruit much beyond the most visible San Juan ensembles for their 1917 sessions. The Puerto Rican Regimental Band, a school chorus, and an orchestra led by Rafael Hernández were recorded. So were speeches and poetry by politician and writer José de Diego, a few small ensembles, and the tenor Francisco "El Paisa" Quiñones.

The repertoire recorded was quite different from that later offered by Puerto Rican groups in New York. Nevertheless, it reflected the multiple outside influences on the Puerto Rican music of the era. The groups sang and played not only the aristocratic Puerto Rican *danza* but also salon dances of Cuban influence, such as *danzones,* and European origin, including *pasodobles, valses,* and mazurkas. On the other hand, the elaborate strophic music of the *jíbaros,* subsistence farmers of the Puerto Rican highlands, and the complex rhythms of the Afro–Puerto Ricans working in the coastal sugar industry were virtually ignored. These recordings thus crystallized a carefully selected diversity of sounds played and heard in Puerto Rico. Choosing what they felt would sell the most, record companies preserved genres and songs based on market concerns.[10]

In making decisions about recording and distribution, which had such important ramifications for their constituents, North American companies were not just culling the most danceable sounds from one particular country. They were also taking into account established trade routes, favorable population demographics, and their political ties with each territory. Close economic links between the United States and Latin America had accounted for reciprocal influences between their popular musics for many years. With the establishment of U.S. cinema, radio, and record company branches in various parts of Latin America, a powerful culture-industry flow dominated by U.S. businesses was well established by the early 1920s.

The activities of U.S. record companies produced their own musical cross-fertilizations between Latin American countries, affecting most heavily the territories over which they had the most economic control. Cuba, for example, had been an important trading partner of the United States since the late eighteenth century. Its land area and population were much greater than those of the other Antilles, and not surprisingly, Cuban records were preeminent within the U.S.-dominated culture industry. In their ongoing attempts to make records as economically as possible while selling as many phonographs as they could, manufacturers relied on Latin America's almost universal use of Spanish to promote a musical interchangeability between countries.[11]

Spanish was not a prerequisite, however, for an unequal distribution based on externally made political and trade decisions. Thus, during the U.S. occupation of Haiti from 1915 to 1934, the Haitians were flooded with both North American and Cuban bands and dance styles, partly via U.S.-produced radios and records.[12] The U.S. occupation of the Dominican Republic formally from 1916–1924, and tacitly thereafter, had much the same result. The Dominican Republic began receiving records from North American companies in 1913. Although these included *danzas, danzones, canciones,* zarzuelas, operas, and two-steps, there was no Dominican-produced material among them. It was not until 1928 that the first records were made of Dominican artists in their homeland. Meanwhile, the Dominican Republic's first famous popular singer, Eduardo Brito, who recorded for Victor in New York in 1929, had grown up imitating the (mostly Cuban) music to be heard on the few record players in his town. Throughout most of his subsequent artistic life, Brito was billed as a Cuban singer, inappropriate to his national origins but appropriate to the mechanical legacy he and his assorted Latin American audiences shared.[13]

The musical environments and tastes of Puerto Rican artists and audiences were formed under similar circumstances. Puerto Rico's ongoing colonial ties to the United States served to make it a guaranteed market for the sounds produced by the North American companies, rather than for a large and representative sampling of its own musical forms. In general, the island's musical resources were tapped much less frequently than those of Cuba, Mexico, Argentina, and many other parts of Latin America. While Puerto Rican musicians were sporadically and almost perfunctorily scouted and recorded, record company dealerships established prior to these local recording efforts assured that Puerto Ricans had already received mechanically reproduced Latin American music from other countries.

This colonialism also bolstered a deliberate underdevelopment of local recording facilities within Puerto Rico. While recording facilities in much of Latin America were initially makeshift, relatively sophisticated studios developed in Mexico, Argentina, and other sites, and they remained primitive at best in Puerto Rico. Francisco López Vidal, for example, recorded for Victor in the 1920s in the studios of radio station WKAQ. All recordings were made after midnight, when the trolleys had stopped running, on fragile acetates; a tiny mistake could make the recording session last all night. The problems of these less than ideal studio conditions were compounded by the technical difficulties of the recording industry in that time period. "We recorded with only two microphones," remembers López Vidal, "one for the orchestra and one for the singer. So what happened was that I played saxophone and violin. The one who played the trumpet played saxophone and violin, and the one who played the guitar also played violin. So when an interlude came with the violins we had to run [to change instruments]." [14] Guitarist Ramón "Moncho" Dávila remembers recording sites that were not even remotely connected to the music industry. During the 1930s he and his Cuarteto Aurora recorded for the Brunswick label in a lodge of the Caballeros de la Verdad (Knights of Truth), in Old San Juan. [15] Predictably, all the recordings made by these North American companies were mass-produced in factories in the New York region.

Just as the possibility of better economic conditions compelled working-class Puerto Ricans to migrate to the metropolitan center of their colonizers, so poor local prospects induced ambitious Puerto Rican musicians to establish themselves in New York. But these hopeful artists entered the city at a time when the major North American phonograph companies were determining to concentrate less on overseas performers and more on local immigrant talent.

ETHNIC RECORDING IN THE UNITED STATES

Two major factors combined to inaugurate the second phase of foreign-language recording by U.S.-based record companies, that taking place on their home turf. First was the companies' ongoing primary concern, the sale of talking machines. Both at home and abroad, these firms had applied most of their energies to enticing the "better classes" to buy phonographs. In the United States this meant producing prestige series of classical recordings as well as ever more elaborate cabinetry for their record-playing equipment. But sales slowed by the second decade of the twentieth century, compelling the companies to find ways to intrigue new classes and groups. Second, World War I cut off American companies' access to Europe as a source of raw musical material or a market, another motivation for turning to the spectrum of ethnic and regional musics within the country.

Ethnic recording activities in the United States were both separate from and mingled with that geared toward a mainstream audience, in ways that would affect both musicians and listeners. As in Latin America, the major American labels created their own categories, cross-fertilizations, and selective criteria for recording and marketing domestic ethnic music. Multiethnic, classical, and popular musicians often crossed paths within a day's work in a single recording studio. These ethnic and regional sounds were not always accessible to the mainstream North American audience, often emerging briefly as fads and then disappearing. Hawaiian music enjoyed a general vogue in the World War I era. Italian opera stars were cross-listed in both general and Italian-language catalogs and were popular with other ethnic audiences as well. Ironically, "hillbilly" music from the American South and Midwest rated a separate catalog as a subculture music. Like much of the "race" music recorded by American blacks, the sounds of Appalachia's residents were virtually inaudible to the majority of citizens from other regions.

Different types of Latin American music in varying states of dilution also wove in and out of the North American consciousness. Ongoing exchanges between Southwestern "cowboy" music and Mexican *corridos,* the nationwide *tango* craze of the pre–World War I era, and the *rumba* infatuation of the 1930s are just a few examples.[16] For other reasons as well, Latino sounds formed a unique subset within a general ethnic framework. Some of the earliest ethnic records made by U.S. companies, for example, were by Mexicans from both sides of the border and predated even African-American and Appalachian recordings.[17] During World War I, Latin America was still a source for immigrants and musicians, as well as an important market for records. While the war and its aftermath cut off the immigration of other groups to the United States, it brought many of the newly naturalized Puerto Ricans to the continent both as soldiers and civilians, providing more potential musicians and audience members for the record companies. The politi-

cal and economic conditions that allowed North American companies
to mass-mediate Puerto Ricans on the island also led to a constant influx
of new migrants who kept alive a separate ethnic music and a demand
for it long after these had disappeared in most other U.S. ethnic communities.

Although the trend toward looking for foreign sounds on domestic
soil extended to Latin Americans as well, the divisions between the domestic and foreign branches of recording were never as clear-cut among
Spanish speakers as they were among members of other ethnic groups.
As a rule, Latin Americans tended to maintain the strongest ongoing
ties to the culture of their home countries, and that included loyalty to
their recording artists on both sides of the border or the ocean. Culturally as well as physically, many of these performers and their audiences
traveled back and forth between the homeland and the new country.

DOMESTIC STRATEGIES

Domestic ethnic recording at first overlapped with overseas ethnic recording, but it also heralded a significant change in audience and orientation. In the decades before the Depression, members of the urban and
rural lower classes of Europe, Asia, and Latin America usually found
steady work in the United States. Bolstered by factory or service-sector
jobs, these immigrants could often buy records and phonographs,
whereas "the impoverished classes they left behind" could not "and thus
did not constitute an audience for their own traditional entertainment,
so far as making and marketing records was concerned."[18] Within the
contours of these three-minute discs, ethnic music was almost by definition a genre by and for working-class migrants.

Puerto Ricans, of course, fit squarely within this category. The first
phonograph had been received on the island with great fuss and fanfare
in 1892, but only the wealthy could afford to buy this novelty for their
homes.[19] Once on the mainland, it was another story. While Bernardo
Vega remembers the modesty of entertainment possibilities among New
York's boricuas in the World War I era, he also tells us that Puerto Rican
records were already an important presence at their gatherings. They
had been available since at least 1918, when "Columbia was recording
danzas, aguinaldos, and other kinds of music from back home." Records
were both relatively cheap entertainment and a reflection of the local
community. Along with the songs recorded in Puerto Rico, boricuas
could listen to some of their talented local merchants, two barbers who
were among the first migrants to record: "Erasmo Lasalle was particu-

larly memorable, a first-rate singer who was the first man to make a recording of Puerto Rican music. His shop was frequented by another great Puerto Rican guitarist, Salvador Maldonado, who performed successfully in variety shows at the time."[20]

Clearly, phonograph companies had been quick to realize the enormous potential for this untapped market.[21] In their eagerness to cultivate new customers, Victor, Columbia, Brunswick, and their contemporaries created talking machines to fit the factory worker's budget. They also began to produce limited editions of suitable ethnic recordings in order to persuade a multiplicity of groups to buy these machines. As Harold Smith, in charge of the Victor Talking Machine Company's U.S. Foreign Department, observed in his memoirs, "In the great tide of immigration in the early 1900's thousands of the new-comers had settled in the foreign communities of our major cities. These foreign-born residents, confronted with a strange new language and customs, welcomed records of the songs and dances of their early days. . . . They were all prospective Victrola owners, if they could have attractive records in their own tongue."[22]

Company personnel often viewed the foreign-born as naïve and easy to manipulate. They also saw most ethnics as naturally musical and attracted to records. Much depended upon the particular group. The *Columbia Record* characterized Chinese music as an "ear-splitting-clatter" and an "awful pot-pourri of drums and string fiddles, never in tune,"[23] but spoke admiringly of African musicians.[24] Not surprisingly, in an article entitled "Edison Phonographs in Four Corners of the World: Instruments Entertaining and Educating Civilized People and Untutored Savages," *Talking Machine World* affirmed that "The native Cuban, like most of his Spanish-speaking prototypes, is musical by nature."[25] By 1917, Victor's house organ was exhorting retailers to take advantage of the "enormous" and "intensely musical . . . foreign element in our midst," and the company displayed a respectable array of ethnic catalogs in dozens of languages for domestic consumption, including Puerto Rican and Cuban versions.[26] A perusal of these catalogs, however, indicates that much of the material was still being culled from export lists and that most of the musicians either had been recorded on their home turf or had been brought over especially by the company to record. After World War I, Victor turned its eyes to the domestic ethnic market and discovered to its chagrin that its major competitor was already there:

> One sales field Victor had not fully explored and developed was that of domestic foreign languages. The U.S. census of 1920 showed that 13% of our population was foreign born. Fifteen or more years earlier, the company had

issued catalogs of foreign language records . . . but these were far outnum-
bered by the Columbia lists. Columbia had put a special effort behind this
product, with salesmen to contact dealers, and artists to record new foreign
language numbers without delay in their New York laboratory.[27]

Smith and his colleagues discovered that there was more to putting
together record collections to persuade the foreign-born to buy Victrolas
than just juggling existing inventories, since "each foreign language
group was constantly adding new musical hits to its best sellers," just as
mainstream Americans were doing. Emulating Columbia and following
advice from Ralph Peer, who had recruited and recorded artists for Victor's recently established "race" and "hillbilly" catalogs, Smith em-
barked on the extensive fieldwork and delicate community relations necessary to build conduits to ethnic artists and audiences. Starting in New
York and later visiting cities in the Midwest, Smith talked to dealers
already involved with the company and searched for new ones, especially in "foreign communities." However, he and his competitors discovered that the ethnic and class dimensions of this process were quite
different in the United States than abroad. Rather than dealing with
storekeepers who shared the linguistic and class background of their
clients, they found English-speaking vendors and establishments that
were isolated from potential foreign, working-class customers.

The company urged dealers to make surveys of the foreign populations surrounding them and to treat the occasional ethnic customer who
wandered in as an important liaison to his or her ethnic group. The store
proprietor was to ask the "Tony Andrianopolises," as one Milwaukee
dealer wrote, what types of records they would like to see in the store,
order them, and depend upon the word-of-mouth advertising ensuing
from such a conversation to bring in a flock of loyal customers.[28] But
increasingly the company found that

> the man who goes deliberately after foreign trade as the mainstay of his exis-
> tence is in a class by himself. As likely as not he is himself foreign-born,
> and has traveled widely among the people to whom he caters in their home
> countries. He has possibly increased his knowledge by acting as ship's stew-
> ard so that he knows what they eat, how they sleep, what are their political,
> social and economic shibboleths, and what happens to them after they land
> in America and shake down to their proper level in this amazing melting-pot
> of a country.[29]

Perhaps modeling their tactics on those of the urbane character described above, Victor looked to a group of ethnic and multilingual
Americans within its own ranks to help in the aggressive pursuit of new

artists and markets. Smith's "foreign roadmen" were often simultaneously fieldworkers locating new talent and company musicians or artist and repertory (A&R) staff.[30] Tetos Demetriades, a Greek singer for the company, recruited talent and became a producer and consultant in the making of Greek, Turkish, and Albanian records before forming his own Victor-affiliated label and ethnic record store. Alfredo Cibelli was a singer and mandolinist who was promoted to supervise Italian recordings, recruit and recommend Italian talent, and occasionally conduct Victor's International Novelty Orchestra. Working with ethnic record merchants, these agents helped the company discover the size and tastes of particular foreign populations, what records should be ordered, and who in the community was recording material. They translated or paraphrased foreign lyrics into English and found out about recorded music from the homeland worth re-releasing domestically. Working on small budgets in shoestring operations, such ethnic liaisons not only performed multiple tasks but dealt with a variety of ethnic groups. Cibelli, for example, became closely associated with the recruiting and making of Spanish-language recordings as well as Italian ones.

In general, capturing a local ethnic market meant a great deal more community work than did catering to a mainstream North American audience. Smith and his colleagues found that whereas North Americans were more prone to demand famous artists and groups far removed from their circle of acquaintances, "It stimulates interest in various localities to make foreign records of local talent."[31] It was also, of course, cheaper as well, once the record companies had worn enough shoe leather in the initial scouting process. At the same time, the fate of ethnic recording was somewhat independent of recording intended for a mainstream American audience. The often poor development of ethnic entertainment for foreign-born Americans, especially away from large cities, ensured that ethnic recording would flourish even at times when North American popular pressings did not. This activity was especially strong during the twenties, even after radio became a strong competitor for general audiences. While not only the Depression but also economic downturns, strikes, and other labor problems in immigrant-populated industries might noticeably affect record sales, manufacturers and merchants generally experienced a steady, if modest, business in ethnic recordings, and they tailored their expectations accordingly. Whereas a popular record for a general audience might sell several hundred thousand copies or more, a good ethnic record sale might consist of a few thousand or even a few hundred. In turn, the production of such limited

editions shaped manufacturers' attitudes toward ethnic musicians and
their procedures with them.

Ethnic recording was thus a valuable, if small-scale, business for Victor, Columbia, and their colleagues. As they had overseas, these companies utilized domestic ethnic storekeepers as liaisons to artists and audiences while making most of the profits themselves. Within the realm of
music, they made a concerted and basically successful effort to work in
conjunction with such entrepreneurs. In essence, this era's ethnic recording was by and for local people, though it was by no means controlled by them. Nevertheless, the effectiveness of company strategies
depended on the context of developments within particular ethnic
neighborhoods.

BARRIO RECORD OUTLETS

Phonograph company personnel had assiduously courted stores in Latin
America to perform the dual function of dealership and musician recruiting. Now they transferred this strategy to their U.S. territory. Many
merchants in ethnic communities, however, were precariously and im-
permanently just a step above the laboring classes themselves. Instead
of a few large, prestigious department stores serving as conduits between the music industry and elite customers, humbler establishments
served working-class customers with music essentially made by their
peers. Smith and his ethnic-attuned cohorts found that the dealers they
wished to reach were often modest and hidden within ethnic neighborhoods. Such stores, the company found, "are usually operated on small
capital, with a minimum overhead, and come under the head of statio-
nery, drugs, cigar, grocery stores and steamship agencies." [32]

This profile fit Puerto Rican settlement in New York. For the first
years after World War I, music stores were not among the most prominent Puerto Rican commercial entities. During that period, record stores
advertising in La Prensa the Spanish-language wares of Victor, Columbia, Pathé, and Odeon typically were run by non–Puerto Ricans, often
outside the neighborhoods with the largest Puerto Rican populations.
Daniel Castellanos, a Spaniard who advertised himself as the first New
York merchant of Spanish-language records, was established at least by
1922 and probably much earlier. His first shop was located in the South
Ferry area of lower Manhattan; later in the decade he opened three
branches, two of them in Harlem. The vast majority of shops advertising
Spanish-language wares were generally located in either lower Manhat-

tan or East Harlem and bore Jewish surnames. Some explicitly advertised that they had Latino managers for their Spanish departments. As in other businesses in East Harlem, change came gradually as the neighborhood's population shifted, and Jewish merchants sometimes stayed behind and adapted to the times. As late as 1929 Victoria Hernández, who had bought her record store from a Jewish owner for five hundred dollars, could advertise her shop as the only Puerto Rican–owned music establishment in New York City.[33] It was not until the 1930s that a few more Puerto Rican stores became visible among the proliferation of Harlem music shops.

Under these circumstances, various types of Puerto Rican–owned stores became critical conduits to new artists. Vega suggests, for example, that before the 1920s record companies used the Puerto Rican commercial enterprises to find their singing barbers. Despite this early start, in 1925, two years past the 1923 peak for their general foreign business, Victor reported only 25 Puerto Rican records in their catalogs to serve a population of twenty thousand mainland Puerto Ricans. By contrast, their Cuban and West Indian catalogs had a total of 355 records for a population little more than double the size of the Puerto Rican population.[34] This paucity of records was the result of a number of factors, including the record companies' prior musical "colonization" of Latin Americans in their home country with Cuban sounds, the popularity of such records among a general audience, and the lack of a critical mass of Puerto Rican migrant storekeepers who could be aggressive advocates for their musical co-ethnics.

While Victor stepped up its campaign in the late 1920s to gain a stronger foothold in what the company dubbed the "U.S. Foreign" market, neighborhood ethnic dealers sometimes had other ideas. As Smith and his foreign roadmen well knew, Victor's success was threatened not only by the competition of their big-business colleagues but by independent ethnic labels established by the very shopkeepers they sought to incorporate into their network. Some proprietors of small ethnic music store who began by trying to create the special records requested by their local co-national customers decided that their unique understandings of their community's tastes could serve them well financially. Independent pressing plants could be established with a small investment, and a spectrum of ethnic entrepreneurs entered the field in the 1920s.[35] Victoria Hernández was one of these.

When Hernández founded her landmark record store on Madison Avenue in 1927, she hoped to market music she had gathered and pressed herself. Employing her brother Rafael as composer and performer, she produced several records with two groups, Las Estrellas Boricuas (The Puerto Rican Stars) and Los Diablos de la Plena (The *Plena* Devils). The discs, recorded and possibly pressed in New Jersey, were sold for twenty cents, far below the prices charged by the major record companies, in New York, Puerto Rico, and Curaçao.[36]

In musical terms, independent labels such as Hispano had a great deal to offer to their communities. Arguably, some degree of originality as well as fidelity to older ethnic sounds went by the wayside of such short-lived efforts.[37] The songs written by Rafael Hernández and recorded on Hispano revealed in numerous ways the composer's intense sense of pride in his heritage. In these songs, as in many of his other creations, Hernández lovingly detailed Puerto Rican historical figures, towns, types of food, and slang expressions. On his Hispano recordings, however, Hernández was also able to use native instruments not found on many commercial recordings, as well as phrases and harmonic progressions taken from songs much beloved in Puerto Rico.

The best-known song from this phase of Hernández's career, "Pura Flama" (Pure Flame), illustrates how these symbols of national pride were mixed with more generalized conventions of Latino music. It was recorded by Las Estrellas Boricuas, a pickup group made up of some of the finest Puerto Rican musicians of the era. Francisco "El Paisa" Quiñones was the lead singer, and Heriberto Torres lent his virtuoso *cuatro* playing to the effort. The prominent use of *cuatro* and *güiro* gave a country flavor to what was decidedly not a piece of *jíbaro* music. Its use of alternating voices trading verses in a sort of musical argument was also reminiscent of the *controversia,* a style long practiced among the *jíbaros.* "Pura Flama," however, opened with the introductory theme of the *danza* that had become Puerto Rico's national anthem, "La Borinqueña." It continued in the lilting rhythm characteristic of the *danza,* although its harmonized singing style and verse structure were more akin to the *bolero.*

The form of "Pura Flama" simultaneously encapsulated diverse Puerto Rican symbols and was shaped by the popular music of the Hispanic Caribbean in general. At the same time, the song's words drew boundaries between Puerto Ricans and members of diverse ethnic groups living in New York:

Me casé con una china,
me dejó a bofetadas.

Luego una americana
que a mí me engañó.
Luego una japonesa,
y después una alemana.
Las judías están fachadas
pero allí no pico yo.

Yo no sé porque estas mujeres son así,
sólo sé que no me quieren a mí.

Si tú no eres chino ni francés,
ni hablas alemán ni japonés.

Razón que convence
cuando me quiero enamorar
me voy a Borinquén
para sentir el dulce hablar
de mi mulata cuando me dice,
Dame un beso mi papá.
Y yo le digo, Negra santa,
dame un beso mi mamá.

Mamá Borinquén me llama,
este país no es el mío.
Borinquén es pura flama
y aquí me muero de frío.

————

I married a Chinese woman,
she left me with slaps in the face.
Then an American woman
who deceived me.
Then a Japanese woman,
then a German woman.
Jewish women have nice figures
but there I don't sample.

I don't know why these women are that way,
I only know that they don't love me.

But you're not Chinese or French,
nor do you speak German or Japanese.

For that reason
when I want to fall in love
I go to Borinquén
to feel the sweet talk
of my *mulata* when she says to me,
Give me a kiss, my *papá*.
And I say to her, *Negra santa*,
give me a kiss, my *mamá*.

Mamá Borinquén is calling me,
this country is not mine.
Borinquén is pure flame
and here I'm dying of cold.

The mix of humor and patriotism was characteristic of the Hernández style. His comparisons of the Puerto Rican woman to the homeland
interwove thematic concerns in a way common to Puerto Rican popular
music of the era. Where a North American popular song of the era
would never have mixed together these diverse concerns, it made sense
to Puerto Rican listeners to combine politics with humor, romance with
love for the *patria*.

Hernández's imaginative blendings, however, soon had to be transferred to a more conventional commercial format. For once again, as
overseas, the economic power of the major companies shaped the cultural choices of record buyers. Victoria's dreams of a big, successful
company were dashed when her first five thousand dollars of earnings
disappeared in the failure of her bank in 1929. Hispano became a casualty of the Depression, which had hit even the powerful major companies hard. Both the particularities of the Depression and the general state
of the record industry made it difficult for the small ethnic music stores
to compete with the large North American companies, which were in-
tent upon capturing their market. Small companies working out of
record stores simply did not have the manufacturing, distribution, and
publicity channels that the major companies had, and so they had to
face their active challenges. The large firms clearly had superior resources, which could render them more effective than even ethnic "insiders," who ostensibly possessed superior knowledge of their audiences'
cultural needs. Musicians and store owners had to make their peace
with this uneven relationship and get out of it what they could. Victor,
for example, spent tens of thousands of dollars yearly for advertising in
the foreign-language press, in addition to its ad campaigns aimed at the
general audience.

Rather than war against ethnic stores, which were actual or potential
record producers, the large companies used their clout to woo them.
Victor enticed dealers with discounts on foreign records, well-designed
window-display items, and financial collaboration in newspaper advertising, all tempting for small-budget stores. In return, ethnic merchants
provided artists. The advantage for record sellers was that their protégés
were recorded under superior studio conditions, at the cost, however,
of company artistic and financial arrangements. The storekeeper who

wanted to make records outside of the tried-and-true sales formula or for obscure ethnic groups often assumed the risk by paying for production or agreeing to buy a minimum number of copies.

In these and other ways, record companies hoped both to win such stores over to function as exclusive channels for themselves and to make money in the process. Victor gave Victoria Hernández an exclusive dealership that was good for a radius of several blocks. In a densely populated area in which record stores were beginning to emerge and compete with her own, this was significant. It was benefited the company, giving it a guaranteed outlet as well as an excellent contact for recruitment of Puerto Rican musicians.

Such accommodations between the major companies and the small Puerto Rican record stores varied, partly in accordance with the competition between the record stores themselves. Gabriel Oller ran a record store in Harlem, where he set up the label Dynasonic in 1934:

> "With a name like Rafael Hernández to compete against," said Oller, "I had to have a gimmick and the Dynasonic test record was it.". . .
> He recorded the music of the neighborhood trios and quartets, the groups which played the house parties, weddings, and other social functions. Each musician received $3.00 for the session. The recordings were done on an acetate, a test record from which a master would be made for $2.50. Musicians like Caney, Johnny López, Panchito Rizet [sic] and Noro Morales recorded acetates and sold them to one of the three record companies at the time, RCA Victor, Columbia, and Decca.[38]

Oller's "gimmick," which passed audition records on to the major companies, probably started off as an earnest attempt to create an alternative label. He was only able to become independent, however, beginning in the 1940s, when the major companies' interest in specialty recording was waning.

Continued links between the island and mainland Puerto Rican markets meant that even stores in Puerto Rico could have contractual arrangements with the major companies while keeping in touch with their migrant musicians. Arturo Cátala of San Juan inspired the formation of Los Jardineros (The Gardeners), a New York–based group that recorded Puerto Rican country music on traditional instruments as well as the ubiquitous dance rhythms of Cuba and the United States. A protean collection of artists who played in other ensembles rather than an ongoing group, Los Jardineros existed mainly to supply original records to Cátala's store in Old San Juan. Cátala contracted with the major companies and *boricuas* residing in New York to make records to order for his audiences. Paquito López Cruz, who played with this group, remembers that Cátala "had a place in San Juan that was called the Jardín del Arte [Garden of Art]. There the records arrived, and they sold a great deal. Then he paid the musicians [and] ordered more recordings. The director there [in New York], Pedro Berríos, was the one who made the recordings. [Cátala] sent the money to Pedro Berríos, [who] would go to Victor or to Columbia to make the records."[39]

Record companies themselves fostered links between the island and the mainland by their marketing strategies. Victor periodically showcased its artists by sponsoring live and radio concerts in Puerto Rico.[40] Musicians sometimes even traveled back and forth on their own. Francisco "El Paisa" Quiñones, for example, was much in demand as a singer in New York but earned his living as a roving mechanic for Puerto Rican sugar *centrales*. Tied to his job, he could only make occasional trips to New York to record with his colleagues.[41]

BETWEEN STUDIO AND STORE

By the late 1920s, when recording of Puerto Rican artists flourished on a modest scale, such performers took for granted the powerful role of record stores and record store owners. Francisco López Cruz remembers that "Victor, for example, would go to a record shop in El Barrio, and they would say to the store owner, 'We want to make a number of records. Recommend me a group that plays well.'"[42] It is clear from musicians' comments that record stores could play a powerful role even working within the interstices of the major companies. Victor and other companies were dependent on record stores such as Victoria Hernández's to take the musical pulse of the community. In turn, these merchants could cultivate connections with the companies and serve as crucial links between them and the musicians in a multitude of ways. Victoria Hernández, as López Cruz, Mario Bauzá, and she herself remembered, would pay the musicians a cash advance for the recording sessions, the pay for which was usually two weeks in coming. In the event of failed sessions, in which no marketable records were produced, the musicians would still have received the money. In exchange for providing this security and assuming some risk, Hernández would receive a percentage of the musicians' checks. Musicians' accounts suggest that she may also have earned a commission on the artists she recommended to the record companies. In order to maintain her place as such a powerful liaison, Hernández would have been obliged by Victor to select for them the most commercially viable artists. In such a relationship, Hernández played an important role on behalf of the musicians.

Shopkeepers such as Victoria Hernández could thus profit from advancing the interests of both musicians and record companies. Although on the surface those interests were similar and sometimes meshed to the advantage of both, not too far below the surface was a continuation, with modifications, of the exploitive relationship begun overseas.

Both companies and musicians considered their recording activities a sideline, though a necessary one, to the business of selling phonographs and performing live, respectively. But the industry's needs structured this marginality for the musicians. Once the connections were made between artists and companies by shopkeepers or other intermediaries, the companies called the artists only sporadically. Knowing that they were catering to a limited market, manufacturers made only as many ethnic records as it took to sell phonographs. Puerto Ricans were even more marginal within this already marginal field. Companies kept fees as low as possible, as López Cruz remembers: "They paid little money. I don't remember exactly, but for one session of one record that was one song on one side, and one on the other, they paid twelve or fifteen dollars, nothing more, to each musician. But: If I got fifteen dollars, I could pay my room for a week and I could get lunch with thirty-five cents."[43]

The singer Davilita, who made many records with Rafael Hernández's Grupo Victoria, recalls a hierarchy in which Puerto Ricans and Cubans were paid less than other Spanish-language artists: "Victor never treated us like they did the Mexicans, the South Americans, . . . when it came to money . . . Venezuela, . . . and Argentina and all those countries charged a lot of money and [the company] paid them. . . . Cugat was Spanish, [he] charged as if he were an American, wherever he went. But the Puerto Ricans, no."[44]

Compounding these hardships, royalties on recordings were unheard of. Victor and other firms' policy of hiring local musicians was not just a way to please ethnic audiences, as Harold Smith had suggested; it also saved them from doling out fees on published materials. A perusal of logs from Victor recording sessions in the 1920s reveals that many ethnic artists, and particularly Latino ones, brought unpublished manuscripts or no music at all to their recording dates. They then signed a form ceding to the company the rights for the music, for which they would receive a one-time and probably minuscule payment. The recording of original music by local working-class artists was thus an ironic by-product of a pernicious system.

The companies' lack of focused interest in and financing for the ethnic recording department shaped both their work strategies and those of the artists. Since the A&R personnel the firms used to supervise Puerto Rican recording sessions were non–Puerto Rican and often non-Latino, they were less tuned in to the nuances of Puerto Rican and other Hispanic music than they might have been. While this could be a handicap, it also gave the musicians a certain amount of flexibility. Victor's Alfredo Cibelli and his interaction with Puerto Rican musicians provides a perfect example.

Starting apparently in the late 1920s and continuing at least through the 1930s, Alfredo Cibelli, the one-time mandolinist and consultant on Italian recordings for Victor, was the artistic director in charge of Spanish-language recordings. Since the beginning of the U.S. Foreign Department at Victor, Cibelli had worked closely with Smith and with Nat Shilkret, the musical director of a Victor house orchestra formed "to render the latest dance-hits, paso-dobles, danzons, etc., for . . . the Spanish-speaking trade."[45] López Cruz remembers Cibelli as "a good musician [who] knew what was a song well sung."[46]

Part of Cibelli's job was to be in touch with the neighborhood record stores. "He knew what sold because he would go to the stores, he would send his employee. 'What's selling?' 'Listen, the *guarachas* are selling a lot.' 'We're going to make some *guaracha* records.'"[47] According to López Cruz, Cibelli was less concerned with the particular songs within a genre, or who owned them, than with fulfilling a quota of the most saleable genres.[48] After an audition of a new group, Cibelli would say, "'Okay, I like this group. I think it's okay. Two weeks from now, come with a *danza,* with a *guaracha,* with a *vals,* with a *plena,* to record.' It had nothing to do with who the author was. The group leader was in charge of looking for the music."[49] Thus, musicians could cavalierly recycle melodies. As music historian Jorge Javariz describes it, "They had to have four pieces to record. If Pedro Flores, for example, didn't have four new pieces, then, he would change the title of one that he'd already recorded under another title."[50] Few composers went to publishers to protect their work, which meant that leaders whose talents lay more in organizing groups or in interpreting the music of others "borrowed" songs, sometimes giving credit to the composers but often claiming it for themselves and creating a litigious and sometimes violent atmosphere between musicians.

Javariz's portrait of a rather informal society of musicians has been confirmed by those involved. Personnel floated in and out of groups on

what López Cruz called a "vénte tú" (come here) basis; that is, enterprising leaders, not all of them especially musical, would form pickup
groups as recording and performing opportunities arose.

> We'll take a specific group, the Grupo Marcano. Marcano lived in New York,
> so he would call the musicians who made up his group—four, five musicians.
> He would say, "Tomorrow's rehearsal." They would rehearse in Piquito Mar-
> cano's house without sheet music, because they were numbers composed
> within the group, or by Rafael Hernández, because Rafael still didn't have
> copyrighted music. They rehearsed and recorded in a session. That would
> generally be four pieces in the same day. . . . There were Christmas numbers
> that they had [with] women singing in a chorus [who] were their own . . .
> wives.[51]

This casual approach to group formation, which saved the company
money, at times extended to recommendations for artists. Leaders could
bring new musicians into the company in pickup groups or endorse new
talent to Cibelli or other A&R personnel. In this way, not only store
owners but enterprising musician-organizers such as Canario, Julio
Roqué, and the Spanish composer and theater director Leopoldo González became important liaisons between companies and artists.

Because record companies were only lending half an ear to such ethnic artists, songs that would have been censored in English sneaked into
mechanical immortality in Spanish. Songs with sexual double entendres,
such as Rafael Hernández's "Menéalo Que Se Empelota" (Shake It/Stir
It Up, It's Hardening), became enormously popular in various parts of
Latin America. Recorded by Trío Borinquen three times during the
1920s, it was the biggest hit the group had ever had. However, it roused
the ire of the middle and upper classes, particularly those in the Dominican Republic. Since Antonio Mesa, the trío's lead singer, was the first
Dominican popular recording artist, people in his country were particularly sensitive to the image he represented. Dominican critics decried the
crass, commercial motivations of the record companies.[52] "Menéalo"
was not unique: it featured the food and sex metaphors used by many
singers recording in the United States in the early 1920s, Bessie Smith
being prominent among them. Not surprisingly, this bawdy number was
set in *guaracha* time, with a percussive piano, *güiro,* and *bongó* leading
the rhythm section.

Other songs that made it past the censors were those that criticized,
in more or less subtle ways, U.S. political domination of Puerto Rico
and its effects. Dozens of such songs, by Pedro Flores, Rafael Hernández, and other composers, passed unnoticed among innocuous numbers

of love lost and found. As Puerto Ricans and as musicians, these recording artists were embedded within an industrial system over which
they had little control, and they gladly bit the hand that only half-
heartedly fed them.[53]

AUTHENTICITY

As in their overseas work, the North American companies tried to maintain a delicate balance between the authenticity they promised their audiences and their desire to get maximum reuse out of performers, songs,
and recordings. The companies had a sort of compact with their homesick public to provide "authentic" music by "native" talent. The following is an excerpt from a Victor catalog:

> By means of a Victor or Victrola everyone can hear the music of his native
> country, and in this way appreciate in its full value all the most beautiful and
> the best of the land that witnessed his birth. You yourself can revive those
> almost-forgotten memories of childhood, now past in the far away and be-
> loved mother country. The songs that once you used to sing, the music to
> whose chords you danced with all the vigor and enthusiasm of youth, all of
> that which can evoke for you wonderful memories of your country, is repro-
> duced with absolute and inimitable perfection. . . . A magnificent and exten-
> sive collection of pure and unadulterated Spanish and Hispanic-American
> music is immediately within your reach if you own one of our instruments.[54]

On the other hand, Victor's desire to make as much money with as little
outlay as possible meant that it tried to recycle songs and artists and
hire as few outside ensemble members as possible. Harold Smith's description of the history of one "Latin" piece tells us a lot about how
Victor milked some of this music for all it was worth:

> The hit song "that knocked them dead" in 1926 was *Valencia*, by José Padilla
> Sanchez, a Spanish composer who had found success in Paris. He had written
> a popular bullfight song, El Relicario. A brother of mine, returning from
> Paris, brought me a copy of Valencia. Nat Shilkret recorded it in pasodoble
> time for the Latin American trade. Paul Whiteman played it in the approved
> Parisian manner, for our domestic trade. Jesse Crawford made a pipe-organ
> record, movie style. Tito Schipa sang it in Spanish. The Revelers made a vocal
> in English. It had a phenomenal success.[55]

In-house ensembles eliminated the need to bring whole orchestras or
even smaller groupings from Puerto Rico and other parts of Latin
America for extended periods of time. The Victor Salon Orchestra, led
by composer and arranger Nathaniel Shilkret, spent years recording

both the company's American popular dance numbers and those targeted for Latin American audiences in the United States and abroad. The orchestra played a wide range of music from many Latin American nations, at times adding an "authentic" representative from one of these countries in the form of a vocalist fronting the group. Dominican Eduardo Brito, for example, first came to New York to record with Victor's house orchestra. The only problem, as Dominican music historian Arístides Incháustegui notes, was that "the Orquesta Internacional did not handle the percussion in the Dominican style, nor did a written musical transcription exist to guide it." [56] In providing just the gloss of authenticity, companies such as Victor sacrificed a great deal in terms of musical depth and variation.

Where possible, companies marketed musicians to more than one ethnic group, and their categorizations were significant to artists' careers. Recording personnel classified Latin artists based on their versatility and salability. López Cruz, who could be classified as a folk musician, or at best a popular musician playing for a limited, specialized audience, describes modest sales and limited publicity when he recorded: "In three weeks or in a month, they were already selling the records. There wasn't much publicity. What happened is that they put the records on the radio, and the people bought them. A good sale would be, in that era, ten thousand records in the United States only, because they sent more records to the different countries: Puerto Rico, Cuba, and Santo Domingo." [57]

López Cruz's recording milieu was not the only that existed for Puerto Rican musicians. Victor and other companies recorded a variety of performers and ranked them within their marketing strategies, testing out their salability to international Latin and/or North American audiences. Johnny Rodríguez, already famous on Puerto Rican radio, was sent for by Victor to make some recordings and seems to have been treated like a star all along. Under Cibelli's wing, he took voice lessons and began recording with a series of pickup groups, whose members would be selected from the abundant resources of the Barrio Latino in the somewhat casual manner already described. Rodríguez claims to have been well backed up by the company in terms of advance publicity and tours. As it saw that he appealed to his audience as a universalized Latin American crooner, the company began to "lend" him to other groups, often of other genres and nationalities, though always within a Latino setting. Thus, Rodríguez recorded with *tríos* and *conjuntos*, with Cuban Alberto Socarrás's urbane Latin *orquesta* and a Guatemalan *ma-*

rimba band. While highly praising Victor, Rodríguez also notes, "I didn't realize what was happening. If I had realized what I was in that era, I would be a millionaire."[58] As it was, he was being paid $125 per recording session even in the late 1930s.

Within a Latino context, one was a "big star" only relatively speaking, even if he or she was promoted as the foreign equivalent of a contemporary popular American singer. Such musicians still used mechanical media as a means to generate publicity and live, cinematic, or radio opportunities for themselves. Ironically, despite generally terrible conditions for African-Americans in the music industry, those in the most prominent black bands could make a great deal more money, as those Puerto Ricans and other Latino musicians who were unafraid of the social stigma attached to the crossover could attest.

Profiting from the almost inevitably eclectic experience of Puerto Rican musicians trying to make a living in New York, companies even had musicians play in house bands for completely different ethnic groups. In an ironic reversal, Puerto Ricans could be the simulated ethnic backup for the "authentic" facade of vocalists of other nationalities. López Cruz and Manuel Peña remember that Puerto Rican musicians sat in on recordings of Polish, Greek, or Ukrainian genres in addition to playing on Latino records. Peña himself was a "houseman" for Cibelli on a series of international recordings. Peña remembers in particular recording Polish music with a group of musicians from various ethnic backgrounds, including an Italian-American accordionist. In this context, Peña's sight-reading was his most important skill: "Whenever [Cibelli] called, well, we went to record. We wouldn't even know what we were going to record. You had to pick up the music and read it there, rehearse it at once, and record it. You had to read it at first sight and fast."[59]

Clearly, record companies were no strangers to the somewhat cavalier mixing of musicians of different ethnic backgrounds under a facade of authenticity. At the same time, they expected this mixing to be done on their own terms. Just as they would have been shocked at some of the political or double-entendre lyrics that were recorded under their very noses, they were sometimes disturbed by musicians' sabotage of their own notions of authenticity.

For performers, the musical versatility demanded of them by the companies was their bread and butter. They cultivated it with pride and pushed it beyond the limits of where even the company expected them to go. Mixing with other Latino and non-Latino musicians in informal parties and live engagements in New York City, musicians became adept at playing one another's music. Thus, Canario's musicians could sit in on Eduardo Brito's group when his Dominican sidemen became ill, and Rafael Hernández was able to cross his trio over to the Dominican market.[60] While record company personnel may have approved such crossovers, there were others that clearly did not, as the following non–Puerto Rican example illustrates.

Beginning with a radio program in 1930–31, the Argentine musician Terig Tucci worked with the Mexican singer Tito Guizar and his trio. The popular group began to perform at musical parties given by doña Rosita de Rocha, a Colombian musician and artist living in New York, whose guests, Tucci remembers, reflected "the most significant of the Latin American artistic scene in general and the Colombian in particular." Through this association, Tucci got involved in some cross-ethnic recording.

> In one of those get-togethers we got to know the famous Colombian singing duo of Añez and Briceño, who proposed that our trio be in charge of the accompaniment in a session of Colombian recordings that would take place in the Victor studios. The director of the Latin American section of this company, an Italian named Alfredo Cibelli, must have been impressed with our performance, because after Añez and Briceño, he continued to call us for other recordings of Colombian music. Thus I knew that Mr. Cibelli was convinced that we were all Colombians! It never would have occurred to me that he could think such a thing. Of course, in order to get maximum authenticity, I surrounded myself in these recording sessions with Colombian musicians.

Tucci saw no reason to inform Cibelli that he was not really Colombian. But a couple of years later, when Tucci was involved with Carlos Gardel and was back in the Victor studios, his past returned to haunt him in a revealing way.

> When the moment arrived for recording the songs of the films [of Carlos Gardel], Victor suggested that Alfredo Cibelli, our old friend, direct the orchestra. Gardel, grateful, rejected the offer and explained that he already had an Argentine orchestra director. Finally the recording day arrived. Mr. Cibelli was astonished to see me in front of the orchestra! Pointing at me, he faced Gardel and said,
> "This man is an imposter! I know positively that Tucci is Colombian!"
> What amount of work it cost us to convince Mr. Cibelli of his mistake.
> "And to think," he said to us some time afterwards, "that I gave you all the Colombian work in the absolute belief that you were a native of Colombia."[61]

RAFAEL HERNANDEZ AS A COMPANY MUSICIAN

As in live performance, musicians entered into somewhat unpredictable cross-fertilizations in their attempts to earn some income in the

recording studio. In recording, the companies' placement and categorizations of music and musicians added yet another dimension to
the eclectic artistic and economic decisions the performers themselves were making. Even more than in live performance, musicians
worked within acute commercial constraints whose long legacy had its
effects upon the music. At the same time, phonograph company technology made possible the widespread dissemination of the new Puerto
Rican small-ensemble sound developing in New York City. Additionally,
the musicians' and their audience's exile in New York, difficult political
and economic conditions both in the city and back home, and the inat-
tention of the record companies to the content of their performers'
songs all contributed to the development of an intensely patriotic Puerto
Rican recorded music. This music was pressed and consumed in New
York, but it was also exported back to Puerto Rico and other parts of
Latin America.

A look at the recording-related activities of Rafael Hernández shows
how a Puerto Rican artist could simultaneously bow to the constraints
of the music industry and combine them with his own eclectic musical
ideas and experience to come up with a body of works considered by his
audience to be almost folkloric and certainly thoroughly Puerto Rican
masterpieces. In itself, Rafael Hernández's recording career exemplifies
the links between the mainland and the island that were created by the
record company as an industrial entity. Hernández began recording
when the Victor Talking Machine Company came to Puerto Rico in
1917, shortly before he entered the U.S. Army as a member of the 369th
Infantry Band. By 5:00 P.M. on January 12, three *danzones* by the twenty-
five-year-old Hernández had been immortalized by the composer's *orquesta*. Victor ledgers also indicate that other groups were recording
Hernández's *danzas, danzones,* and his *vals* "Miprovisa" at least by the
previous year. Hernández's music was thus among the first offered by
Victor "Porto Rican" catalogs. Hernández also played in the Banda Municipal de San Juan, another entity recorded by the company, which used
some of his works. Clearly, when he left Puerto Rico Hernández was no
stranger to American recording companies and their ways of functioning, nor to playing a variety of genres in different group configurations.

From early in his recording career, Hernández's music reflected the
range of ethnic influences to be found on the island. Although a *vals,*
for example, "Miprovisa," had a distinctly Italian flavor, it used the
mandolin, arpeggiated chords, and grace notes characteristic of the ma-
zurka. Now these diverse sounds were compressed into the three-minute
format of the 78-rpm records.

When Rafael Hernández formed his Trío Borinquen in 1926, *tríos* and other small ensembles were a relatively new phenomenon in popular music. Aided by new microphones and recently developed electrical recording techniques, the sound of such groups' delicate guitar and hand-held percussion could now be preserved on disc. Whereas previously they had recorded large Puerto Rican bands and operatic soloists, record companies were undoubtedly delighted to be able to get an acceptably full ethnic sound by hiring such small groups, to which they could add house personnel or freelance Latino musicians as needed.

Trío Borinquen's eclectic recording history with Columbia undoubtedly reflected the company's desire to get the most work it could out of as few musicians as possible, as well as Hernández's own incredibly varied experience. His work with numerous ensembles in Puerto Rico, James Reese Europe's army band, and several years in Cuba just prior to forming Trío Borinquen all contributed to the repertoire of this remarkable composer. With Trío Borinquen, Hernández recorded songs, virtually all written by him, in Colombian, Argentine, and the all-important Cuban genres, such as the *bolero* and the *son*. When Dominican Antonio Mesa became the group's first voice after Canario's departure, they began to cross over to his country's market. Indeed, the first recordings the Dominican Republic received that remotely resembled their native music came from Trío Borinquen, renamed Trío Quisqueya on such discs to give them more authenticity. Hernández's Grupo Victoria, which began recording in 1932, featured some numbers as Conjunto Panameño, undoubtedly part of another crossover attempt. During most of that decade, moreover, Hernández was establishing himself in Mexico, and his periodic recording trips to New York reflected his new home's growing influence upon his music.

Hernández's eclectic career and abundant talents combined with the demands of a commercial market to make him an opportunist as well as an artist. His activities were sponsored not only by record companies but by his sister Victoria, Sánchez Morales, and the Mexican company Sal de Uvas Picot, all of whom helped finance and coordinate his musical tours. The structure of the music industry and the demands of the audience it had cultivated shaped his repertoire and contributed to changes in instrumentation and procedure in the recording studio.

The group's style differed markedly from that of Trío Borinquen. The *trío* had used little more than guitar combined with *claves, maracas,* or *güiro*. Borinquen's songs often used an operatic intermingling of voices singing different melody lines and took liberties with the rhythm. Prolonging certain musical notes and phrases, the *trío*'s sound was almost dreamy, clearly made for listening rather than for dancing. Grupo Victoria, however, bowed to the new styles of first and second voices singing in perfectly synchronized harmonies, as well as to the metric precision needed to make songs danceable. Increasing sophistication of recording technology in this period also enabled the record companies to engineer a complex sound with the use of a few additional instruments, while retaining the title and flavor of a small, intimate ensemble. Clarifying the difference between "Victoria"'s live and recorded work, the group's lead vocalist, Davilita, explained, "Cuarteto Victoria was a lot of people—we were like nine or ten. It wasn't a *cuarteto:* what recorded was Grupo Victoria."[62]

Whereas on tour the group might actually be a quartet with two guitars and a couple of vocalists with *claves* and/or *maracas,* in the studio it was often augmented with instruments such as piano, bass, trumpets, flutes, traps, *marímbula,* and clarinet and several vocalists or a chorus of voices. Using Cuban and international Latin genres such as the *son,* the *rumba,* the *guaracha,* and the *bolero* even in the records marketed to Puerto Rico and Puerto Ricans on the mainland, Grupo Victoria depended at times upon Cuban session musicians. For a number of Hernández's quickly immortalized recordings, Alberto Socarrás furnished the flute, and Mario Bauzá the trumpet. "They were recording Cuban music. They wanted a sound, like a Cuban. So they get Mario there, Mario give it that flavor, Mario rehearse it with them and give them some idea about it. I'm the one that improvise, and the improvisation gotta be Cuban. They don't want no Puerto Rican improvisation, they want to imitate."[63] According to Bauzá, the Cubans such as himself who worked on these recordings were more than just session musicians; they functioned as informal music directors and used their firsthand expertise to get the right ethnic sound. Just as Puerto Ricans could be session musicians for other ethnic groups, and Latinos were placed, particularly in the percussion sessions, in North American groups to impart a Latin flavor, Grupo Victoria and other small ensembles strove to create a commercially viable sound using important musical additions and advisers.

Boricuas created songs featuring the dance rhythms that appealed to Latinos from all nationalities but often employed verbal, harmonic, and melodic references that only resonated with Puerto Ricans. *Boricuas* found themselves to be a subculture within a subculture, dancing to the Cuban and Argentine sounds that outsiders associated with all "Latins." Nevertheless, they could insert in-jokes and private messages into the songs they composed within these genres. Lacking a country or even a

widely recognized national music, Puerto Ricans on island and mainland were still aided by their musicians in carving out a cultural space
for themselves. It is perhaps for this reason that Rafael Hernández's
songs were quickly adopted by many Puerto Ricans as their musical heritage. It was as if the songs had always existed, as if they had nothing to
do with the North American industry that had put them before their
consumers.

HERNANDEZ AS FOLKLORIC
AND THE RISE OF THE PATRIOTIC SONG

"In order to rigorously classify the music and lyrics of Rafael Hernández's songs, one has to establish a fine distinction between the popular
and the folkloric," wrote Margot Arce admiringly in 1939. "It's quite
possible that we're witnessing the process of transformation of Hernández's songs into authentic folklore."[64] Arce's were not the only words
to that effect written while Hernández was still active within the New
York–based small-ensemble milieu. And yet the composer, who had already written hundreds of songs, rarely used indigenous instruments or
worked within native Puerto Rican folk musical genres, aside from an
occasional *aguinaldo* written and recorded near Christmastime. Moreover, the man who proudly called himself a *jíbaro* grew up in a coastal
town, hopped between Latin American cities, and quite possibly never
spent a day in the country in his life.[65] Given the context of his life and
work within a broad range of popular genres, what accounts for Rafael
Hernández's powerful reputation as a quintessential Puerto Rican composer, and even more paradoxically, of folk music?

Javariz claims that the Puerto Ricanness celebrated in Hernández's
songs and those of his contemporaries is based on, "more than anything
else, the lyrics of the songs. . . . These lyrics are encased in musical forms
which . . . are common to the entire Caribbean area."[66] It is clear that
both audiences and artists were aware of the tremendous symbolic
power that song lyrics could possess. "Linda Quisqueya," recorded by
Trío Borinquen in 1928, was originally "Linda Borinquen," but Hernández changed the words as part of his attempt to pay homage to the Dominicans, to whose market the group was appealing. The tune, a Cuban
habanera, was the same in both versions. Conversely, years later, an attempt to change one word critical of the United States in Hernández's
1935 "Preciosa" led to an uproar from which the composer's reputation
never fully recovered.[67]

Coexisting with the standard odes to love unrequited or fulfilled were legions of songs that praised the physical wonders of Puerto Rico, narrated the life of its people, and, increasingly, complained of its ongoing domination by the United States. A quiet *independentista*, Rafael Hernández set his sentiments to beautiful melodies that captured the hearts of Puerto Ricans, many of whom felt their "jibarito insigne" (renowned peasant) was expressing sentiments they were unable or afraid to express.

"El Buen Borincano" (The Good Puerto Rican), recorded by Grupo Victoria in 1939, exemplified Hernández's use of a popular sound for dancing together with words containing bittersweet humor. In a slow *rumba*-like rhythm of *claves, bongós,* and staccato trumpets, Hernández calls attention to his nationality in an odd manner:

> Si no hubiera yo nacido
> en la tierra en que nací,
> estuviera arrepentido
> de no haber nacido allí.
>
> ---
>
> If I had not been born
> in the land in which I was born,
> I would regret
> not having been born there.

He goes on to tell the listener that given where he was born, he cannot help being patriotic:

> Yo no tengo la culpita,
> oigan queridos hermanos,
> de nacer en esa islita
> y de ser buen borincano.
>
> ---
>
> It's not my fault,
> listen dear brothers,
> that I was born in this island
> and that I'm a good Puerto Rican.

After saying that he wants to be buried in Borinquén, he establishes a sense of kinship with other Latin American countries and their independence movements:

> Bolívar en Venezuela,
> en Cuba Maceo y Martí,
> y en república Argentina
> el glorioso San Martín.

Y le dieron a Quisqueya
Duarte bella libertad,
y a mi tierra borinqueña
sólo Dios se la dará.

———

Bolívar in Venezuela,
in Cuba Maceo and Martí,
and in the Argentine republic
the glorious San Martín.

And to Quisqueya
Duarte gave beautiful liberty,
and to my land of Borinquén
only God will give it [liberty].

Under the apparently pious resignation lurks a not so hidden criticism of the United States. The situation of Puerto Rico is so critical, the song implies, that only divine help can rescue it.

Rafael Hernández had a unique way of blending humor and irony, patriotism and pathos, but he was not the only composer from this unrecognized country writing nationalistic songs during the 1920s and 1930s. Two songs, Pedro Flores's "Sin Bandera" (Without a Flag), recorded in 1935, and Julio Roqué's "La Llave" (The Key), recorded in 1939, also expressed passionate feelings about the *patria*. The Flores song, which was especially popular, decries Puerto Rico's lack of sovereignty and of patriots such as those of the nineteenth century to bring it about:

¡Ay! si mi patria tuviera
su propia bandera
desplegada al sol.
¡Ay! Si existieran patriotas,
como eran Barbosa,
de Diego, y Muñoz,
tal vez mi patria
no fuera tan pobre,
y esclava de extraña nación.
Hoy no tienen las boricuas,
en la tierra ni un rincón.
No les queda
más que un grito
que se ahoga en el corazón.

———

Ay! if my homeland had
its own flag
unfurled in the sun.

Ay! If patriots existed,
like Barbosa,
de Diego, and Muñoz,
perhaps my homeland
wouldn't be so poor,
and slave to a strange nation.
Today the *boricuas* don't have
in their own land even a single corner.
Nothing remains to them but a cry
that drowns in the heart.

Flores denied any political affiliation, but it is clear that such songs were important symbols to their composers, performers, and audiences whether or not they professed to be *independentistas*. Johnny Rodríguez sang the song on network radio at the beginning of World War II and considered it to be the major act of political defiance in his youth.

> They didn't let people sing that song on U.S. radio, because before you could sing a song on American radio you had to bring the words to the censor, and if he approved it, it went on the air, otherwise no. [But] I said, "I'm going to sing it." It's a very beautiful song and very suggestive, but it has something pretty strong against the Americans. But it's a song that's an expression of the people. And in my youth I had *independentista* ideals.[68]

Members of the working class such as Flores or Rodríguez did not have a monopoly on such sentiments. Julio Roqué and his orchestra recorded "La Llave" with the fifteen-year-old Myrta Silva passionately singing the words. These powerful lyrics, written by Gonzalo O'Neill, a playwright who was also part of New York's Puerto Rican business and organizational elite, protested U.S. plans to build a military base in Puerto Rico with the express purpose of making the island the "key" in guarding U.S. interests in the Panama Canal Zone. In ironic contrast to Flores's song, with its high-flown poetry, "La Llave" tries to capture Puerto Rican speech patterns. It mocks typical American diplomatic euphemisms and refers to a Tío, who is, of course, Uncle Sam.

Such songs took on an intensity not to be found in Puerto Rican music before or since.[69] Since they were written under conditions of exile, both the indifference of the record companies to ethnic song lyrics and ongoing and current political and economic conditions in New York and Puerto Rico sharpened what might have been gentle nostalgia into fierce patriotism and more or less open criticism of the United States. During the 1930s the Depression hit hard on both the mainland and the island, and tensions were high. Puerto Ricans in New York experienced deteriorating living conditions, constant discrimination, and rampant unemployment. There were riots in Harlem, and Puerto Rican labor union locals and community organizations joined with the Harlem branch of the Communist Party and Congressman Vito Marcantonio to stage protests against evictions, poor job conditions, and unemployment. Many of these organizations also supported the simultaneous struggles of dock and sugar workers in Puerto Rico and made common cause with the island's resurging nationalist movement.

Such patriotic music developed in this volatile era, when many were decrying the plight of Puerto Ricans at home and abroad and the political and economic role of the United States. Music was an important form of expression for the working classes. It could be an inspiration to struggle or a sublimated form of protest during a violent era. At a time when the U.S. government was taking fierce countermeasures against Puerto Rican independence and labor-related activities, it took no notice of these inspirational songs.[70]

During this time period one song was especially meaningful for Puerto Ricans: Rafael Hernández's "Lamento Borincano" (Puerto Rican Lament). Bernardo Vega remembers that this song literally filled the air in East Harlem: "At around that time Rafael Hernández was making the rounds in New York. These were his bohemian days, when he was hard at work. His song 'Lamento Borincano' began to fill the air in El Barrio. . . . We were on the eve of the most serious economic depression ever to hit the United States of America."[71]

"Lamento Borincano," also known as "Lamento Jíbaro," was first recorded in 1930 by Canario y Su Grupo. It quickly became an enormous hit and an unofficial Puerto Rican national anthem, and it still has that status today. "Lamento Borincano" tells the story of a Puerto Rican *jíbaro,* a subsistence farmer from the mountainous interior of the island who goes into town to sell, as author Edward Rivera somewhat facetiously puts it, the "bag or two of tubers" that "his scrappy patch of land has thrown up."[72] Unfortunately, when he gets to the town, he discovers that it is closed up, a casualty of the Depression and increasingly difficult subsistence for Puerto Rican small farmers since the American invasion in 1898. The *jíbaro* returns to his home crushed, his dreams of a better life shattered.

Despite its setting in island conditions, the song was purely a New York product. In one poignant account Rafael Hernández tells us:

I found myself together with a group of friends in a Harlem restaurant. All of us were artists in the same boat. It was a December cold such as can only exist in New York, a day in which you're broke [se está bruja] and it is raining a lot outside. One of our companions had a bottle of Puerto Rican rum. While we were passing the bottle, the memories of our little island rushed in, and our minds flew to the sunny beaches of the faraway land. The palm trees and all the beautiful things there appeared to us that day like the image of Paradise. The nostalgia of that cold, sad, and melancholy afternoon drew my fingers to the almost-falling-apart piano in a corner, and I began to play the melody of "Lamento Borincano." It emerged spontaneously.[73]

Descriptions of the circumstances of the song's recording once again stress the competitive, inbred society in which the mostly working-class musicians found themselves and the lack of protection their work received. Hernández claimed in a 1963 interview: "I was playing in the store [Victoria's] about nine in the morning and Canario came, and he heard me playing. . . . 'Come here, Canario, listen, listen well.' He came close to the piano and I began to sing and play the number, and . . . he grabbed the number and left running, carrying it in the street. . . . In a short time, Canario . . . had recorded it."[74] Whether or not the above is apocryphal, the first known recording of "Lamento Borincano" was done by Canario for Victor on July 14, 1930. It featured a simple instrumentation—guitar, *maracas,* and *clave.* The eighteen-year-old lead singer, Davilita, was recording for the first time. The way this came about also underscores the casualness of the musicians' world and their intersection with a recording studio that, though strict with time schedules, did not distinguish between the artists. According to Davilita,

> Victor assigned a Monday for the recording, and the Sunday before, all of Canario's group went on an excursion to Rockaway Beach and they sang and drank a great deal. . . . [Ramón] Quirós, who was going to sing "Lamento Borincano" with Fausto [Delgado], was completely hoarse in the morning. They had to record the song, and I, who had gone to the studio only to be with them there, was the only person who knew it. There was a huddle and then Canario came to me and said, "You're going to record 'Lamento Borincano.'" And right there I almost died of fright. My stomach was turning over. This was going to be a profound experience for me, and besides, they took me by surprise, but there they encouraged me and joked with me, and I calmed down, and thus musical history was made in New York, since that was the first recording of "Lamento Borincano." It was also my first recording.[75]

The song became an instant hit, and later an instrumentally slightly more elaborate version was recorded by Brunswick. López Cruz remembers that it came out about the same time as the popular "El Manisero." "'El Manisero' had the saving grace of rhythm, but 'Lamento Borincano' had the poetry."[76] While Hernández's song, meant more for reflection than for dancing, never achieved the popularity among North Americans that Simóns's work did, it was, López Cruz tells us, famous throughout Latin America:

> "Lamento Borincano" was the greatest success not only of Canario [but of]
> all the groups and orchestras, because it represents the sadness of the *jíbaro,*
> and his miserable life without money, in that difficult period in which there
> was little work, the Depression. And this number was tremendous at that
> time. So tremendous that it sold a great deal in all of America. Because the
> Venezuelans, the Colombians, the Argentines, all had the same problem of
> the *campesino* who lived in misery. . . .
> That song was tremendous. In that time, it made people cry.[77]

Called by José Luis González "the first 'protest song' composed in
Latin America," this number was a big hit among the peasant and working classes of the region, who were quite unlike the rarefied audiences
for most overtly political music composed today.[78] The song spoke to
international problems and used an internationally recognized genre,
the *bolero,* rather than a traditional Puerto Rican folk style such as the
complex *décima* of the *jíbaros* themselves, to articulate one symbolic
farmer's experience. Ironically, its use of a popular rather than a folk
mode probably facilitated the regional crossover of its potent message.
Like many of Hernández's songs, "Lamento Borincano" both used the
conventions of popular music and wove together strands of the island's
diverse ethnic and musical cultures. The song had a verse-and-chorus
structure typical of much North American–influenced popular music.
Major and minor modes alternated in the verses (one of Hernández's
trademarks), but in a way that was more coordinated with the symmetry
of popular song structure than with the song's emotional highs and
lows. Nevertheless, "Lamento Borincano" blended this light opera and
danza-derived minor-to-major transition with a folkish singing style and
simplicity of instrumentation that were reminiscent of the *jíbaro* tradition. Additionally, the song's guitar lines both savored of Spanish dance
styles and were propelled by a slight Afro-Caribbean syncopation, while
imparting a sense of melancholy and foreboding.

Sale, loco de contento,
con su cargamento
a la ciudad, ay,
a la ciudad.

 Lleva en su pensamiento
todo un mundo lleno
de felicidad, ay,
de felicidad.

Piensa remediar la situación
del hogar, que es toda una ilusión.

Y alegre, el jibarito va
cantando así, diciendo así,

pensando así por el camino,
Si yo vendo la carga, mi Dios querido,
un traje a mi viejita voy a comprar.

Y alegre también su yegua va,
al presentir que aquel cantar
es todo un himno de alegría.
En eso le sorprende la luz del día
y llegan al mercado de la ciudad.

Pasa la mañana entera
sin que nadie pueda
su carga comprar, ay,
su carga comprar.

Todo, todo está desierto
y el pueblo está muerto
de necesidad, ay,
de necesidad.

Se oye este lamento por doquier
en mi desdichada Borinquén, sí.

Y triste, el jibarito va
pensando así, diciendo así,
llorando así por el camino,
Que será de Borinquén, mi Dios querido.
Que será de mis hijos y de mi hogar.

Borinquén, la tierra del edén,
la que al cantar el gran Gautier
llamó la Perla de los Mares.
Ahora que tú te mueres con tus pesares
déjame que te cante yo también,
yo también.

———

He departs, beside himself with joy,
with his load
for the city, ay,
for the city.

He carries in his thoughts
a whole world filled
with happiness, ay,
with happiness.

He plans to remedy the situation
in his home, which is a complete illusion.

And happy, the *jibarito* goes
singing this way, speaking this way,
thinking this way, on the road,

If I sell my goods, dear God,
I'm going to buy a dress for my old lady.

And his mare goes happily too,
sensing that this song
is an anthem of total joy.
With that the light of day surprises her
and they come to the city market.

He passes the entire morning
without anyone being able to
buy his goods, ay,
buy his goods.

Everything, everything is deserted
and the town is dead
of necessity, ay,
of necessity.

This lament is heard everywhere
in my wretched Borinquén, yes.

 And sadly the *jíbarito* goes
thinking this way, speaking this way,
crying this way, on the road,
What will become of Borinquén, my dear God.
What will become of my children and my home.

Borinquén, the land of Eden,
that which upon singing the great Gautier
named the Pearl of the Seas.
Now that you're dying of your troubles
let me sing to you too,
me too.

Once again, the song showed an artful blending of the personal and
the national, linking together the fate of one farmer and his family with
the fate of his country. Despite the fact that its narrative dealt with
Puerto Rico, the song's New York origins remained a salient part of even
its reception overseas. The first live performance of "Lamento Borincano" in Puerto Rico, in which López Cruz took part, did not occur
until 1931. After careful rehearsal in New York and on the boat, Canario and his group, all of whom had lived away from the island for several
years, donned white outfits and *pavas*, the straw hats of the *jíbaros*, and
caused a sensation paying homage to an occupational group that had
virtually disappeared. It was a group from which they themselves, literally or figuratively, had also disappeared. The generalized experience of
the farmer in the song could be taken to represent the ongoing economic

struggles of Puerto Ricans on the island and, as part of that, their serial
displacement first to the island cities and then to places such as New
York, a phenomenon of which the musicians and their music had been
a part. Thus, the song, diffused through the mechanics of the record
industry, was deeply meaningful to its performers and audiences.

The record companies persisted through the years in treating Puerto
Ricans and other ethnic audiences as dumb animals with an unreason-
ing instinct for music, or at best as mere sales ciphers. According to
Harold Smith, "Music means more to them [than Americans] at any
time, and the music of their homelands means still more. They love it as
they love food. They like gypsy music, and they like it as loud as they
can get it." [79] While they saw music as a powerful medium of communication that reached across language barriers, it was to further their own
commercial ends, as this statement from the *Columbia Record* shows:
"One distinct advantage of demonstrating Columbia records to people
from across the ocean is that while they may not understand your language they will instantly understand favorite marches, love lyrics, dance
numbers and comic songs, sung in their mother tongues on musical Columbia Records." [80] Members of such populations took seriously the music issued by them and for them as a means of communication, but on
very different terms, as Puerto Rican bandleader Augusto Rodríguez
passionately pointed out in 1935:

> "Lamento Borincano" is a historical document: it's the optimistic, hardwork-
> ing *jíbaro*, who dreams of the day he'll have the happiness he deserves, whom
> reality changes into an intense pessimist, it's the faithful portrait of today's
> colonial tragedy; with its sad, interesting, plaintive cadence, it captures the
> stoic resignation of our *jíbaro* and paints his situation with more efficacy
> and intensity than the sterile efforts of the everlasting commissions to the
> metropolis in demand of justice. [81]

When we look at the music and the circumstances of its production
and reception, the "spendthrift" ethnics who in company portraits can
be easily coaxed out of their scant funds all of a sudden become passionately nationalistic and homesick exiles. They looked at music as a way
to articulate deep feelings and sometimes disguised political sentiments,
unacceptable in a more blatant form. Mechanically diffused songs such
as "Lamento Borincano" spoke to their existence and validated it in a
way no popular art form had ever done before. Within the three dimensions of such lives, López Cruz's claim that his *compatriotas* would
rather buy records than eat seems no idle boast.

CHAPTER FIVE

"El Home Relief"

Canario and the New York *Plena*

Canario, I admire him because he's given the *plena* stature, but on the other hand, he's not a serious *panderetero* or *plenero*. He was a singer of *boleros* and pretty songs of yesterday. He sang well in that time period. He did quite a number of *plenas,* but they weren't true *plenas* like the old ones, and I remember that he didn't use *pandereteros*. He made the *plena* to his taste, and if he put in a *pandereta* it was a mediocre one.

Marcial Reyes, *plenero,* 1974[1]

Canario was the author of other beautiful compositions of a popular character, but his memory will live on associated with the *[plena],* in which he was a brilliant creator and interpreter and of which he was the greatest publicist.

C. Orama Padilla, 1975[2]

Manuel "Canario" Jiménez Otero (1895–1975) was best known for singing and recording the *plena.* This human canary's musical legacy lives on, and so do the passionate and contradictory arguments surrounding his career. Depending upon one's point of view, Canario was either a musical artist or a nonmusical hustler for performers much more adept than himself. Some see Canario as an informal ethnic middleman, while others see him as a popularizer who skimmed the cream from the creativity of others. Detractors and admirers agree, however, that Canario has a place in the history of Puerto Rican music as the man who made the *plena* an internationally famous popular sound.

Within the life history of the *plena* and of this particular artist are contained significant questions about and insights into the multiple meanings of music produced by Puerto Ricans in New York City. Who owned the *plena*—those who created it or those who popularized it? Was it necessary or sufficient to be a Puerto Rican to stake a proprietary claim to the music, or did one have to be a black resident of one of the lower-class districts from which it emanated?

It is futile to try to objectively measure Canario's "authenticity" as the practitioner of a form of "traditional" Puerto Rican music. It is more fruitful to examine how such loaded terms were understood and used by members of the Puerto Rican community, to explore the contradictions between their perceptions and the actual contours of Canario's career. Many of Canario's colleagues felt that he was not a real *plena* musician, but Canario's fans on both sides of the ocean saw him as the very personification of the genre. Audience and record company perceptions went a long way toward the folklorization of Canario and his version of the *plena*. And yet Canario's permanent historical association with the genre was based on his recording activities in New York City in the late 1920s and the mid-1930s; the *plena* formed a relatively small part of his long musical career.

To complicate matters, both the music and its context were constantly changing. Through Canario's recordings, we can hear how the *plena*'s topicality evolved to suit new environments and how its instrumentation metamorphosed to suit new performance situations. The *plena* came into popular prominence through a process of serial migration that spanned decades, regions, and continents. The history of the *plena* in New York City during the 1920s and 1930s is a history of this migration. It is also a case study of an ethnic music that developed within, and in dialogue with, a broader entertainment context. During an era when African-American and Cuban dance music had an explosive popularity among diverse New York audiences, the *plena* was one of the few homegrown forms that Puerto Rican musicians got a chance to play. Within this musical hierarchy, the *plena*'s fame meant a great deal to expatriate Puerto Rican musicians and audiences. It is puzzling, therefore, that the *plena*'s acerbic commentary on everyday life and its lively rhythm did not catch on as widely or for as long as the *bolero*, the *son*, and the *rumba* did. The *plena* fever among Spanish speakers in New York and Latin America was sporadic and short-lived, and the form was never adopted by North American audiences.

In order to adequately study the development and reception of the New York *plena*, we need to understand the background of the form and its social connotations in Puerto Rico. The *plena*'s history has been far from neutral, and a complex of motives led Puerto Ricans to either reject the music or embrace it as their own. Ongoing links between the *plena*'s island and mainland evolution make its chronology especially complicated.

THE BIRTH OF THE *PLENA*

The *plena* is a primarily Afro–Puerto Rican music that originated in the lower-class neighborhoods of turn-of-the-century Ponce and its out-skirts. Most performers and observers agree that the impetus for this musical form, now considered by many Puerto Ricans to be the quintes-sential island sound, actually came from outside Puerto Rico. Constant contact between port cities such as Ponce and the islands of the English-speaking Caribbean promoted musical exchanges between sounds of African descent. According to Juan Flores, the migration of former slaves from the English-speaking Caribbean to La Joya del Castillo (the Jewel of the Castle), a lower-class Ponce neighborhood, encouraged the mixture of Anglophone Caribbean rhythms with "traditions and styles native to Puerto Rico. Though it is not known how or why, it is clear that the 'English' sound caught on in Ponce and sparked the emergence of a new genre of Puerto Rican popular music."[3] Augusto Coen, who became a folklorist when he returned to the island after his New York big band career, attributed the *plena*'s beginnings to a specific pair who were new migrants to Puerto Rico: "Back then in the dawn of our cen-tury, a couple came to Ponce from Saint Kitts. The two were accustomed to play guitar and tambourine through the streets of Ponce to earn a living. . . . A little afterwards, the plena began to be very popular in Ponce, in a place known as La Joya del Castillo."[4] Elderly *pleneros* con-firm the existence of "Los Ingleses," as John Clark and Catherine George were popularly known, though some cite Barbados as their island of origin. The couple played in the streets and *cafetines* of lower-class Ponce, inspiring a generation of musicians in the city and the sur-rounding rural areas. Within this milieu they created a fusion between "Anglo" and Puerto Rican sounds, a fusion which quickly became the *plena*.[5]

Plenas were "musical newspapers," with all the biting topicality of editorial pages and gossip columns.[6] Their four-line, often repetitive verses unfolded the latest neighborhood, national, or international events. Performers sang in unison and in call-and-response format, using vibratoless, often nasal voices, and danced to the music as well. Origi-nally the instrumentation was made up entirely of percussion instruments, but over time and after passing through many hands, it became more elaborate.

The *plena*'s lyrics and music adapted to changing social circumstances, in large part the result of the serial migrations of its lower-class practitioners. These *pleneros,* along with their nonmusical cohorts, were subject to the changing rhythms of Puerto Rican plantation agriculture and construction and, ultimately, to the job opportunities of New York City. Ernesto Vigoreaux, an Afro–Puerto Rican musician and composer from the southern part of the island, remembered the spread of the music's geographical base with the movements of these laborers:

> The origin of the *plena* is in the towns of the south. When an engineer appeared, he was damming the southern rivers. There were people on the island who didn't have aqueducts, irrigation. . . .
>
> In those times there wasn't anything mechanical. Everything was by hand, with dynamite, pick and shovel. And the office where they paid, where the American engineers were, was in Guayama, the town where I was born. Well, there was a lot of work over there, and all of those workers, the poor sugarcane cutters and laborers, went there to work in that job. And among those people emerged the *plena,* in 1902.[7]

Workers often improvised *plenas* that reflected their lives and interpreted the world around them:

> When they were making the dams they made a tunnel, they crossed a mountain underneath, and a *plena* emerged that nobody knows and nobody has recorded, that was the first *plena* heard, and it said,
>
> Pa'l tune, pa'l tune, me voy pa'l tune.
> Pa'l tune, pa'l tune sábado, domingo y lunes.
>
> [To the tunnel, to the tunnel, I'm going to the tunnel.
> To the tunnel, to the tunnel, Saturday, Sunday and Monday.]
>
> This was [sung] in a *cafetín* in Guayama that was called Africa. There the *plena* was danced, and that *plena* was in style, and no one recorded it. If Canario had learned it, he would have recorded it, because Canario appropriated all the *plenas* without having composed any.[8]

Black workers on rural farming and construction projects formed a growing audience for this music. Elderly musicians say that the *plena* evolved from a casual form played by wandering individuals and couples to an increasingly formalized *conjunto* music. By the second decade of the twentieth century, professional musicians who devoted themselves mostly or solely to the *plena* began to form *conjuntos* in the Ponce area. They added melodic instruments such as the accordion and the guitar to the percussive *panderetas* and *güiros* used by the *plena*'s original per-formers. The most famous musician of that era was Joselino Oppenhei-mer (1884–1929), commonly known as "Bumbún," an agricultural worker descended from slaves.[9] A *panderetero* and singer, Bumbún com-posed many *plenas* and performed with his own group.

Like any living musical form, the *plena* changed in response to a change in setting. During the World War I era, the increasing numbers of black workers inside the island's cities inspired variations on the ur-ban *plena*. Among Afro–Puerto Ricans all over the island it began to displace the *bomba,* the African-descended musical form that was one of the *plena*'s direct ancestors. Through the movement of workers the *plena* made its way to San Juan, where it quickly became associated with the city's poorest neighborhoods. As in Ponce, it was influenced by sounds coming in from outside the island. During Marcial Reyes's youth in Santurce in the early part of this century the *plena,* influenced by the Cuban *son,* was played in a rhythm that was more lively ("más movido") than its Ponce equivalent.[10]

Plenas dealing with the war inevitably emerged within this highly topical form. Vigoreaux recalled that "in the First World War, when the *Carolina* was sunk, [the cane cutters] came out with the *plena* that said: 'El submarino alemán, el submarino alemán, / lloraban los marineros, lloraban hasta el capitán' (The German submarine, the German submarine, / the sailors cried, everyone cried, even the captain)."[11]

THE *PLENA* AND SOCIAL STIGMA

> They didn't know how to read or write, [they had] low morals, and women came from that same category as well, from the happy life, prostitutes, and they made a race of such people. So those people would give their dances, and the police and the populace didn't allow this music, the music of bad people.[12]

Ernesto Vigoreaux remembered this as the climate in which the *plena* developed in southern Puerto Rico. Quite often, police invaded the dances where the *plena* was played, breaking them up by force. The *plena* was the music of poor people, whose way of life was distasteful to those looking on, so much so that they tried to put an end to their off-hour celebrations in "small wooden houses, *cafetines* and supply stores."[13]

Such tensions moved northward with the spread of the *plena*. In San

Juan the music was a constant source of friction between the lower and upper classes. Marcial Reyes remembers that "the liberal party, which was that of society, didn't like the *plena* because it said that it came from the lowly people, from brawlers and lost women. According to the higher-ups, it caused disorder among the people. So when [the police] encountered you [i.e., the *pandereteros*] at night, they jailed you."[14]

What was it about the *plena* that made municipal governments, police forces, and upper-class people so angrily punitive? Upper-class and official mistrust of Afro–Puerto Rican music dated from the times of slavery. Under cover of the *bomba* and other percussive musics, slaves had sometimes planned and carried out rebellions. Even in the period after emancipation, light-skinned Puerto Ricans tended to look at areas of dense black settlement as exotic worlds with questionable cultural practices. Vigoreaux's own town, Guayama, was an important center of sugarcane cultivation, and many former slaves still lived and worked in the area. By the first decade of the twentieth century, Guayama was known throughout the island as "La Ciudad Bruja" (The City of Witches) because a large proportion of its African descendants supposedly practiced witchcraft.

Related to the *bomba,* the *plena* existed in a sphere apart from the sounds emanating from white elites. The music was stigmatized by its lower-class and Afro–Puerto Rican origins, and feelings about it were bound up with a national ambivalence regarding race and self-identity. The *plena* was a percussive music whose use of instruments and rhythm showed clear African roots. Although *panderetero* Marcial Reyes was a white man, he was the exception who proved the rule. An enthusiastic *plenero* who learned from black musicians and made his own *panderetas,* he remembers: "They called me 'El Blanquito' [The Little White Man] because all of them were of the black races; there weren't whites. The whites were divided between lawyers and doctors at that time."[15]

The punitive measures officials took against the *plena* not only reflected past and present associations with slaves, rebellions, and poor people of color in general but were in response to the form's off-color or harshly critical words. Branded immoral because of the taint of its origins, the *plena* was a bit like ragtime or the *tango,* other early-twentieth-century musical forms that were "stained" by their associations with the lower classes, blacks, and brothels. However, there were important differences between the *plena* and the *tango* that made the former more threatening still: "While the *tango* is explicitly plaintive, burdened with emotions, laments, and rejections, the *plena* almost al-

ways is lacking in nostalgia, weeping, and sorrow, being an effective ve-
hicle to promote criticism, to ridicule, to accuse, to fantasize. . . . Its
repertoire includes attitudes and sentiments such as pleading, animosity,
advice, and warnings."[16]

Once the *tango* was excised from its original setting, its lyrics seemed
relatively innocuous. The *plena,* however, was an unsentimental form
whose verses contained explicit social critiques issuing from the lower
classes. In terms of its forms, social roles, and repression by authorities,
the *plena* was similar to topical and satirical genres from other parts of
the Caribbean, including the Cuban *son,* the Dominican *merengue,* and
the calypso of Trinidad. Like its Caribbean cousins, the *plena* lampooned people of wealth and position, criticized government policies,
and satirized powerful institutions. Vigoreaux recalled many Puerto Rican examples of strong lyrics' stirring up controversy: "When there was
a criticism of something that happened, a piece of news, a *plena* came
out, among the people themselves. For example, when rum was prohibited here during the First World War, they came out with a *plena.* And
then when a Spanish bishop came to Ponce, all the women were in love
with the bishop.[17]

Vigoreaux remembered hearing "El Obispo" (The Bishop) when he
was six years old, in 1912, coinciding with the actual arrival of a Spanish bishop to Puerto Rico. The song was ingenious in its apparent ingen-
uousness, narrated from the point of view of an innocent, starstruck
child. Satirizing the cleric's unpriestly appearance and behavior, "El
Obispo" caused a huge scandal and was officially banned. The following is just one version of a song that had countless communally improvised verses, some even more scandalous:

Mamita, mira el obispo,
el obispo llegó de Roma.
Mamita, si tú lo vieras,
¡qué cosa linda, qué cosa mona!

Dicen que no bebe ron,
pero lo bebe por cuarterolas.
Mamita, si tú lo vieras,
¡qué cosa linda, qué cosa mona!

El obispo juega topos,
se emborracha y se enamora.
Mamita, si tú lo vieras,
¡qué cosa linda, qué cosa mona!

Tiene los dientes de oro,
y en los de abajo tiene coronas.

Mamita, si tú lo vieras,
¡qué cosa linda, qué cosa mona!

Y dicen las hermanitas
del Sagrado Corazón:
Muchachas, tengan cuidado,
que ese obispo es un león.

El obispo se emborracha,
juega topos y se enamora.
Mamita, si tú lo vieras,
¡qué cosa linda, qué cosa mona!

Mommy, look at the bishop,
the bishop arrived from Rome.
Mommy, if you could see him,
how pretty, how cute!

They say he doesn't drink rum,
but he drinks it by the quarter-cask.
Mommy, if you could see him,
how pretty, how cute!

The bishop shoots crap,
he gets drunk and he chases women.
Mommy, if you could see him,
how pretty, how cute!

He has gold teeth,
and the bottom ones have crowns.
Mommy, if you could see him,
how pretty, how cute!

And thus say the sisters
from Sacred Heart:
Girls, be careful,
because that bishop is a lion.

The bishop gets drunk,
he shoots crap and he chases women.
Mommy, if you could see him,
how pretty, how cute!

The *plena* was also used to attack important secular institutions. In the 1920s, for example, the North American lawyer from the Guanica Central, the largest and most notorious United States–owned sugar-refining company, went swimming in the ocean and was reportedly eaten by a shark. The gleeful "Tintorera del Mar" (Sea Shark) was the musical result of that event. Working-class people in Puerto Rico certainly had difficulties gaining direct control over the economic and social institutions shaping their lives. They must have witnessed the rise of the

American-dominated sugar industry, for example, with great frustration, as it displaced diversified production and small landowners and turned many into poverty-level wageworkers in the first decades of the twentieth century. Laborers had limited success in strikes and other collective actions staged to protest these steadily worsening work conditions. On the other hand, they could always lampoon those institutions.

Other songs threatened the upper classes as directly as they did the powerful economic institutions, such as the Catholic Church or the sugar *centrales*. Vigoreaux remembered that wealthy people used to bribe musicians not to perform *plenas* that lampooned them and their families: "A person would fall into disgrace, [and] they would come out with a *plena* on him, and he would say, 'Look, don't sing that *plena* to me.' He would give money so that they wouldn't sing it. For example, in Salinas there was a man, Guillito Godreau. The Godreaus were millionaires. And so Godreau had bad hair, and there was a pomade that stretched the hair." [18] Somehow the *pleneros* were privy to such secrets as a wealthy man's use of a preparation to hide the "bad hair" connoting a partly African heritage, and they made the most of such knowledge. By "censoring" the *plena* that reported this intimate fact, Godreau simultaneously suppressed both his physical African roots and the African-based contribution to the island's musical heritage.

Meanwhile, the *plena* had followed the ongoing migration of many of its practitioners and was developing a life of its own in New York City. As the center of both the North American recording industry and the Puerto Rican migration, New York City would have an effect on the trajectory of the *plena*. In turn, the *plena*'s development in New York City would influence its cultural role on the island, feeding back into ongoing debates regarding Puerto Rico's cultural identity.

CANARIO AND THE NEW YORK *PLENA* SCENE

The development of an important *plena* scene in New York City had everything to do with the United States' relationship to Puerto Rico. The very processes that sent musicians and their working-class compatriots into economic "exile" in New York were also responsible for the city's highly developed record industry. This industry in turn preserved, disseminated, and to an extent legitimized the *plena* as an acceptable representative of one facet of Puerto Rican culture. It also, inevitably, changed the music, leading to its "commercialization . . . with an attendant departure from *plena* roots." [19]

The history of the popularization of the *plena* in New York City is tied up with the life of Canario, a man who grew up far from the ambiance in which the *plena* developed. Born in Orocovis, Puerto Rico, Manuel "Canario" Jiménez spent his childhood in Manatí, where he worked from an early age in the sugar industry. While still a child he migrated to San Juan, paying his way by singing, and became an apprentice tobacco worker in the city. In 1914 he stowed away on a boat to Spain but was caught and deported to Cuba. Shortly thereafter, he stowed away again and found himself in New York. In that metropolis he joined the merchant marine, a trade he alternated with music. Canario's seafaring experience not only shaped the contours of his musical career but also earned him his professional moniker. One day the captain of a boat Canario was painting caught him idling and said, "You, always singing like a canary, and you don't work!"[20] Canario was dismissed that very day from the job, but the nickname stayed with him the rest of his life.

Canario's greatest fame lies with the *plena,* but he spent years singing other types of music before he devoted himself to this particular genre. In fact, Canario may well have been the first Puerto Rican singer to record music in New York. By his own account, Canario spent the second decade of the twentieth century singing *corridos* and other Mexican songs for Pathé, Odeon, and other labels.[21] He even recorded for Daniel Castellanos, the Spaniard who probably had the first Latin music store in the city.[22]

Accounts of Canario's career in the years after World War I show that he spent the time alternating sea voyages and performing live and for records. In 1925, he became the lead singer of Rafael Hernández's Trío Borinquen, with whom he sang *boleros, canciones,* and other popular forms. Canario's frequent trips with the merchant marine interrupted his career with Trío Borinquen. When he returned from one of his numerous voyages, Canario found the Dominican Antonio Mesa in his place as lead singer for the *trío.* While it would be hard to substantiate Vigoreaux's claim that Canario formed a *plena* group as a competitive revenge against Rafael Hernández, it is clear that he formed Canario y Su Grupo within a relatively short time after his dismissal from Trío Borinquen.

Canario's introduction to the *plena* was in itself rather fortuitous. By his own admission, he first heard the genre in New York in the late 1920s. According to one account, Canario first heard the music played by Jarea, a young man from La Perla, a slum area of San Juan. During the 1920s Jarea performed around New York City with his own *plena* group. Vigoreaux believed that Canario used his record company contacts to get Jarea's sound recorded, but on the condition that Canario himself be the leader of the group.[23] According to another account, Mateíto Pérez, a famous accordionist from Ponce, brought his group to New York before Canario had any notion of what the *plena* was. Canario's nose, however, told him that both the group and the form had commercial potential: "Once established in the big city, [Pérez] visited Manuel Jiménez (Canario), who persuaded him to take up *plenas,* to be recorded by a corporation headquartered in Manhattan. Eventually, many musicians who belonged to Pérez's group joined Canario and his group, who, apparently, maintained Mateíto Pérez as an adviser for some time."[24]

After some months of knocking on doors with this new discovery in hand, Canario finally obtained a contract with the Victor Talking Machine Company. Although conflicting accounts make it difficult to pinpoint an exact date, it is clear that before the decade was over, Canario had immortalized some of the most popular *plenas* from Puerto Rico, such as "Cuando las Mujeres Quieren a los Hombres" (When Women Love Men), "Santa María" (Saint Mary), "Qué Tabaco Malo" (What Bad Tobacco), and "El Obispo" (The Bishop).[25]

Within a short time, Canario and his *plenas* were the toast of Puerto Rican New York. Catalino Rolón, at the time a teenager just beginning to play with Plácido Acevedo and other Puerto Rican group leaders, marks the late twenties as the time "when Canario came with his *plena,* that they played records here, the *plena,* the *plena,* and as they were Puerto Ricans, everybody liked the *plena.*"[26] This ethnic-based identification with the newly commercialized form apparently crossed class lines, at least in New York:

> By 1929, when that early commentary appeared in the New York weekly *El Nuevo Mundo,* *plena* had struck firm roots in the emigrant community: "accompanying the continual stream of Puerto Ricans to the city of the dollar," it says there, "like a ghost, or like some leftover that it's impossible to get rid of, there sound the chords of the *plena.* And at night in our Latin 'Barrio,' oozing out of the cracks in the windows and blasting from the music stores, there is the sound of the Puerto Rican *plena,* which has taken over everywhere, from the poorest and filthiest tenements of East Harlem to the most comfortable middle-class apartments on the West Side."[27]

By 1930 Canario was embarking on triumphal Latin American tours, following the general success of his records in all the Spanish-speaking parts of the hemisphere.[28] Francisco López Cruz, who joined up with

Canario for his 1930 tour, recalled: "Those numbers, from the 1920s, were a sensation. I still wasn't in Canario's group, but every number that reached the streets sold. It was so much that way that when I came to know Canario, he was astonished that I knew everything he'd recorded. But everybody knew it, it was sung on the radio so much, in Puerto Rico and in El Barrio even more."[29]

Canario performed in ethnic halls and clubs and on radio in New York. He recorded with a constantly changing group of some half-dozen players and singers, including several who would become famous as leaders, instrumentalists, and vocalists with other celebrated Puerto Rican groups. He continued touring and recording for Victor, Brunswick, and Columbia throughout the 1930s, with both small groups and a larger *orquesta*. According to one source, Canario, together with other popular Latino artists, even went to the White House to sing for President Roosevelt in 1934.[30]

The context within which the *plena* developed represented a mixed blessing for a Puerto Rican population that was anything but uniform. For the New York musicians and for Puerto Ricans in the city in general, Canario's success had both practical and symbolic dimensions. Virtually no Puerto Rican artists were recorded in New York for the better part of the 1920s. When they were, they were immortalized within the largely Cuban genres dominating the Latin music industry. Canario's recording of the *plena* both opened the doors for other Puerto Rican groups and finally put one type of Puerto Rican sound on the musical map, however briefly. Closely following Canario's success, other groups also began to record *plenas* with the major companies. Small ensembles recording for Victor, Columbia, and Brunswick were staples of the *plena* scene that developed in New York City in the late 1920s. Indeed, the first recording efforts of future group leaders such as Pedro Flores, Pedro Marcano, and Plácido Acevedo were in playing the *plena*.

Canario was important as an intermediary with the record companies and as an incubator of Puerto Rican talent. By all accounts, he was more of a shrewd businessman, manager of groups, and record company adviser than an accomplished artist. Musicians who played with Canario remember him as a generous man who treated them well and got them work. Paquito López Cruz describes his experience with Canario y Su Grupo in 1930 as follows:

> Canario was the only one [in the group] who wasn't a musician. . . .
> Canario didn't know how to read or write. His wife taught him. He got married old. But when we were together, he didn't know how to read or

write. He didn't direct [the group] in that sense. He was the man who would look for the contracts, who would talk to Mr. Cibelli. One time we went to play for King Beer. I remember we took a subway till the end of the line, and from there they took us in cars to another place. And there was a huge party with hundreds of people. Those kinds of things he got us. . . .

And I remember that when we came to Puerto Rico [on tour in 1930], my uncle, who was a great musician, waited for us with my father on the dock. So my uncle asked me, "And which is Canario? He must be a great musician, right?" I didn't want to tell him. . . .

We were grateful that he got us work. There were never fights, because Canario was a generous man and a man who was always happy. If there was little money, little money was shared; if there was a lot of money, a lot was shared.[31]

If López Cruz's response is representative of the feelings of most musicians, it was enough that Canario was a good administrator, a hustler who got jobs; indeed, this was more important than musicianship to the group's survival and to the livelihood of its members. In a sense, both Canario and the musicians in his group were adopting the *plena* and wilfully collaborating in the making of a legend for their own benefit.

Scrutiny of such a history puts notions of ethnic insiders and outsiders in a new light. In assessing the place of an ethnic artist, there are multiple motives to consider, those of his or her close cohorts, the music's original practitioners, a diverse audience, and the record companies dealing with the music. There was nothing particularly natural or inevitable about Canario's "adoption" of the *plena,* though record companies and audiences may have chosen to think otherwise. Like W. C. Handy's commercialization of the rural blues, with which he had become familiar relatively late in life, Canario's ethnic "ownership" of the *plena* was only such relative to the perceptions of outsiders to the ethnic group.[32] Outsiders such as the personnel of the Victor Talking Machine Company, however, had the power to solidify and mythologize this ownership, to make Canario *the* representative of the *plena* for the contemporary Puerto Rican record-buying public. A September 1929 dealer order blank for Victor, for example, had nothing but *plenas* by Canario listed in its "Porto Rican" section. "Here are the latest novelties made to suit the tastes of our Cuban and Porto Rican customers," the copy gloated. "Play these up to your Spanish trade who hail from the islands, and watch your sales grow!"[33]

Although Canario was Puerto Rican, and thus to record companies a fitting representative of an island-based folk-to-popular genre, he was an outsider to the circumstances and expressive needs that led to the

development of the *plena*. An astute musical popularizer who appro-
priated the *plena* from its original practitioners, he commercialized and
recontextualized it within a broader musical career. A light-skinned man
with straight hair, Canario became an important mediator between a
North American–run record industry and its ethnic audience. He was
an effective liaison between the "unacceptable" original practitioners
and consumers of this music and a potentially broader Puerto Rican and
Latin American audience. Arguably, Canario's superior knowledge of
the New York recording industry led him to exploit those who supplied
him with much of his musical material.[34] Prolific composers and *pleneros* such as Mateíto Pérez and Bumbún knew nothing about copy-
righting and protecting their work. As happened with many other
"folk" compositions from the spectrum of ethnic groups recording for
the major labels, the songs were copyrighted by the recording artist and
the company. Thus, Canario became the "author" of many immortal
compositions.

Canario's virtual canonization as the first important *plenero* is under-
standable within this industry structure but puzzling within the context
of his career. Discographies show that Canario never devoted himself
exclusively to *plena,* and the periods in which he concentrated on it were
relatively brief. Canario's recording history, at least beginning with Victor as Canario y Su Grupo in 1929, was a musically eclectic one. After
that year his repertoire no longer consisted primarily of the *plena* but
included the *bolero,* the *guaracha,* the *seis,* and the *aguinaldo* and even
the *son,* the *rumba,* the *corrido,* and the *guajira* as he moved into the
1930s.[35] That is, Canario recorded a mixed "folk" and "popular" repertoire that included song forms not only from Puerto Rico but from Cuba
and Mexico as well. Undoubtedly encouraged by his record companies,
the singer was trying to adapt to diverse audiences and changing times
in which the *plena* was a short-lived commercial phenomenon.

CHANGES IN THE NEW YORK *PLENA*

As Canario and his contemporaries recorded favorites of the genre, these
plenas underwent still another series of alterations. Combining *pleneros*
from the island and musicians experienced in other genres, these groups
augmented the *plena*'s traditional instrumentation. On the *plenas*
emerging from New York's recording studios could be heard trumpets,
flutes, and clarinets.[36] Voices might sing in harmony, and instrumental
roles might be more tightly arranged. The three-minute format of the

78-rpm discs in itself imposed a drastic change on the *plena*. The pre-recording conventions of the form had encouraged many participants and almost limitless invention of verses. On records *pleneros* could perform only three or four verses, usually sung by one pair of designated first and second voices.

In New York, *pleneros* took advantage of a changed social context. They showcased old songs and adapted or invented lyrics to fit new conditions and new attitudes toward the music. Despite the controversial genesis of "El Obispo," for example, Canario had no problems when he recorded this *plena* in the late 1920s. Taken out of historical and geographical context, songs that had been bitingly satirical in Puerto Rico now became nostalgic classics, sources of ethnic pride within multicultural New York City. In fact, whereas in Puerto Rico such *plenas* had been suppressed by the upper classes because of both social context and scandalous words, in the New York setting these attributes seem to have given the form a sort of voyeuristic fascination for those seeking an exotic primitivism. Many of Canario's *plenas* capitalized on the very reputation that originally had made for police confrontations. They emphasized the "happy life" among the lower classes to the point of great distortion. A *plena* that in Puerto Rico spoke of a woman as "la reina de las mujeres" asked why she was now alone. A "cosmetic operation" by a New York "arranger" altered that crucial line and changed the protagonist from "the queen of women" to a woman who had had seven husbands and was now alone. The new version was based on "the premise that the women immersed in that [lower-class] atmosphere must be promiscuous."[37] Many *plenas* recorded in New York immortalized the Puerto Rican lower classes as perpetually violent and sexually undiscriminating, without the deeper feelings and reactions attributed to those higher on the social scale. This exaggeration now capitalized on the scandalous reputation of the *plenas* and the *pleneros'* society, providing Puerto Rican record buyers with a highly distorted picture of the lives of one sector of their population. It is surely no coincidence that "Cortaron a Elena" (Elena Got Cut), a song about a woman who is either injured or killed in a dance by a jealous man, is probably the best-remembered *plena* of all time. Clearly, it was not only ethnic "outsiders" who were prone to stereotyping and sensationalizing the ethnic group. Ethnic "insiders," divided by class, region, and race, were involved in the process of reinventing their cultural heritage.

The *plena* inevitably changed as a result of both the new circumstances of its practitioners and audiences and the influence of the record companies. At the same time, knowing who controlled the development of the music and its distribution is critical to understanding other possible alternatives. Musical alternatives that enterprising businesspeople such as Victoria Hernández, who struggled to establish small independent labels, offered were never given the opportunity to fully develop. These musical alternatives were not necessarily either more inventive or more traditional than those of the large record companies, but they sometimes broke out of the safe formulas of a Victor, a Columbia, or a Brunswick.

Among the handful of songs recorded by doña Victoria on her short-lived Hispano label were the works of an ensemble called Los Diablos de la Plena (The *Plena* Devils). This group was undoubtedly masterminded by Rafael Hernández. Its personnel included Pedro Marcano and Pastor Villa, who later went on to work for Canario, as well as the Jarea whom Vigoreaux credited as the man who brought the *plena* to New York. Two of the *plenas* the group recorded, "Mi Guagua" (My Bus) and "Cuando las Mujeres Quieren a los Hombres" (When Women Love Men), show a slightly different approach to the music than do those recorded by Canario and other groups on the mainstream labels. "Cuando las Mujeres," for example, a standard of the *plena* repertoire, more prominently featured the traditional *panderetas* and other percussion instruments in a slow, sinuous beat that sounds as though it was influenced by the Cuban *son* as well as the calypso of the English-speaking Caribbean. A brass trio that includes a tuba punctuates the percussion, and the accordion so characteristic of Canario's and other *plena* groups is nowhere in evidence. The verses of the song, a tribute to the homemade magic women supposedly performed in order to keep their men faithful, are somewhat less sensationalistic here than in Canario's version.

Such attempts at creative recording, as we have seen, died with the onset of the Depression and the powerful competition of the major companies. Nevertheless, *plena* groups recording with the major companies continued the genre's topical and satirical role. The *plenas* coming out of the New York record industry articulated Puerto Rican concerns both on the island and within the metropolis. Not surprisingly, the songs were released simultaneously with critical time periods and events. "Arizona," recorded by Canario in 1929, chronicled the departure of Puerto Ricans contracted to pick cotton in the Southwest. "Temporal, Temporal," written by Rafael Hernández and recorded by Canario, simply and colorfully lamented Hurricane San Felipe, which had recently devastated the island, while "Están Tirando Bombas" (They're Throwing Bombs), in 1935, criticized Governor Blanton Winship and his role in the recent police massacre of four *independentistas* in Río Piedras. Other *plenas,* such as "El Home Relief" (1935) and "Qué Vivío" (What a Way of Life) (1936), dealt with conditions in New York during the Depression.

In both "El Home Relief" and "Qué Vivío" Canario sings in the cynical tones of a man who has come to New York solely to enjoy its welfare benefits. He provides a simultaneously facetious and anguished insider's commentary on what was undoubtedly the way many North Americans viewed the singer's compatriots. In "Qué Vivío," as in many Puerto Rican songs of the era, the singer also makes reference to other ethnic groups. The word *vivío* itself was an example of a Newyorican adaptation of Spanish:[38]

> Qué vivío, qué vivío,
> qué vivío tiene la gente aquí en Nueva York.
>
> Ayer tarde llegó
> de la China, sabe Dios.
> El lunes por la mañana
> temprano se dirigió
> a donde daban el guiso
> y en seguida se reportó
> . . . .
>
> No me voy, no me voy,
> no me voy de Nueva York.
> Aquí me pagan la casa,
> me dan ternera con papa,
> y carne de lata que es un primor.
>
> Papacito, son las nueve,
> el reloj ya sonó.
> Muchacha, déjame y véte,
> que a las doce viene el cheque
> y ahora sigo durmiendo yo . . .
>
> _____
>
> What a way of life, what a way of life,
> what a way of life the people have in New York. (chorus)
>
> Late yesterday she arrived[39]
> From China [or] God knows.
> Monday morning
> she went early
> to where they give out the free stuff
> and at once she reported
> . . . .

I'm not leaving, I'm not leaving,
I'm not leaving New York.
Here they pay for my house,
they give me veal and potatoes,
and canned meat that is exquisite.

Papacito, it's nine o'clock,
the alarm went off.
Girl, leave me and get lost
the check comes at twelve
and meanwhile I'll keep sleeping . . .

Plenas from 1929 by Rafael González Levy's group, Los Reyes de la
Plena (The *Plena* Kings), described the difficulties of Prohibition ("La
Prohibición Nos Tiene" [Prohibition's Got Us]) and the difficulties of
children of Puerto Rican–born parents running their own romantic life
("En la Ciento Diez y Seis" [On One Hundred Sixteenth (Street)]). On a
lighter note, Los Reyes chronicled the Dempsey-Tunney fight ("La Pelea
Dempsey-Tunney").

In roughly the same period during which the *plena* became well
known in New York City, it enjoyed a corresponding popularity in
Puerto Rico. *Panderetero* Ramón Cepeda, for example, remembers playing on the prestigious radio program of Rafael Quiñones Vidal in 1935
as an important turning point in the *plena*'s history in Puerto Rico.[40] The
plena even found its way into some of the *casinos* of the upper classes.[41]

Canario's ascendance as a media star in the metropolis, and the legiti-
mization of his music through altered words, recording, and touring,
undoubtedly had a great deal to do with the music's diffusion through
the island's different social strata. At first a suppressed or ignored form,
the *plena* in this period became symbolically important as virtually the
only homegrown popular sound to take its place among the Latin music
recorded by North American record companies and efficiently distributed in Puerto Rico.

Relations between the island and the mainland continued to be criti-
cally important for musical development and cultural image-making in
both places. The *plena*'s popularity was brief in both Puerto Rico and
New York. In both places it figured in the ongoing debates over the
cultural components of Puerto Rican identity.

THE DECLINE OF THE *PLENA*

The New York *plena* developed primarily through records. There is very
little evidence of Canario or other *pleneros* playing live in elegant caba-

rets or even the neighborhood theaters of El Barrio. Dependent on a fickle mainstream record industry ever in pursuit of short-term "novelties" and long-term safe bets, the artists who had started off with *plenas* had all switched to *boleros, sones, guarachas,* and *rumbas* by 1930. The *plena* was now recorded only occasionally by Canario and by *orquestas* led by Puerto Ricans such as Julio Roqué and Augusto Coen. In the same period, the *plena* also suffered a decline on the island. A number of celebrated though unrecorded Ponce musicians abandoned their *plena* activities for nonmusical work after 1935, probably owing to decreasing public interest in the music.[42]

Why did the *plena* not take hold as a more permanent part of the musical landscape of New York City or Puerto Rico? Some suggest that even in New York City the *plena* could not escape the taint of its lower-class and African-influenced origins. Yet the *plena* was historically analogous to Latin and North American dance forms that later acquired general popularity. The Cuban *son* and the Dominican *merengue,* which had equally stigmatized origins, became enduringly popular song forms, transcending their pariah status by the 1930s.

Vigoreaux felt that the musical and instrumental simplicity of the *plena* offended the pride of Puerto Rican dancers, who by now were accustomed to the highly arranged and orchestrated music of Latino and North American bands. By contrast the *plena* remained rhythmically simple and rather repetitive in its harmonic and verse structure. Yet the *plena,* like its social equivalents in Cuba and Trinidad, was adaptable to a more complex instrumental format and to new formal arrangements. Through the years, a series of orchestras made such adaptations, but the *plena* never transcended its novelty status even among many Puerto Ricans.

More satisfying explanations for the development and decline of the *plena* are to be found both within the music industry and in the debates over national identity taking place among Puerto Ricans. The very conditions of Puerto Rican colonialism made the island's music subordinate to the Latino forms promoted most heavily by a U.S.-dominated music industry. As was the case in other industries, musical reception and distribution in Puerto Rico was shaped by North American government and corporate policies. In New York, cabarets, theaters, and record companies were owned by non-Latino whites; Hispanic managers and supervisors, when there were any, were virtually never Puerto Ricans. In order to survive, Puerto Rican musicians made a virtue of adaptability to international musical genres. It is possible that if more Puerto

Rican–owned clubs and record companies had existed, the fate of the *plena* and other indigenous sounds might have been different. Then again, it might not have been.

The very topicality of the *plena,* which spoke to events in Puerto Rico, made it a short-lived and culturally specific form. *Plena* lyrics usually spoke to immediate events and conditions, not universalized human emotions. The songs could be quickly relegated to historical or folkloric categories, which is exactly what happened to Canario himself in his later career. Indeed, writer Monserrate Deliz places the *plena* on a continuum with other Puerto Rican storytelling forms that are now considered folkloric, such as the *seis con décima,* dating from the Spanish colonial period.[43]

The *plena* was also caught up in a heated national debate. The genre emerged and developed at a time when the island's upper- and lower-class populations experienced increasingly divergent political interests and cultural practices. The struggle over Puerto Rican national culture and class versus national interests reached a crescendo in the 1930s. Many island elites advocated an independence tied to their class interests, ignoring the economic needs of the working population. Threatened by increasing working-class political awareness and labor activism, members of Puerto Rico's upper classes tried to promote a national unity whose cultural components were based on a nostalgic backward glance to Spain.

Despite the *plena*'s ethnically specific contours, continuing controversy over its cultural connotations prevented it from being adopted as a national symbol. The *plena* continued to be a source of symbolic contention throughout the 1930s, a time when middle-class Puerto Ricans in particular were trying to define the island's national identity. As an African-based form, the *plena* may also have posed a cultural threat to those New York Puerto Ricans who were anxious not to be seen by North Americans as "Negroes."

Similar sentiments surfaced in Puerto Rico. Many writers and observers of the "better classes" were dismayed that the *plena* was increasingly *the* music that ethnic outsiders identified with Puerto Ricans in New York. As late as 1935, when the *plena* had already enjoyed considerable recorded popularity, writer Tomás Blanco could complain that such prejudices led Puerto Ricans to reject a unique cultural product, perhaps the only musical form that they could truly call their own:

> "The *plena* is a thing of savage Negroes," a good gentleman told me one time, indignant that I was defending it. . . . In that belief is based, to my eyes,

the secret of our timidity before the *plena* and in front of strangers. That sentence seems to prove right a perceptive North American visitor who saw in the contempt for the *plena* indications of racial antagonism. . . . I think our racial prejudice, in the majority of cases, can be reduced exclusively to the irrational horror of being taken for a *mulato*.[44]

From the early twentieth century, Hispanophile intellectuals had spoken of the *danza* as the logical foundation of a Puerto Rican artistic culture that they were struggling to form in spite of the island's legacy of political and cultural colonialism. The comments of writers such Braulio Dueño Colón, flutist, composer, and band director, suggest that middle- and upper-class Puerto Ricans felt that there was a war between island forms and invading foreign sounds. Lamenting particularly the popularity of Cuban and North American genres, such writers tended to frame their complaints in racist terms. Decrying African elements from abroad, they applied their criticisms to Afro–Puerto Rican music as well. Now the *danza* was measured as much against the *plena* and the *bomba* as against the threat of North American cultural infiltration.[45] Dueño's notion of regional music, for example, both pandered to elitist aesthetic criteria and studiously ignored the contributions of the island's African and indigenous populations. In fact, he mentions the incorporation of elements of the *bomba* during one phase of the *danza*'s development as leading to the degeneration of the latter by "imposing a grotesque and therefore anti-aesthetic rhythm on the *danza*."[46] Ironically, the corps of professional black and *mulato* musicians on the island were far more likely to work within white-oriented forms such as the *danza* to further their careers than to develop black musical styles for general popular consumption. Some scholars have even suggested that Cuba's very racial segregation and large black population were the keys to the widespread popularization and diffusion of the *son* and the *rumba* as opposed to the *plena*.[47] It is certainly true that Cuban blacks and *mulatos* manifested more cultural and organizational racial consciousness than did their Puerto Rican counterparts. The *afrocubanismo* movement so important in Cuba in the 1930s, for example, had no equivalent in Puerto Rico.

Undoubtedly, bourgeois thinkers of the 1930s were also terrified by the strong manifestations of working-class protest in the 1930s, which was often accompanied by topical *plenas*. The *plena* was a unique form that represented a consolidation of working-class musics from different regions into a universally accessible sound.[48] While the gap was widening between the interests of Puerto Rico's upper and lower classes, bourgeois writers continued to advocate the *danza* and *música jíbara* as part of the cultural repertoire needed to unify Puerto Ricans.[49] It is likely that Margot Arce's and Augusto Rodriguez's rhapsodizing over Rafael Hernández's "Lamento Borincano" was as much about its primarily European musical structure, and its use of the *jíbaro* rather than the Afro–Puerto Rican as a central national figure, as it was about the song's own compelling charms.[50]

CONTEXTUALIZATION OF THE *PLENA* ·

When the stormy 1930s were safely over, both Canario and the *plena* found themselves safely tucked away into a nostalgic cultural niche. When Canario returned to Puerto Rico to live in 1949, he performed and recorded the *plena* sporadically until 1968. Self-conscious preservationists, represented by the Instituto de Cultura Puertorriqueña, crowned Canario the *plena* king and also celebrated *jíbaro* music as representative of a collective national past. Now an islandwide institution, a sort of elder statesman of the *plena,* Canario made a "folkloric" album for the Instituto in 1964. In 1975, blind from diabetes, Canario died. He received a final tribute from the Instituto and an honorific burial in Viejo San Juan. The same Instituto, however, which concentrated on "traditional" music (i.e., popular music of the past, now detached from its vital popular roots and political meaning), barred the outspoken *independentista* singer Davilita from performing his still politically relevant and provocative songs on its premises. In the meantime, the *plena* continued to exist, not just as a folkloric relic, but as part of a repertoire of evolving popular forms that continued to express the concerns of a lower-class and often dark-skinned population.

Conclusion

Son de Borinquén, Son del Barrio

People sometimes forget that jazz was built not only in the minds of the great ones but on the backs of the ordinary ones—ordinary musicians from down South who carried the music to the corners of the country, to little speakeasies in little towns where they played honky-tonk music for $5 a night. Or less. Sometimes they played for drinks, and the sheer love of it.

Cab Calloway[1]

Cab Calloway's words about jazz and its artists could well describe the labor of Puerto Rican musicians or just about any other group of popular performers. Within a market-oriented society, it is perhaps inevitable that the taproots of musical production are much more extensive than the few leaves and flowers that show themselves on the surface. The performers and composers described in these chapters, while important in their own right, are also symbolic of a much larger group of artists. There were undoubtedly hundreds of amateur or semiprofessional Puerto Rican musicians in New York during the 1920s and 1930s who were not lucky enough to have their talents recognized or immortalized through records. We are unlucky as well to have missed them.

The Puerto Rican musicians described here continued to produce music well beyond the 1930s. Throughout their careers, most of these emigrant *boricuas* stayed closely in touch not only with Puerto Rico's musical currents but also with its economic conditions. Just as the island and the mainland were always connected for most of them, so were the economics and the aesthetics of music. Indeed, many of these artists spent years watching for a favorable island climate in which they could practice their craft. When they found it, they usually returned home.

As they returned to the island, many of the musicians who had sojourned in New York became active in the Puerto Rican musicians' union, formed in 1938 and affiliated with the American Federation of Musicians in 1951. Through their efforts, they created conditions that became incentives for others to return. By the late 1940s Plácido Acevedo, Pedro Marcano, and Rafael Hernández were among those returnees who had helped island musicians get fixed minimum rates for hotel and radio work, standardized contracts, and a health insurance plan. At the same time, the union experienced some difficulty over just how to deal with the status of Puerto Rican musicians who were constantly in transit or who had been away for a long time. After much discussion, the membership decided that musicians coming from outside, including Puerto Ricans with years of experience in New York, needed to reside in Puerto Rico for six months in order to join the union without restrictions. The circumstances under which nonresidents could work were extremely limited so that those who had chosen to make their musical fortune on the island, which still was not an abundant source of opportunities, would be protected.

A related important development was the rise of the tourist and hotel trade during and after World War II. Although a few elegant hotels had existed in San Juan as early as the 1920s, Puerto Rico had always been overshadowed by Cuba as a Caribbean tourist site. The large-scale construction of hotels in Puerto Rico began during the war, when many American troops were stationed on the island's proliferating military bases. This development continued throughout the 1940s and 1950s as part of the island industrialization program known as Operation Bootstrap, implemented under the insular government of the recently formed Partido Popular Democrático (Popular Democratic Party), or PPD. Along with the mostly U.S.-owned garment factories, petrochemical plants, and pharmaceutical companies lured to the island by generous tax abatements and low local wages, Hilton Hotels International built the Caribe Hilton. Other companies followed suit, while the insular government cooperated to promote Puerto Rico as an attractive island resort area.

The circumstances surrounding hotel development and employment suggest once again that musicians and other members of the working-class population often have somewhat different interests and life paths. Operation Bootstrap's sprawling industrial development displaced thousands of agricultural workers without creating the large numbers of stable factory positions that the insular government had hoped for. While the reasons for this are too complicated to explain here, it is clear that massive out-migration became intrinsic to the success of the island's economic development program and was encouraged by government officials. Thus, as performers were returning from their long exile to take advantage of new opportunities, other *boricuas* were just beginning to leave in huge numbers. New York's Puerto Rican population was probably less than 100,000 in 1940; by 1950 it comprised about 187,000 first-generation migrants and 58,000 mainland-born children of Puerto Rican parents.[2] During the 1950s and 1960s tens of thousands of Puerto Ricans continued to migrate from the island to New York City.

Puerto Rican musicians who returned to the island did not always escape the economic woes of their compatriots. Many had difficulty getting jobs in the new resorts, which were mostly geared to a North American tourist trade that grew even more in the aftermath of the Cuban Revolution. Perhaps fortunately for them, others went back to the island independently of this new show-business scene. A few became folklorists by trade or through the public's imagination, which often converted yesterday's popular styles to the category of timeless, traditional music. We have already seen how Canario became the elder statesman of the *plena*. Augusto Coen, who had spent the 1940s in New York recording for two new companies specializing in Latin music, Seeco and Ideal, was back in Puerto Rico by the end of the decade.[3] On the island he became a school bandleader and a founding member of the Sociedad Puertorriqueña de Autores, Compositores y Editores de Música (Puerto Rican Society of Music Authors, Composers, and Publishers), and he wrote books and articles about *plenas, danzas,* and longstanding Puerto Rican religious ceremonies. Paquito López Cruz, who decided to leave the New York music scene after Cuarteto Victoria's triumphant 1934 tour of Puerto Rico, got a doctorate in music in Madrid, wrote books on Puerto Rican vernacular music, and almost single-handedly revived the teaching and playing of the *cuatro,* which had all but died out on the island.

In the meantime, Rafael Hernández, ever the curious, itinerant, and versatile musician, went to Mexico for a month in 1932 and ended up staying, making short visits to New York and Puerto Rico, for fifteen years. He graduated from the National Conservatory of Music in Mexico City and wrote a number of classical works, some based on *plenas* and other "folk" music. At the same time, Hernández kept up with his times and with eclectic Latin American tastes, writing not only *boleros* and *rumbas* but *cha-chas,* Mexican *corridos,* and twists. He led radio bands and orchestras in Mexico and returned to Puerto Rico in 1947 as a national hero. Hernández remained an active composer and ensemble leader until his death from cancer in 1965.

As I have tried to show throughout this work, it is pointless to argue over the exact time of the golden age of Latino or Puerto Rican music and crucial to avoid summing up a period of time as either a return to some sort of cultural authenticity or a plunge into cultural decline and corruption. Rather, it is important to examine both the continuities and changes from one period of time to another. In the 1940s, Puerto Rican musicians were still choosing eclectic survival strategies based on their historical circumstances, particular skills, and expectations. Most of them never received much financial reward. Latin music was still weaving in and out of the mainstream American consciousness in ways that affected these musicians and their *compatriotas.* Finally, the multifaceted nature of music, with its economic, social, technological, and aesthetic aspects, meant that it continued to elude easy categorizations or cultural readings. Whatever the period, it is equally difficult to make sweeping statements about class, race, gender, geography, or generation with regard to a living cultural form such as music. It is equally hard to classify musicians' output as pop, folk, or classical, "authentic" or "diluted."

Music among Puerto Ricans on both the island and the mainland was a living synthesis of many disparate forms, layered and pieced together over time. The ways in which members of this ethnic group characterized and utilized music were usually diverse, based on individual, class, racial, occupational, and many other factors. In other words, Puerto Ricans of diverse backgrounds made and used music as they saw fit. If they chose to call a genre or a song their own, this decision was not based on a musicological analysis of the actual provenance of the music. Their classifications took on a life of their own, colored more by their own needs and feelings than by what any strictly musicological analysis could tell them. Such definitions varied not only between individuals and groups but over time. In the early and even mid-nineteenth century, for example, elite European settlers and their descendants still viewed the *danza* as a suspect hybrid. But with the growth of nationalist sentiment, the "invasion" of Cuban and North American dance forms, and the growing presence of Afro–Puerto Rican popular music from "below," by the late nineteenth and early twentieth century the upper classes had positively sanctified the *danza* as the national music of Puerto Rico. Over time and in defensive reaction to rapid social, economic, and political change, the *danza* became a potent national symbol.

The years between the world wars were both a unique period for Puerto Rican music, musicians, and audiences in New York City and part of this ongoing, ever-changing history. It was an era when Puerto Rican, Latino, and other explicitly ethnic musicians and musical forms had a distinct place on the stage, in cabarets, and in the grooves of 78-rpm records. At the same time, historical scrutiny of the period yields certain lessons and examples that could well be applied to other eras, ethnic groups, and cultural forms. The conclusions drawn from such historical work also might help us understand ethnic conflicts taking place today within the United States and all over the world.

If this study has been successful, it will have shaken loose from their moorings preconceptions of ethnic identity and cultural expression. But if cultural symbols such as music are constantly in flux, how can we bemoan the loss of "traditional" music, presumably attenuated over generations in a new land? What is it that we study as ethnic historians, and how do we evaluate the cultural experience of our subjects? I would suggest two major areas of focus: first, a historical tracing of the actual process of the making and remaking of these cultural symbols, the ongoing renegotiation of their meaning; and second, a scrutiny of the power relations within which the music is created and consumed.

If we start with the premise that ethnic identity has no fixed symbols and is one of a range of identities that people can hold simultaneously or successively, the ethnic experience takes on a new complexity. At the same time, the preconceptions of many of the actors involved imposes certain categories on this experience that must be taken into account. The lives and careers of dark-skinned Puerto Rican musicians, for example, show ethnicity both in constant formation and subject to powerful stereotypes. While Puerto Ricans *de color* (as they were euphemistically called) had been subject to discrimination on the island, the bipolar racial classification scheme of the United States recast them in a new identity. Within a discriminatory music industry, Afro–Puerto Rican musicians found themselves traveling along very different career paths than their lighter-skinned compatriots. Barred from most white American groups, Afro–Puerto Rican musicians nevertheless served musical apprenticeships with some of the finest black jazz bands of the era. These musical *boricuas* were neither black nor white and were indeed often connected by family, godparent, and island or uptown work ties with lighter-skinned Puerto Rican musicians. Like other ethnic Americans, they simultaneously held several identities as members of various communities. Thus, both their presence and their music injected new variables into a society accustomed to thinking in dichotomies of black and white, ethnic and assimilated. Indeed, the history of the careers of these musicians challenges the typical ethnic-to-American stereotype. These musicians did not journey on a relentless path toward assimilation into a vaguely defined "mainstream"; they traveled "backwards" to form Latin bands. They also traveled "laterally," utilizing artistic elements from several subcultures within the United States. Rather than a simple, romanticized return to roots, their musical creations were actually new syntheses of jazz and Latino, mainly Cuban, music. Afro–Puerto Rican musicians were joined by their musical *compatriotas* in this eclecticism. Spurred by economic urgency as well as creative temperament, virtually all of them pieced together a living in diverse spheres and allowed multifarious influences to shape their compositions. Puerto Rican musicians amassed a wide-ranging repertoire that in turn had an effect on the music they brought before their co-ethnics.

Thus, the complexity experienced by these musicians also affected the lives of nonmusical Puerto Ricans in New York City between the world wars. Rather than being isolated, *boricuas* actively coexisted with other ethnic groups in their work, social, and cultural lives. These groups ranged from a variety of Spanish speakers to assorted Europeans, Caribbeans, and African-Americans. In the entertainment sphere, as in other spheres of daily life, this coexistence gave Puerto Ricans multiple models and choices to draw upon in deciding what was "their" music. The music enjoyed by Puerto Ricans at their local clubs, for example, drew from a number of Spanish-speaking and North American traditions and had both practical and symbolic functions for its audiences, performers, and promoters. Puerto Ricans might, and did, attribute national content to musical forms that were actually hybrids of styles from numerous Latin American and North American–based subcultures. They continually looked back to the island and region of their birth for cultural inspiration, just as they drew upon the artistic expressions surrounding them in multiethnic New York. As Latinos, Puerto Ricans, and migrants to North America, they enjoyed a variety of musical forms that symbolized these simultaneous identities. At the same time, as Puerto Ricans they were in a peculiarly hierarchical position. Living in a society that made them a subculture within a subculture, many drew cultural boundaries defensively, investing their music with a nationalistic passion rarely found in the music of other groups.

Music had symbolic power, and Puerto Ricans did at times debate over what sounds genuinely represented them or who was an "authentic" practitioner of the music. We need to examine these debates more closely rather than impose our own measures of good artistry or ethnic group membership. Categories of ethnic insideness and outsideness seem to dissolve as we examine such controversies and the historical circumstances surrounding them, since who belongs to an ethnic group becomes ambiguous. Manuel "Canario" Jiménez, chief exponent of the *plena* in his times, is a case in point. A music associated with lower-class blacks in southern Puerto Rico, the *plena* moved with its practitioners to the island's urban slum areas and finally to New York City. Canario came from outside this musical milieu but saw the commercial potential of the genre in the late 1920s. He forthwith adopted the music, popularizing it through his New York record company connections. Although some considered Canario a mercenary hustler and others considered him a true folk artist, it is clear that his recording of the *plena* made it one of the few Puerto Rican forms to enjoy even a brief popular vogue among Latinos.

Was Canario a representative Puerto Rican artist, a "folk" artist? Did he have a more genuine claim upon this music that he did not grow up with than did the numerous non-Latinos of his time who played Latin music? Was an artist such as the Spaniard Leopoldo González, for example, a Puerto Rican musician because he composed anthems, much loved by *boricuas,* to an island he had never seen? Conversely, was a Puerto Rican musician who never played island sounds a member of the group or part of another? Explicit or implicit controversies within an ethnic group regarding what constitutes membership to that group cut to the heart of ethnic studies and need to be explored.[4]

The commercial world in which such music has been produced inevitably introduces complications into these areas of debate. Like other ethnic musicians and music industry personnel, the *boricuas* chronicled in these pages shaped their activities according to the demands of the market. In the process of selling themselves and their music, Puerto Rican musicians made diverse and sometimes difficult choices about where and what they would play. At times they self-consciously catered to stereotypes of Puerto Ricans or Latinos and their music that were held by ethnic outsiders or even members of their own group. Musicians were often supported in their careers by each other as well as by local merchants who, like them, were interested both in promoting Puerto Rican culture and in making money. Both musicians and their intermediaries worked within an industry in which Puerto Ricans and their music were generally subsidiary to other dominant Latino and North American popular sounds and industry figures. They had to tailor their output to such conditions.

Inescapably, issues of power came into play in the shaping of old and new musical "traditions." If Puerto Ricans were choosing stereotyped songs such as "The Peanut Vendor" and making them their own, were they not then genuine expressions of the "folk"? Conversely, when Theodore Roosevelt, Jr., decided to naysay the Puerto Rican conservatory plan and elevate *jíbaro* music, did the democratic, grassroots origins of the music make his action less autocratic? I would argue that such power relations are the inextricable context within which we must evaluate not only the development and reception of musical forms but the very way they are named. As the study in these pages indicates, for example, the North American record industry had a huge impact on the classification, marketing, and even the migration of Puerto Rican musicians. Penetrating Puerto Rico and other parts of Latin America and the Caribbean early in the century, U.S.–based record companies played an important role in the shaping and cross-fertilization of musical tastes in these areas. Moreover, the North American industry's development of good distribution outlets but poor recording facilities in Puerto Rico encouraged musicians to migrate to New York to try their luck. Both technological developments peculiar to the recording industry and the political and economic structures grew out of the colonial relationship between Puerto Rico and the United States are part of the story of this ethnic music. Puerto Rican musical production on both the island and the mainland needs to be compared with similar phenomena developing within a variety of political and economic arrangements in other parts of the Caribbean and Latin America. A number of Cuban and Puerto Rican writers have even suggested that the Gulf Coast area should be studied as part of a continuum with the Caribbean, since similar histories of slavery and European migration have often produced similar social structures and analogous musical forms in these areas.[5]

The complex structure of the recording industry itself makes it difficult to attribute power and responsibility to one quarter. It also brings up issues of interethnic contact once again. Once Puerto Ricans stepped into New York recording studios, for example, they were not absorbed into a faceless North American mainstream. Intermediaries, who were often first- or second-generation ethnic Americans themselves, tried to package and sell "authenticity" while crossing their artists over to as many different audiences as possible. Meanwhile, the artists themselves exercised their own notions of authenticity and appropriate music. During a politically and economically troubled era, composers such as Rafael Hernández and Pedro Flores grafted intensely nationalistic Puerto Rican words onto commercially acceptable Cuban forms, creating masterpieces that were almost instantly accepted by *boricuas* as pieces of native folklore.

All of these questions need to be considered, of course, and there also needs to be a more stringent analysis of the development of the musical forms themselves. The very gaps between how members of an ethnic group describe "their" music and the "actual" evolution of such genres can reveal a great deal about economic, political, and cultural processes and the relationships between them. The skills of a historical-minded ethnomusicologist are needed for detailed explorations of how and why musical genres change over time and between classes, genders, races, regions, and countries. The subtleties of new influences in orchestration and instrumentation and changing uses of voice, rhythm, harmony, and melody are all worth exploring. Even an exploration, through period photographs, of the formations in which musicians have been arranged may be historically significant.[6]

One of the problems with discussion and classification of music is, of course, the terminology used, often in an abbreviated, unreflective way. As I have suggested throughout this book, a group of people can decide that a piece of music is a folk song even if they know who wrote it and when it was written. Indeed, some scholars believe that defining "folk music" as a collective product without a discernible author is itself ideologically suspect. They suggest that songs always have composers, whether we can identify them or not.[7] Others feel that academic studies privileging what is known as "traditional" music, which often consists of earlier popular styles frozen in time, do not leave room for exploring the sorts of creative new combinations often invented, to paraphrase Juan Flores, John Attinasi, and Pedro Pedraza, at the intersection of two or more cultures.[8]

Recently a number of writers have also called into question the use of blanket terms to describe certain genres of music. Separately but consistently, they have come to the conclusion that terms like *polka, salsa,* and *son* refer to, not genres with specifically describable characteristics, but umbrellas under which many types of music fit. Such blanket terms for genres have an ahistorical weakness as well. There is no reason to suppose, for example, that Cuban *rumbas* from the nineteenth century were the same as the ones played even for Latino audiences in New York City in the 1930s. Moreover, such classifications often occur within the ear of the individual listener.[9] I would argue that scholars need to do more oral history work not just with musicians but with their audiences as well, regarding what songs they remember, how they classify them, what was most popular in a historical period and why.

In fact, the individual and collective hopes and fantasies that feed into the creative process of musical activity go far beyond what any technical analysis can uncover, no matter how precise the terminology. Although it is not embedded in the explicitly religious contexts of many nonindustrial societies, the popular music of the so-called developed world often has not only ritualistic but also spiritual characteristics. In Puerto Rico and New York much of the music composed, played, and listened to by the subjects of this study had a symbolic, almost magical quality. Puerto Rican musicians migrated for many of the same reasons that their nonmusical compatriots did, and they held many of the same working-class jobs, but their musical skills gave them a special status. The musicians who formed *tríos, cuartetos,* and *orquestas* were both community culture-bearers and people who could sometimes take themselves or their music across the class, geographical, and racial barriers their *compatriotas* could not transcend.

And yet many people persisted in believing that where their music and entertainers could travel, so could they. As Langston Hughes remarked in the aftermath of the Harlem Renaissance, "I was there. I had a swell time while it lasted. But I thought it wouldn't last long. . . . For how could a large and enthusiastic number of people be crazy about Negroes forever? But some Harlemites thought the millennium had come. They thought the race problem had at last been solved through Art and Gladys Bentley."[10] Hughes's acid tongue notwithstanding, some African-Americans sincerely believed that bringing their music before white audiences and patrons in the 1920s would eradicate prejudice against their group. Even during World War I, the Puerto Ricans who played in Jim Europe's army band were part of an experiment enacted on this principle, their experience the concrete manifestation of an attempt to change society through the universalization of ethnic cultural forms. African-Americans were by no means alone, however, in seeing general acceptance of "their" music as a passport to gain social acceptance for themselves. As David Whisnant points out, there is often a politics to cultural movements taking place among essentially disempowered people, in which artistic expressions become "a diversion, a substitute for engaging with . . . political and economic forces, processes and institutions . . . altering the entire basis of individual identity and social organization."[11]

Similarly, Puerto Ricans on both the island and the mainland fought for respectability and power through music. Upper- and middle-class *boricuas* tried to use music to create the national identity that they did not have in political and economic terms. Like their counterparts in numerous parts of the Caribbean, they tried to suppress local musical practices of African descent and privileged European-based forms as their characteristic music. Working-class composers created songs that were powerful symbols of Puerto Rican identity, using snippets of old and beloved tunes and lyrics that lovingly described local towns, the beauty of the countryside, agricultural products, and national heroes.

The music of these composers not only had a significant context of creation but also flourished independently after its birth. People who listened to these songs drew multiple meanings from them that they passed along among themselves. While Rafael Hernández sojourned in various parts of Latin America, for example, his music took on a life of its own, ever susceptible to infinite interpretations as a powerful patriotic and ethnic symbol. In the late 1930s and early 1940s, Alfredo Méndez, née Mendelsohn, a Jewish pianist who assumed a new identity as a Latin bandleader for a New York radio program, *La Hora Hispana*, used "Lamento Borincano" as his theme song. Simultaneously, the head of Puerto Rico's new Partido Popular Democrático, who, like Rafael Hernández, had been a *bohemio* in New York during the Depression, used it as the symbol of a better way of island life in his campaign. As the ex–Greenwich Village poet and former *independentista* Luis Muñoz Marín would explain in his memoirs,

> Lamento Borincano, composed in 1930 by my friend Rafael Hernández and generally known as *El Jíbarito*, faithfully reflected the situation that we wanted to change. We wanted to break the circle of misery that surrounded the life of the Puerto Rican *jíbaro*, to put an end to the defeat of his good intentions. We proposed to discover the magnitude of [the *jíbaros*'] electoral strength. It was necessary to create militancy among the destitute, to unite them in a common cause, and to impress upon them the vote's potential as a peaceful weapon, capable of converting legitimate demands into the country's law.[12]

Thus, 1939 and 1940 found Muñoz and his fellow PPD members cruising up and down the backroads of the island in a Ford, playing "Lamento Borincano" on a loudspeaker and displaying the slogan "Pan, Tierra, y Libertad" (Bread, Land, and Liberty) to the *jíbaros* they were trying to persuade to endorse the new party. And indeed, in 1940 the PPD won substantial victories in the insular legislature, based in large part on this careful populist campaigning. Eight years later Muñoz himself became the first elected governor of the island. In the meantime, he and the new party were instrumental in creating and implementing the Operation Bootstrap program that would pave over that rural world evoked by Hernández's song.

As Muñoz Marín changed from fierce *independentista* to staunch ally of U.S. government and corporate interests, tying the economic and political fate of the island ever closer to theirs, inevitably, his relationship to the songs of Rafael Hernández changed as well. Several accounts suggest that Muñoz Marín actually tried to delete several words from "Lamento Borincano" but was unsuccessful.[13] It was another story with "Preciosa," however. A *bolero* composed by Hernández and first recorded in 1935 by his Grupo Victoria, "Preciosa" had reached the informal but nevertheless important status of an unofficial national anthem, much as "Lamento Borincano" had a few years earlier. Like "Lamento Borincano," it expressed not only feelings of love and nostalgia for Puerto Rico but discontent for conditions on the island. In "Preciosa," however, the references were more direct and political:

Preciosa te llaman los bardos
que cantan tu historia.
No importa el tirano te trate
con negra maldad.
Preciosa serás sin bandera, sin lauros, ni gloria.
Preciosa, preciosa, te llaman
los hijos de la libertad.

Precious you are called by the bards
who sing your history.
It's not important that the tyrant treats you
with black evil.
Precious you'd be without a flag,
without laurels, or glory.
Precious, precious, you are called
by the children of liberty.

No one who heard the song, written during the rumblings of an intensely nationalist era, doubted to whom *el tirano* (tyrant) referred. Muñoz himself was uneasy about the sentiments of the song in light of

Puerto Rico's dependence upon the United States and the possibility of a more official Commonwealth status for the island. He had the word *tirano* officially changed to *destino* (destiny), probably in the late 1940s. No one is quite sure of Hernández's relationship to this decision. Nevertheless, the composer's silence lent the impression of at least tacit acceptance, and he fell into disgrace in the huge public outcry that followed. Although Hernández formally reestablished the word *tirano* to the song, which had become larger than the composer himself, the two versions have continued to circulate and remain the source of intense debate even today. Independence-inclined audience members in Puerto Rican clubs are likely to ask for the song, and singers are just as likely to refuse to sing it, for the sake of their careers. When the song is performed in Puerto Rico, New York, or wherever expatriate Puerto Ricans are gathered, audiences of all political persuasions wait in suspense for that all-important lyric. Most cheer passionately if the original words are sung. Like "Lamento Borincano" and many other songs created by Puerto Ricans sojourning in the Iron Babel more than fifty years ago, "Preciosa" remains a living part of the Puerto Rican cultural repertoire and a multidimensional national symbol.

Notes

PREFACE

1. Jeremy Brecher, "A Report on Doing History from Below: The Brass Workers History Project," in *Presenting the Past*, ed. Susan Porter Benson, Stephen Brier, and Roy Rosenzweig (Philadelphia: Temple University Press, 1986).

INTRODUCTION

1. Cab Calloway and Brian Rollins, *Of Minnie the Moocher and Me* (New York: Thomas Y. Crowell, 1976), 71.

2. A notable work, and still, sadly enough, the exception, is Virginia Sánchez-Korrol, *From Colonia to Community: The History of Puerto Ricans in New York City, 1917–1948* (Westport, Conn.: Greenwood, 1983).

3. Nathan Glazer and Daniel Moynihan, *Beyond the Melting Pot: The Negroes, Puerto Ricans, Jews, Italians, and Irish of New York City* (Cambridge, Mass.: MIT Press, 1963), 88.

4. See, e.g., Linda Chávez, *Out of the Barrio: Towards a New Politics of Hispanic Assimilation* (New York: Basic, 1991).

5. Peter Manuel, *Popular Musics of the Non-Western World: An Introductory Survey* (New York: Oxford University Press, 1988), 46; John Storm Roberts, *The Latin Tinge: The Impact of Latin American Music on the United States* (1979; reprint, Tivoli, N.Y.: Original Music, 1985), 89. This is not to suggest that the overall history of Cuban popular music has been adequately covered, especially in English. Aside from brief references to the *rumba* era of the 1930s, chronicles of Cuban music in New York usually focus on its development from the 1940s to the present. Nevertheless, enthusiasts of Cuban music have at least some resources to turn to.

., Oscar Handlin, *The Uprooted* (New York: Grosset and Dunlap, :hez-Korrol, *From Colonia to Community;* Virginia Yans-, *Family and Community: Italian Immigrants in Buffalo,* (Ithaca: Cornell University Press, 1977); and Rudolph Vecoli, i in Chicago: A Critique of the Uprooted," *Journal of American* ɪ, no. 1 (1964): 404–17.

7. Micaela di Leonardo, *The Varieties of Ethnic Experience: Kinship, Class, and Gender among California Italian-Americans* (Ithaca: Cornell University Press, 1984), 96.

8. John Bodnar, *The Transplanted* (Bloomington: Indiana University Press, 1985), 185.

9. See, e.g., Roberts, *Latin Tinge;* Max Salazar, "History of Afro-Cuban Music," *Sonido* 1, no. 1 (1981), 2–5; and Isabelle Leymarie, "Salsa and Migration," in *The Commuter Nation: Perspectives on Puerto Rican Migration,* ed. Carlos Torre, Hugo Rodríguez-Vecchini, and William Burgos (Río Piedras: University of Puerto Rico Press, forthcoming).

10. Bogdan Denitch, quoted in Jeremy Brecher, John Brown Childs, and Jill Cutler, eds., *Global Visions: Beyond the New World Order* (Boston: South End, 1993), 21.

11. See Fredrik Barth, ed., *Ethnic Groups and Boundaries* (Boston: Little, Brown, 1969); di Leonardo, *Varieties of Ethnic Experience;* David Whisnant, *All That Is Native and Fine: The Politics of Culture in an American Region* (Chapel Hill: University of North Carolina Press, 1983); Adelaida Reyes-Schramm, "The Role of Music in the Interaction of Black Americans and Hispanos in New York City's East Harlem" (Ph.D. diss., Columbia University, 1975); and Felix Padilla, *Latino Ethnic Consciousness* (Notre Dame: University of Notre Dame Press, 1985).

12. Eric Hobsbawm and Terence Ranger, eds., *The Invention of Tradition* (New York: Cambridge University Press, 1983).

13. Mark Slobin and Richard Spottswood, "David Medoff: A Case Study in Inter-Ethnic Popular Culture," *American Music* 3, no. 3 (1985): 261, 263.

14. Charles Keil, "Slovenian Style in Milwaukee," in *Folk Music and Modern Sound,* ed. William Ferris and Mary L. Hart (Jackson: University of Mississippi Press, 1982), 32–59.

15. Advertisement, *La Prensa* (New York City), 13 June 1930.

16. William Roseberry, *Anthropologies and Histories* (New Brunswick: Rutgers University Press, 1989), 26.

17. Manuel Peña, *The Texas-Mexican Conjunto: History of a Working-Class Music* (Austin: University of Texas Press, 1985).

18. di Leonardo's *Varieties of Ethnic Experience,* particularly chapters 4 and 5, has helped me to draw such conclusions based on my own research in New York and Puerto Rico. So have my multiethnic musical research and organizing in Waterbury, Connecticut, shared and interpreted with Jeremy Brecher.

19. Howard S. Becker, *Art Worlds* (Berkeley and Los Angeles: University of California Press, 1982).

1. "IN OUR HOUSE, MUSIC WAS EATEN FOR BREAKFAST"

1. *Viejo* means "old" and refers to the original walled city established by the Spaniards. The Governor's Palace and many official and historic buildings are still there, even though the city has expanded far beyond its original area.

2. Héctor Campos Parsi, "Unos bailan, otros lloran: Crónica de la música puertorriqueña durante la gran depresión (1928–1931)" (master's thesis, Centro de Estudios Avanzados de Puerto Rico y el Caribe, 1992), 260–65.

3. Ibid. The delegation included the composers and ensemble leaders Arístides Chavier, Augusto Rodríguez, and Joaquin Burset.

4. *Boricua* is the Taino Indian term for a resident of the island of Borinquén, as Puerto Rico was called in precolonial times. These terms are still common among Puerto Ricans.

5. Pedro Malavet Vega, *Historia de la canción popular en Puerto Rico (1493–1898)* (Santo Domingo: Editora Corripio, 1992), 224–25.

6. There were, however, many songs that were critical of the conditions of migrants' lives both in Puerto Rico and on the mainland, as we shall see.

7. See, e.g., Micaela di Leonardo, *The Varieties of Ethnic Experience: Kinship, Class, and Gender among California Italian-Americans* (Ithaca: Cornell University Press, 1984), 49.

8. John Bodnar's *The Transplanted* (Bloomington: Indiana University Press, 1985) is a synthesis of many such works and in itself provides an example of in-depth examination of all these realms except the cultural.

9. For a useful outline of these regions, see Jorge Duany, "Popular Music in Puerto Rico: Towards an Anthropology of Salsa," *Latin American Music Review* 5, no. 2 (1984): 187–216.

10. For more information, see Fernando Picó, *Historia general de Puerto Rico* (Río Piedras, P.R.: Ediciones Huracán, 1988); James Dietz, *Economic History of Puerto Rico: Institutional Change and Capitalist Development* (Princeton: Princeton University Press, 1986); and History Task Force, Centro de Estudios Puertorriqueños, *Labor Migration under Capitalism: The Puerto Rican Experience* (New York: Monthly Review, 1979).

11. The relatively low percentage of slaves in Puerto Rico as compared with other Caribbean societies has been cited by Hispanophile thinkers throughout the past two centuries as "proof" that there has been little African influence on Puerto Rican culture. See, e.g., Campos Parsi, "Unos bailan, otros lloran"; and Noel Allende Goitia, "Por la encendida calle antillana: Cultura musical y discurso histórico en la sociedad puertorriqueña en la década del treinta (1929–1939)" (master's thesis, University of Puerto Rico, 1992).

12. Duany, "Popular Music in Puerto Rico," 191.

13. Malavet Vega, *Historia de la canción popular,* 131.

14. Ibid., 129, 177; José Emanuel Dufrasne, "Los instrumentos musicales afroboricuas," *La tercera raíz: Presencia africana en Puerto Rico* (San Juan: Centro de Estudios de la Realidad Puertorriqueña and Instituto de Cultura Puertorriqueña, 1992): 57–62.

15. Although the term *Afro–Puerto Ricans* is not generally used by Puerto

Ricans, I use it to denote Puerto Ricans of clear African descent, particularly if they have made conscious use of that heritage.

16. Dufrasne, "Los instrumentos musicales afroboricuas," 59–60; Donald Thompson, "A New World Mbira: The Caribbean Marímbula," *African Music Society Journal* 5, no. 4 (1975–76): 140–48.

17. Angel Quintero Rivera, "Music, Social Classes, and the National Question in Puerto Rico" (Río Piedras: Centro de Investigaciones Sociales, University of Puerto Rico, February 1987, photocopy); Duany, "Popular Music in Puerto Rico."

18. Peter Manuel, *Popular Musics of the Non-Western World: An Introductory Survey* (New York: Oxford University Press, 1988), 26.

19. Duany, "Popular Music in Puerto Rico," 190.

20. Haydée E. Reichard de Cancio, *Memorias de mi pueblo. . .Aguadilla* (1990; reprint, Quebradillas, P.R.: San Rafael, 1991), 33.

21. Donald Thompson, "El ambiente musical en Puerto Rico en la década de 1880," *Cupey* 6, nos. 1–2 (1989): 123, 125, 129.

22. Malavet Vega, *Historia de la canción popular,* 172–73, 303–5.

23. It is important to remember, however, that these were not wholesale borrowings or forms entirely alien to Puerto Ricans. Puerto Rican, Cuban, and other Latin American societies with sizable African populations experienced somewhat parallel syncretisms between musical forms. Moreover, Puerto Rican musicians and audiences adapted such genres to their own purposes, with unique instrumental combinations, musical phrases, and lyrics. In fact, Puerto Rican composers such as Rafael Hernández pushed genres such as the *bolero* to their limit, in turn influencing the form's development in Cuba and Mexico.

24. However, Edgardo Díaz Díaz and Peter Manuel point out the ways in which people of color in Puerto Rico and Cuba used the *guaracha* and the *rumba* for their own purposes, class solidarity and/or political satire. See Díaz Díaz, "Social Meaning of the *Guaracha* in Two Puerto Rican Urban Contexts (1871–1926)" (Paper, University of Texas, Austin, n.d.), 11; and Manuel, *Popular Musics,* 30.

25. I am indebted to Edgardo Díaz Díaz for bringing some of these points to my attention.

26. Angel Quintero Rivera, "Music, Social Classes, and the National Question in Puerto Rico," 34.

27. Malavet Vega, *Historia de la canción popular,* 292.

28. Ibid., 424.

29. Héctor Campos Parsi, *Música,* vol. 7 of *La gran enciclopedia de Puerto Ric* (Madrid: Ediciones R, 1976), 221.

30. Ibid., 23.

31. Ibid., 25.

32. Malavet Vega, *Historia de la canción popular,* 250, 265–74.

33. Ibid., 369.

34. There is inadequate information in secondary sources regarding the cultural formation of each town or its social history to establish such links and patterns, so I am only able to suggest them here.

35. Pepito Arvelo, interview by author, Santurce, P. R., 30 November 1988.

36. Francisco López Vidal, interview by author, Río Piedras, P. R., 15 December 1988.

37. Manuel Peña, interview by author, Bayamón, P. R., 12 December 1988.

38. Victoria Hernández, interview by author, New York, 11 May 1989.

39. The *bombardino* is a valved horn slightly higher in range than a tuba.

40. Victoria Hernández, interview by author, New York, 27 March 1989.

41. Francisco López Cruz, interview by author, San Juan, 4 December 1988.

42. Charles Rogler, *Comerío: A Study of a Puerto Rican Town* (Lawrence: University of Kansas Press, 1940), 178.

43. There are, of course, some exceptions, possibly more than current research shows. A history of Aguadilla, for example, shows that Carmen Sanabia, who later married composer and municipal bandleader Jesús Figueroa, actually played piano not only in a San Juan movie theater but also in other pubilc settings. See Nestor A. Rodríguez Escudero, *Hijos ilustres de Aguadilla* (Caparra Heights, P.R.: Centro Gráfico del Caribe, 1986), 135–37.

44. López Vidal, interview.

45. Johnny Rodríguez, interview by Gustavo Batista and Juan Mora Bosch, 12 February 1985, transcript, Instituto de Cultura Puertorriqueña, San Juan.

46. Ibid.

47. Arvelo, interview, 30 November 1988.

48. López Cruz, interview, 4 December 1988.

49. Ibid.

50. Ibid.

51. Miguelito Miranda, interview by Edgardo Díaz Díaz, tape recording, 13 April 1984, Hato Rey, P. R., transcript, 2.

52. *La música en Aguadilla,* booklet of the Décimocuarto Festival de la Música de Rafael Hernández (N.p., 1988), 10.

53. José Pastrana, "Case History #14," Box 3710, Works Progress Administration, Historical Records Survey, New York Municipal Archives, New York.

54. Peña, interview.

55. Máximo González Negrón, "La Orquesta Happy Hills," *La canción popular* 3, no. 3 (1988): 27.

56. Ibid., 28.

57. Efraín Vaz, interview by Edgardo Díaz Díaz, tape recording, Villa Carolina, P. R., 30 May 1985, transcript, 13.

58. Malavet Vega, *Historia de la canción popular,* 261.

59. Tito Henríquez, interview by author, San Juan, 26 November 1988.

60. Ernesto Vigoreaux, interview by Edgardo Díaz Díaz, tape recording, Río Piedras, P. R., 10 April 1985, transcript, 10; Angelica Duchesne, interview by author, Caparra Heights, P. R., 5 January 1993.

61. Juanchin Ramírez, interview by Gustavo Batista, tape recording, 2 February 1985, Instituto de Cultura Puertorriqueña, San Juan; Rafael Portela, "Compositores del Viejo San Juan," *La canción popular* 5, no. 5 (1991): 54.

62. Vigoreaux, interview, 10 April 1985, 31.

63. Catherine Dower, *Puerto Rican Music following the Spanish American War* (Lanham, Md.: University Press of America, 1983), 64, 68.

64. González Negrón, "La Orquesta Happy Hills," 27–31.

65. Allende Goitia, "Por la encendida calle antillana," 139.

66. Dower, *Puerto Rican Music*, 87.

67. Nicholas Slonimsky describes this process of acclimation of European forms throughout Latin America, just as he shows Latin, particularly Cuban, music spreading throughout Europe and North America. See Slonimsky, *Music of Latin America* (New York: Thomas Y. Crowell, 1945).

68. Sidney Mintz, *Worker in the Cane: A Puerto Rican Life History* (1960; reprint, New York: W. W. Norton, 1974), 72–74.

69. Vaz, interview, 30 May 1985, 2, 4.

70. Rogler, *Comerío*, 176.

71. Campos Parsi, *Música*, 244.

72. José Enrique Ayoroa Santaliz, "La trompeta mágica de Puerto Rico," *La canción popular* 5, no. 5 (1990): 58.

73. Edgardo Díaz Díaz, "Música para anunciar en la sociedad del siglo XIX," *Revista musical puertorriqueña* 1 (January–June 1987): 7–13.

74. Portela, "Compositores de Viejo San Juan," 54.

75. Campos Parsi, "Unos bailan, otros lloran," 257–58.

76. Ibid., 38–39.

77. See Kathy Peiss, *Cheap Amusements: Working Women and Leisure in Turn-of-the-Century New York* (Philadelphia: Temple University Press, 1986); Roy Rosenzweig, *Eight Hours for What We Will: Workers and Leisure in an Industrial City, 1870–1920* (New York: Cambridge University Press, 1983); and Robert Sklar, *Movie-Made America: A Cultural History of the American Movies* (New York: Random House, 1975).

78. Pablo Marcial Ortíz Ramos, *A tres voces y guitarras: Los tríos en Puerto Rico* (Santo Domingo: Editora Corripio, 1991), 41.

79. Rafael Portela, interview by author, Río Piedras, P. R., 3 December 1988.

80. Campos Parsi, *Música*, 214.

81. López Cruz, interview, 4 December 1988.

82. Campos Parsi, "Unos bailan, otros lloran," 204.

83. López Vidal, interview.

84. Angélica Duchesne, interview.

85. Ibid.

86. Ernesto Vigoreaux, interview by author, Río Piedras, P. R., 17 November 1988.

87. Campos Parsi, "Unos bailan, otros lloran," 135, 136.

88. Pío López Martínez, *Historia de Cayey* (San Juan: Cooperativa de Artes Gráficas Romualdo Real, 1972), 123.

89. Campos Parsi, *Música*, 214.

90. Ernesto Vigoreaux, interview by Gustavo Batista, 30 September 1980, transcript, Instituto de Cultura Puertorriqueña, San Juan, 24.

91. Campos Parsi, "Unos bailan, otros lloran," 147–48.

92. Ibid., 85.

93. Vigoreaux, interview, 10 April 1985, 29.

94. History Task Force, *Labor Migration under Capitalism,* 121; José Luis Torregrosa, *Historia de la radio en Puerto Rico* (Hato Rey, P.R.: Esmaco, 1991), 95.

95. American Social History Project, *Who Built America? Working People and the Nation's Economy, Politics, Culture, and Society,* vol. 2 (New York: Pantheon, 1992), 283.

96. Johnny Rodríguez, interview, 12 February 1985, 18–19.

97. Ibid., 19.

98. Tito Henríquez, interview by Gustavo Batista, 1985, transcript, Instituto de Cultura Puertorriqueña, San Juan, 23.

99. Antonio Moreno Caldero, "El Cuarteto Mayarí," *La canción popular* 4, no. 4 (1989): 17–18.

100. *Limber* is actually *lindbergh,* flavored ices named for the North American aviator, who had visited Puerto Rico in 1927.

101. Moreno Caldero, "El Cuarteto Mayarí," 17–18.

2. FROM "INDIANOLA" TO "ÑO COLÁ"

1. Emmett J. Scott, *Scott's Official History of the American Negro in the World War* (1919; reprint, New York: Arno and New York Times, 1969), 306.

2. Some of the Puerto Ricans who fought and played in the 369th and other regiments were Rafael Hernández, Jesús "Pocholo" Hernández, Rafael Duchesne, Ceferino Hernández, Eligio Rijos, Gregorio Félix Delgado, Antonio González Cancel, Froilán Jiménez, Eleuterio J. Meléndez, Nicolás Vázquez, José Rosa, Genaro Torres, Leonardo Cruz, Pablo Fuentes Más, Arturo Ayala, Sixto Benítez, Angel Carrión, and Francisco Meléndez (courtesy of Donald Thompson, Río Piedras, P. R., and the National Personnel Records Center, Division of Military Records, St. Louis, Missouri).

3. Though Puerto Ricans were citizens under the law and therefore draftable, they could not vote in presidential elections and could not create binding legislation without the approval of the U.S. Congress.

4. See, e.g., Eduardo Seda Bonilla, *La cultura política de Puerto Rico* (Río Piedras, P.R.: Ediciones Amauta, 1976); and Clara Rodríguez, *Puerto Ricans: Born in the U.S.A* (Boston: Unwin Hyman, 1989), chap. 3.

5. Seda Bonilla, *La cultura política,* 179.

6. There is some debate over whether the orchestra was known as Los Jolly Boys (Victoria Hernández, interview by author, New York, 27 March 1989; Rafael Aponte Ledée, "Una fotografía y . . . unos chuscos," *El Nuevo Día,* 7 January 1987) or as the Sombras de La Noche (Night Shadows) (Jorge Javariz, "Trayectoria artística y discográfica de Rafael Hernández," in *El disco en Puerto Rico 1892–1965* [Ponce, P.R.: Museo del Arte, 1992], 27). Aponte Ledée claims that the Jolly Boys was formed by Hernández to compete with the Sombra de la Noche [*sic*], an orchestra directed by Carmelo Díaz Soler.

7. Noble Sissle, "Happy in Hell: Memoirs of Lieutenant James 'Jim' Europe [October 1942]," Manuscript Division, Arthur A. Schomburg Center for Research in Black Culture, New York, New York, 18.

8. Recording ledger, Victor Talking Machine Company, 1917, Radio Corporation of America Archives, New York.

9. Reid Badger, "James Reese Europe and the Prehistory of Jazz," *American Music* 7, no. 1 (1989): 48–67.

10. Arthur W. Little, *From Harlem to the Rhine* (1930; reprint, New York: Haskell House, 1974), 112.

11. Reid Badger, "The Conquests of Europe: The Remarkable Career of James Reese Europe," *Alabama Heritage* 1 (Summer 1986): 44.

12. "From the island," or *de la isla,* refers to people from outside the San Juan area. The phrase is used by San Juan residents to imply that these people are provincial, unsophisticated.

13. Lynn Abbott, "'Play That Barber Shop Chord': A Case for the African-American Origin of Barbershop Harmony," *American Music* 10, no. 3 (1992): 289–325.

14. This was true at least until the 1930s, when the municipal bands faded out of the picture and music became a more lucrative business, in which whites could make money without the stigma previously associated with being a musician.

15. Little, *From Harlem to the Rhine,* 120.

16. Natalie Curtis, "The Negro's Contribution to the Music of America," *Craftsman,* February 1913, reprinted in *Harlem on My Mind: Cultural Capital of Black America,* ed. Allen Schoener (New York: Random House, 1968), 28.

17. Sissle, "Happy in Hell," 24.

18. Ibid., 25–26.

19. Little, *From Harlem to the Rhine,* 46.

20. Scott, *Scott's Official History,* 199.

21. Sissle, "Happy in Hell," 55.

22. Ibid., 54–55.

23. Javariz, "Trayectoria artística y discográfica," 27.

24. *Rafael Hernández vive . . . y siempre está en nosotros* (Aguadilla, P.R.: Publicaciones Año Centenario, 1991), 14.

25. Little, *From Harlem to the Rhine,* 130.

26. See, e.g., Leonardo Acosta, *Música y descolonización* (Havana: Editorial Arte y Literatura, 1982), 183.

27. John Santos, notes for *The Cuban Danzón: Its Ancestors and Descendants,* Ethnic Folkways FE 4066; Edward A. Berlin, *Reflections and Research on Ragtime* (Brooklyn: Institute for Studies in American Music, Conservatory of Music, Brooklyn College of the City University of New York, 1987); William J. Schafer and Johannes Riedel, *The Art of Ragtime* (1973; reprint, New York: Da Capo, 1977).

28. Berlin, *Reflections and Research on Ragtime,* 77.

29. Little, *From Harlem to the Rhine,* 350.

30. David Levering Lewis, *When Harlem Was in Vogue* (New York: Alfred A. Knopf, 1981), 171.

31. Ray Coen, interview by author, Río Piedras, P. R., 9 January 1989. Although Coen says that Escudero played bass, discographies and jazz dictionaries generally describe him as playing *brass* bass, i. e., tuba.

32. For example, an account of a Puerto Rican musician's death, "La muerte de Yeyo," *El Nuevo Mundo,* 29 December 1928, mentions flowers being sent to the funeral home by the Blackbirds Orchestra and McKinney's Cotton Pickers, indicating Yeyo's probable firsthand acquaintance with these black North

American groups. Since only the most famous Puerto Rican–born jazz players are found in jazz dictionaries, and only those who actually recorded with jazz and popular groups are found in discographies, there were probably many lesser-known musicians involved in this scene who are invisible to us.

33. Robert Kimball and William Bolcom, *Reminiscing with Sissle and Blake* (New York: Viking, 1973): 127.

34. Brian Rust, *Jazz Records, 1897–1942* (Essex: Storyville, 1982); Leo Walker, *The Big Band Almanac* (Pasadena: Ward Ritchie, 1989); Leonard Feather, *The Encyclopedia of Jazz* (New York: Horizon, 1960); Barry Kernfeld, ed., *The New Grove Dictionary of Jazz* (London: Macmillan, 1988).

35. Usera was an extremely important Puerto Rican musician and arranger who deserves detailed research. He worked with many groups and was for a long time the arranger for the musically nonliterate Pedro Flores, mentioned in chapter 3 below.

36. Mario Bauzá, interview by author, New York, 2 June 1989.

37. Bernardo Vega, *Memoirs of Bernardo Vega,* ed. César Andreu Iglesias, trans. Juan Flores (New York: Monthly Review, 1984), 107; American Social History Project, *Who Built America? Working People and the Nation's Economy, Politics, Culture, and Society,* vol. 2 (New York: Pantheon, 1992), 240.

38. Javariz, "Trayectoria artística y discográfica," 28.

39. Kimball and Bolcom, *Reminiscing,* 93.

40. Ibid., 116.

41. See the account in Thomas Hennessey, "From Jazz to Swing: Black Jazz Musicians and Their Music—1917–1935" (Ph.D. diss., Northwestern University, 1973). While there were many highly trained African-American and Creole musicians in New Orleans, many musicians in the post-ragtime jazz world were not reading musicians.

42. Duke Ellington, *Music Is My Mistress* (Garden City, N.Y.: Doubleday, 1973), 34.

43. Samuel B. Charters and Leonard Kunstadt, *Jazz: A History of the New York Scene* (Garden City, N.Y.: Doubleday, 1962), 153.

44. John Hammond with Irving Townsend, *John Hammond on Record: An Autobiography* (New York: Summit, 1977), 68.

45. John Hammond [Henry Johnson, pseud.], "The Negro in the Jazz Band," *The New Masses,* 17 November 1936, 15.

46. Jack Schiffman, *Uptown: The Story of Harlem's Apollo Theater* (New York: Cowles, 1971), 152–53.

47. Esperanza Delgado, interview by author, New York, 21 October 1988.

48. Lawrence Chenault, *The Puerto Rican Migrant in New York City* (1938; reprint, New York: Russell and Russell, 1970), 150.

49. Seda Bonilla, *La cultura política,* 237, cites a 1957 study of Puerto Ricans living in New York. Bernardo Vega notes in his *Memoirs,* 97, that Puerto Ricans sometimes claimed they were Spaniards or avoided speaking Spanish entirely in order to avoid problems.

50. Vega, *Memoirs,* 195.

51. Bauzá, interview, 2 June 1989. Ironically, Bauzá uses the racist term

"better hair." Classifying people of color according to "good" and "bad" hair seems to have been as prevalent in the Spanish-speaking Caribbean as it was in the United States.

52. Mario Bauzá, interview by author, New York, 8 May 1989.

53. Ibid.

54. Angélica Duchesne, interview by author, Caparra Heights, P. R., 5 January 1993.

55. Mario Bauzá, interview by author, New York, 2 June 1989.

56. Bobby Capó, interview by author, New York, 22 April 1988.

57. Bauzá, interview, 2 June 1989.

58. Ibid.

59. Ibid.

60. Ray Coen, interview, 9 January 1989.

61. "Músico portorriqueño que triunfa en Nueva York," El Mundo, 24 November 1940.

62. Ray Coen, interview, 9 January 1989.

63. Ibid.

64. Ibid.

65. Ibid.

66. Max Salazar, "History of Afro-Cuban Music," Sonido 1, no. 1 (1981): 4.

67. A pandereta is an Afro–Puerto Rican tambourine. It comes in various sizes and is made by stretching a skin over a round frame. It does not have the metallic disks or the jingling sound that characterize the tambourine commonly used in the United States.

68. A tribute to what Charles Keil has called the hall-of-mirrors-like dynamics of musical exchange, in this case between Latinos and African-Americans, is the fact that when Calloway issued "Minnie the Moocher" in 1931 it was backed by a number called "Doin' the Rhumba." See John Storm Roberts, The Latin Tinge: The Impact of Latin American Music on the United States (1979; reprint, Tivoli, N.Y.: Original Music, 1985), 93.

69. Ellington, Music Is My Mistress, 491.

70. For a brief account of the afrocubanismo movement, see Alejo Carpentier, La música en Cuba (Mexico: Fondo de Cultura Económica, 1946), chap. 16.

71. Salazar, "History of Afro-Cuban Music," 3.

3. PIPE WRENCHES AND VALVE TROMBONES

1. Francisco López Cruz, interview by author, San Juan, 4 December 1988. Puerto Rico was experiencing an economic decline years before the New York stock market crash. López Cruz, who left Puerto Rico two years before the Great Depression, seems to be equating the 1920s depression on the island with the 1930s one in the United States.

2. José Pastrana, "Case History #14," Box 3710, Works Progress Administration (WPA), Historical Records Survey, New York Municipal Archives, New York.

3. Ibid.

4. Jorge Javariz, "Rafael Hernández: El hombre y su música," program no. 5, WPR Radio, Puerto Rico, October 1992–January 1993.

5. Victoria Hernández, interview by author, New York, 11 May 1989.

6. Flores was not a musician in Puerto Rico. He was born in Naguabo in 1893 or 1894 and died in 1979.

7. Jaime Rico Salazar, *Cien años de boleros* (Bogotá: Centro de Estudios Musicales y La Academia de Guitarra Latinoamericana, 1987), 124.

8. Héctor Campos Parsi, *Música,* vol. 7 of *La gran enciclopedia de Puerto Rico* (Madrid: Ediciones R, 1976), 131.

9. López Cruz, interview, 4 December 1988.

10. Rumor has it that Caney himself was Jewish, possibly a Cuban but possibly not.

11. Antonio Moreno Caldero, "Don Plácido Acevedo Sosa," *La canción popular* 6, no. 6 (1991): 35.

12. Campos Parsi, *Música,* 127.

13. Jorge Javariz, "Cincuenta años de música en Puerto Rico," *La canción popular* 2, no. 2 (1987): 5.

14. For one example of the modern perpetuation of these images, see John Storm Roberts, *The Latin Tinge: The Impact of Latin American Music on the United States* (1979; reprint, Tivoli, N.Y.: Original Music, 1985): "Cuarteto Caney, Cuarteto Victoria, and Cuarteto Machín . . . were strictly local" (90).

15. The *tres* is a nine-stringed Cuban guitar with a sound distinct from the ten-stringed, mandolinlike Puerto Rican *cuatro.* The *marímbula* is a wooden box with metal prongs that makes bass sounds, more or less the Cuban equivalent (in both socioeconomic and musical terms) of the North American washtub bass.

16. Clara Rodríguez coined the useful metaphor "snapshot approach" in *Puerto Ricans: Born in the U.S.A.* (New York: Unwin Hyman, 1989), 43.

17. *Directorio hispano de la ciudad de Nueva York* (New York: Alpina, 1929), 75.

18. Virginia Sánchez-Korrol, *From Colonia to Community: The History of Puerto Ricans in New York City, 1917–1948* (Westport, Conn.: Greenwood, 1983), 29.

19. Victoria Hernández, interview by author, New York, 27 March 1989.

20. "Recuerda composiciones grabadas Trío Borinquen," *El Mundo,* 18 January 1964, suppl.

21. Mike Amadeo, interview by author, Bronx, N.Y., 31 May 1988.

22. Catalino Rolón, interview by René López and Jorge Pérez, 1979, transcript, Centro de Estudios Puertorriqueños, New York.

23. Nathan Glazer and Daniel Moynihan, *Beyond the Melting Pot: The Negroes, Puerto Ricans, Jews, Italians, and Irish of New York City* (Cambridge: MIT Press, 1963), 91; Box 3737, WPA, Historical Records Survey.

24. Bernardo Vega, *Memoirs of Bernardo Vega,* ed. César Andreu Iglesias, trans. Juan Flores (New York: Monthly Review, 1984), 9–10.

25. Lawrence Chenault, *The Puerto Rican Migrant in New York City* (1938; reprint, New York: Russell and Russell, 1970), 104.

26. Rolón, interview.

27. Johnny Rodríguez, interview by author, Santurce, P. R., 21 December 1988.

28. Vega, *Memoirs*, 73.

29. Box 3737, WPA, Historical Records Survey.

30. Ibid.; Glazer and Moynihan, *Beyond the Melting Pot*, 91.

31. Box 3737, WPA, Historical Records Survey; Caroline Ware, *Greenwich Village, 1920–1930: A Comment on American Civilization in the Post-War Years* (Boston: Houghton Mifflin, 1935), 227.

32. Vega, *Memoirs*, 101.

33. Pedro Malavet Vega, *La vellonera está directa* (Santo Domingo: Editora Corripio, 1985), 164.

34. Esperanza Delgado, interview by author, New York, 21 October 1988.

35. Amadeo, interview.

36. Vega, *Memoirs*, 101.

37. Josean Ramos, *Vengo a decirles adiós a los muchachos* (San Juan: Sociedad de Autores Libres, 1989), 24.

38. López Cruz, interview, 4 December 1988.

39. Ibid.

40. Johnny Rodríguez, interview, 21 December 1988.

41. Box 3737, WPA, Historical Records Survey.

42. *La Prensa* (New York), 1 August 1919.

43. López Cruz, interview, 4 December 1988.

44. "Guia del lector," *La Prensa*, 13 May 1924.

45. "Sociedades hispanas," ibid., 13 February 1928.

46. Ibid., 28 July 1919.

47. Ibid., 12 March 1927.

48. Box 3737, WPA, Historical Records Survey.

49. López Cruz, interview, 4 December 1988.

50. "Sociedades hispanas," *La Prensa*, 25 September 1926.

51. "Programa del Día de las Madres," *El Nuevo Mundo* (New York), 10 May 1930.

52. Victoria Hernández, interview, 11 May 1989.

53. López Cruz, interview, 4 December 1988.

54. Victoria Hernández, interview, 27 March 1989.

55. *Inspirado* means, more or less, one who is naturally inspired, and *enamorado,* one who is susceptible to falling in love or who has many love interests. Although Victoria Hernández did not say this, it is clear that these were roles that required a spontaneous and loose lifestyle that men, but not women, could get away with.

56. Victoria Hernández, interview, 11 May 1989.

57. Javariz, "Rafael Hernández."

58. Victoria Hernández, interview, 11 May 1989.

59. *Manhattan Address Telephone Directory,* summer 1930, 87. This directory gives a block-by-block rather than an alphabetized listing of addresses and telephone numbers.

60. John J. Bukowczyk, *And My Children Did Not Know Me: A History of the Polish-Americans* (Bloomington: Indiana University Press, 1987), 36–37.

61. F. Arturo Rosales, "Spanish Language Theater and Early Mexican Immigration," in *Hispanic Theater in the United States*, ed. Nicolás Kanellos (Houston: Arte Público, 1984), 18–19.

62. Sánchez-Korrol, *From Colonia to Community*, 81.

63. Max Salazar, "First in the Groove: Gabriel Oller, Aguinaldos to Salsa," pt. 1, *Latin New York*, February 1974, 2.

64. Efraín Vaz, interview by author, Río Piedras, P. R., 4 January 1989.

65. Rafael Portela, interview by author, Río Piedras, P. R., 3 December 1988.

66. *Revista Roqué* (radio magazine), n.d..

67. Terig Tucci, *Gardel en Nueva York* (New York: Webb, 1969), 121.

68. Evidence indicates that the black writers, artists, and show producers of the 1920s received a great deal of help from wealthy white patrons. With the onset of the economically difficult 1930s and the shift in focus of these patrons from black cultural expression to other artistic concerns, blacks had an extremely difficult time getting funding for artistic projects and entertainment ventures. While in the realm of music, bands such as Cab Calloway's and Duke Ellington's were thriving, most African-American ensembles were not (see chapter 2). A strong and supportive black merchant class might have helped to offset some of the problems of economic and social discrimination described in chapter 4.

69. Ted Fox, *Showtime at the Apollo* (New York: Holt, Rinehart and Winston, 1983), 60.

70. See Harold Cruse, *The Crisis of the Negro Intellectual* (New York: William Morrow, 1967), 73–83, for an account of a strike by black theater operators against the Lafayette Theater management that became a communitywide issue of white versus black labor.

71. On the demographic changes, see the population reports in Box 3737, WPA, Historical Research Survey; Sánchez-Korrol, *From Colonia to Community*; Vega, *Memoirs*; and Nicolás Kanellos, *A History of Hispanic Theater in the United States: Origins to 1944* (Austin: University of Texas Press, 1990), 127, 135.

72. "Los bufos cubanos en el teatro Park Palace," *El Nuevo Mundo*, 22 March 1930.

73. Ibid.

74. Ibid., 13 June 1938.

75. *The Scandals* was the name of a popular Broadway show produced a few years earlier by George White.

76. Advertisement, *La Prensa*, 12 November 1932.

77. "Tres mil personas ovacionaron a Carlos Gardel en la 'Premiere' del 'Campoamor,'" ibid., 13 August 1934; Tucci, *Gardel en Nueva York*, 69.

78. "Por los teatros," *La Prensa*, 13 April 1934.

79. Roberts, *Latin Tinge*, 89.

80. Amadeo, interview.

81. Manuel Peña, interview by author, Bayamón, P. R., 12 December 1988.

82. Pepito Arvelo, interview by author, Bayamón, P. R., 12 December 1988.

83. Francisco López Cruz, interview by author, Río Piedras, P. R., 6 December 1988.

84. Francisco López Vidal, interview by author, Río Piedras, P. R., 15 December 1988.

85. Charlie Palmieri, interview by Centro de Estudios Puertorriqueños, 19 June 1974, transcript, Centro de Estudios Puertorriqueños, New York.

86. Rolón, interview.

87. Roberts, *Latin Tinge*, 76.

88. Chenault, *Puerto Rican Migrant*, 129.

89. Box 3737, WPA, Historical Records Survey.

90. Chenault, *Puerto Rican Migrant*, 129.

91. López Cruz, interview, 4 December 1988.

92. Tucci, *Gardel en Nueva York*, 22–23.

93. Johnny Rodríguez, interview, 21 December 1988.

94. Ibid.

95. Palmieri, interview.

96. López Cruz, interview, December 4, 1988.

97. Tucci, *Gardel en Nueva York*, 93–99.

98. Box 3737, WPA, Historical Records Survey.

99. Advertisements, *La Prensa*, 1927–39, passim.

100. Advertisement, ibid., 13 December 35.

101. Tucci, *Gardel en Nueva York*, 224.

102. Arvelo and Peña, interviews by author, 12 December 1988.

103. Desi Arnaz, *A Book* (New York: William Morrow, 1976), 50.

104. Roberts, *Latin Tinge*, 91.

105. López Cruz, interview, 6 December 1988.

106. Vaz, interview, 4 January 1989.

107. Johnny Rodríguez, interview, 21 December 1988.

108. Ibid. A *guayabera* is a loose-fitting, often embroidered cotton shirt worn by men in Cuba, Puerto Rico, and other parts of Latin America.

109. López Cruz, interview, 6 December 1988.

110. Ibid.

111. Bobby Capó, interview by author, New York, 22 April 1988.

4. "VÉNTE TÚ"

1. Francisco López Cruz, interview by author, Río Piedras, P. R., 6 December 1988.

2. Richard Spottswood, "Ethnic and Popular Style in America," in *Folk Music and Modern Sound,* ed. William Ferris and Mary L. Hart (Jackson: University of Mississippi Press, 1982), 60–70.

3. "Spanish Records: Mexican Specialties," *Columbia Record* 2, no. 1 (1904): 2; Pekka Gronow, "Ethnic Recordings: An Introduction," in *Ethnic Recordings in America: A Neglected Heritage,* ed. American Folklife Center (Washington, D.C.: Library of Congress, 1982), 16.

4. Cristóbal Díaz Ayala, *Música cubana del areyto a nueva trova* (San Juan: Editorial Cubanacán, 1981), 233; Pedro Malavet Vega, *El tango y Gardel* (Barcelona: Zip Editora, 1975), 92; "Making Records in Porto Rico," *Talking Machine World* 5, no. 6 (1909): 14.

5. "Making Records in Porto Rico," 14.

6. Jorge Javariz, "Cincuenta años de música en Puerto Rico," *La canción popular* 2, no. 2 (1987): 4.

7. Recording ledger, Victor Talking Machine Company, 1917, Radio Corporation of America Archives, New York.

8. Ibid., 27 January 1917.

9. Díaz Ayala, *Música cubana*, 233.

10. Gronow, "Ethnic Recordings," 5.

11. Curiously, Spanish-language catalogs from this and later periods advertise music in Italian, German, and English and have music from Trinidad, France, and Hawaii, but there is no evidence of Brazilian or Portuguese records. Yet Rio de Janeiro was certainly an early recording base for the large North American record companies.

12. Gage Averill, "Haitian Dance Bands, 1915–1970: Class, Race, and Authenticity," *Latin American Music Review* 10, no. 2 (1989): 212.

13. Arístides Incháustegui, *El disco en República Dominicana* (Santo Domingo: Amigo del Hogar, 1988), 12; Wilson Roberts Hernández, *Eduardo Brito* (Santo Domingo: Ediciones de Taller, 1986).

14. Francisco López Vidal, interview by author, Río Piedras, P. R., 15 December 1988.

15. Ramón Dávila, interview by author, Levittown, P. R., 29 December 1988.

16. John Storm Roberts, *The Latin Tinge: The Impact of Latin American Music on the United States* (1979; reprint, Tivoli, N.Y.: Original Music, 1985).

17. Spottswood, "Ethnic and Popular Style," 63–64.

18. Richard Spottswood, "Commercial Ethnic Recordings in the United States," in *Ethnic Recordings in America*, ed. American Folklife Center, 63.

19. Edgardo Díaz Díaz, "El impacto del fonógrafo en la sociedad puertorriqueña del siglo XIX," *La canción popular* 4, no. 4 (1989): 40.

20. Bernardo Vega, *Memoirs of Bernardo Vega*, ed. César Andreu Iglesias, trans. Juan Flores (New York: Monthly Review, 1984), 101, 98.

21. Harold Smith, "SUBJECT: Foreign Record Situation," memo, 28 May 1925, 5, Box 4, File 20, Music Division, Harold D. Smith Collection, National Library of Canada, Ottawa.

22. Harold D. Smith, "The Thing Talked: Some Memories of Days Spent Inside and Outside the Phonograph Business" (1963), 214, Box 7, Files 15–16, ibid.

23. "Around the World with Our Record Makers: In China," *Columbia Record* 6, no. 3 (1908): 3–4.

24. Frederick Starr, "Making Graphophone Records in Central Africa," ibid. 7, no. 10 (1909): 10–13.

25. "Edison Phonographs in Four Corners of the World: Instruments Entertaining and Educating Civilized People and Untutored Savages," *Talking Machine World* 24, no. 1 (1928): 42.

26. Harold Smith, "Going After the Foreign Business," *Voice of the Victor* 12, no. 9 (1917): 173.

27. Smith, "The Thing Talked," 214.

28. Harry A. Goldsmith, "The Buyer of Foreign Records," *Voice of the Victor* 13, no. 5 (1918): 87.

29. Smith, "Going After the Foreign Business," 173.

30. Smith, "The Thing Talked," 268.

31. Smith, "SUBJECT: Foreign Record Situation," 5. In his introduction to Maurice Waller and Anthony Calabrese's *Fats Waller* (New York: Schirmer, 1977), Michael Lipskin notes that blacks in Harlem in the 1910s had no ethnic outlet besides piano rolls, and when they heard Mamie Smith's "Crazy Blues" floating out of local record stores, they were transfixed by "the sound of one of their own, singing the blues with a band that was definitely from the neighborhood" (xiv). The idea that groups of people systematically ignored or abused in the media would react more positively to recordings by local artists is an interesting one and worth exploring. Undoubtedly, the aesthetic issues are also bound up with the fact that for poor people, achievement in the arts represents an escape from poverty.

32. Smith, "SUBJECT: Foreign Record Situation," 8.

33. See, e.g., Hernández's advertisements in *La Prensa*, 13 April and 13 December 1929.

34. Smith, "SUBJECT: Foreign Record Situation," 2. Cristóbal Díaz Ayala claims that only Argentina and Uruguay had more records than Cuba in Victor's 1923 Spanish-language catalog (*Música cubana*, 147).

35. Gronow, "Ethnic Recordings," 7.

36. Victoria Hernández, interview by author, New York, 27 March 1989.

37. Gronow, "Ethnic Recordings," 7.

38. Max Salazar, "First in the Groove: Gabriel Oller, Aguinaldos to Salsa," pt. 2, *Latin New York*, March 1974, 2.

39. López Cruz, interview, 6 December 1988.

40. Héctor Campos Parsi, "Unos bailan, otros lloran: Crónica de la música puertorriqueña durante la gran depresión (1928–1931)" (master's thesis, Centro de Estudios Avanzados de Puerto Rico y el Caribe, 1992), 210.

41. Ovidio Dávila, interview by author, Vega Alta, P. R., 16 December 1992.

42. Francisco López Cruz, interview by author, San Juan, 4 December 1988.

43. Ibid.

44. Pedro Ortíz Dávila, interview by Edgardo Díaz Díaz, Cataño, P. R., 31 May 1985, transcript, 24–26.

45. Smith, "The Thing Talked," 215.

46. López Cruz, interview, 4 December 1988.

47. Ibid.

48. The best-selling genres were the popular, usually danceable ones. Forms that were undanceable or whose dances were outmoded, such as the *seis, aguinaldo,* and *mapeye* of the mountainous interior of Puerto Rico, became "Christmas music," recorded by a few groups every October and November and sold in December.

49. López Cruz, interview, 4 December 1988.

50. Jorge Javariz, interview by author, Bayamón, P. R., 13 December 1988.

51. Ibid.

52. The song title really means "Stir/shake it up or it will set/harden" and can refer either to a food that has coagulative properties or to sexual arousal.

53. John Hammond, no follower of Marx or Gramsci, claims that record companies in a racist society did exercise a certain degree of politically motivated censorship: "Every so often one can find a note of mild protest in a few of the Negro blues records which are tucked away in the 'race' catalogs. . . . But in general the studio supervisors are careful to see that the blues sound a note of defeat and futility, for it is middle class whites and large chain stores that distribute records to Negroes in the south" (John Hammond [Henry Johnson, pseud.], "Music: New Recordings," *The New Masses,* 31 March 1936, 27).

54. *Discos Victor Portorriqueños* (catalog), Victor Talking Machine Company, July 1920, 1, Sound Recordings Collection, Record Catalogs Collection, Rodgers and Hammerstein Division, Lincoln Center Branch, New York Public Library, New York.

55. Smith, "The Thing Talked," 249.

56. Incháustegui, *El disco en República Dominicana,* 15.

57. López Cruz, interview, 4 December 1988.

58. Johnny Rodríguez, interview by author, Santurce, P. R., 21 December 1988.

59. Manuel Peña, interview by author, Bayamón, P. R., 12 December 1988.

60. Incháustegui, *El disco en República Dominicana,* 15, 41.

61. Terig Tucci, *Gardel en Nueva York* (New York: Webb, 1969), 212–13.

62. Pedro Ortíz Dávila, interview by Gustavo Batista, 1985, transcript, Instituto de Cultura Puertorriqueña, San Juan.

63. Mario Bauzá, interview by author, New York, 2 June 1989.

64. Margot Arce, "Puerto Rico en las canciones de Rafael Hernández," *Isla* 1, no. 4 (1939): 4–5.

65. Jorge Javariz, "Trayectoria artística y discográfica de Rafael Hernández," in *El disco en Puerto Rico, 1892–1965* (Ponce, P.R.: Museo del Arte, 1992), 30.

66. Javariz, "Cincuenta años de música," 3.

67. For a more extensive discussion of this 1940s event, see the conclusion.

68. Johnny Rodríguez, interview by Gustavo Batista and Juan Mora Bosch, 12 February 1985, transcript, Instituto de Cultura Puertorriqueña, San Juan.

69. Jorge Javariz, interview, 13 December 1988.

70. This is true even today. José Salinas, who organized the annual Rafael Hernández Festival in Aguadilla, noted: "When you say to people 'independentista,' they don't view it very well, but when you say 'Lamento Borincano,' they do. . . . Our culture is undeniable" (José Salinas, interview by author, Aguadilla, P. R., 3 November 1988).

71. Vega, *Memoirs,* 157.

72. Edward Rivera, *Family Installments: Memories of Growing Up Hispanic* (New York: Penguin, 1983), 244.

73. Ma Dhyan Elsa Betancourt, *Hasta siempre Rafael Hernández* (Río Piedras, P.R.: Yaravi, 1981), 18–19.

74. *Tiempos Viejos,* WPR Radio, Puerto Rico, March 1963.

75. Pedro Zervignon, "Cantor que cante a los pobres, ni muerto se ha de callar," *El Reportero,* 10 July 1986.

76. López Cruz, interview, 6 December 1988.

77. Ibid.

78. José Luis González, "La protesta jíbara en el Lamento Borincano," *El Nuevo Día* (San Juan), 18 April 1982.

79. Smith, "Going After the Foreign Business," 173.

80. "What International Department Is Doing," *Columbia Record* 15, no. 3 (1917): 5.

81. Augusto Rodríguez, "Rafael Hernández: El cantor puertorriqueño," in *Antología del pensamiento puertorriqueño,* ed. Eugenio Fernández Méndez (1935; reprint, Río Piedras: University of Puerto Rico, 1975), 989.

5. "EL HOME RELIEF"

1. Marcial Reyes, interview by Centro de Estudios Puertorriqueños, 11 December 1974, transcript, Centro de Estudios Puertorriqueños, New York. A *pandereta* is a type of tambourine used in the *plena,* and *pandereteros* are those who play them. Throughout this chapter I often quote or use the word *plenero* to generally denote a practitioner of this musical genre.

2. C. Orama Padilla, "En la muerte de plenero mayor 'Canario,'" *Revista del Instituto de Cultura Puertorriqueña* 18, no. 69 (1975): 1–3.

3. Juan Flores, "Bumbún and the Beginnings of the Plena," *Centro de Estudios Puertorriqueños Bulletin* 2, no. 3 (1988): 20.

4. "Fue en Ponce . . . Augusto Coen nos relata el origen de la plena," *Alma Latina,* 5 May 1951, 5.

5. Félix Echevarría Alvarado, *La plena: Origen, sentido y desarollo en el folklore puertorriqueño* (Santurce, P.R.: Express Offset and Printing, 1984); Flores, "Bumbún," 16–25.

6. Jorge Duany, "Popular Music in Puerto Rico: Toward an Anthropology of *Salsa,*" *Latin American Music Review* 5, no. 2 (1984): 192.

7. Ernesto Vigoreaux, interview by author, Río Piedras, P. R., 26 December 1988.

8. Ernesto Vigoreaux, interview by Gustavo Batista, 30 September 1980, transcript, Instituto de Cultura Puertorriqueña, San Juan.

9. Flores, "Bumbún," 18.

10. Reyes, interview.

11. Vigoreaux, interview, 30 September 1980.

12. Vigoreaux, interview, 26 December 1988.

13. Flores, "Bumbún," 20.

14. Reyes, interview.

15. Reyes, interview. Ramón Cepeda, another elderly *plenero,* from a family that is still famous throughout Puerto Rico for practicing the form, concurs that very few whites or light-skinned people were involved in the music (Ramón Cepeda, interview by author, Bronx, N.Y., 30 July 1990). Nevertheless, Eduardo Seda Bonilla, Charles Rogler, and others cite the relatively high incidence of interracial marriage and residence among lower-class Puerto Ricans.

16. Echevarría Alvarado, *La plena,* 61.

17. Vigoreaux, interview, 26 December 1988.

18. Ibid.

19. Flores, "Bumbún," 17.

20. Ovidio Dávila, interview by author, Vega Alta, P. R., 16 December 1992.

21. José Enrique Ayoroa Santaliz, "Manuel Jiménez Otero ('Canario')," *La canción popular* 4, no. 4 (1989): 7–8.

22. *Plenas: Manuel "Canario" Jiménez y Su Conjunto Típico,* liner notes, L. P. ICP/MP-5, Instituto de Cultura Puertorriqueña, 1964; Héctor Campos Parsi, *Música,* vol. 7 of *La gran enciclopedia de Puerto Rico* (Madrid: Ediciones R, 1976), 73; Ovidio Dávila Hernández, "¿Quién fue el primer cantante puertorriqueño en grabar música popular?" *El Mundo,* 11 October 1981, *Telerevista* section. Dávila Hernández calls the store owner Manuel Castellanos, but it is clear from the context and from supporting documentation that he is in error about the first name.

23. Vigoreaux, interview, 26 December 1988.

24. Echevarría Alvarado, *La plena,* 151.

25. María Luisa Muñoz, *La música en Puerto Rico: Panorama histórico-cultural* (Sharon, Conn.: Troutman, 1966), 93.

26. Catalino Rolón, interview by René López and Jorge Pérez, 1979, transcript, Centro de Estudios Puertorriqueños, New York.

27. Flores, "Bumbún," 24.

28. "El Canario," *El Nuevo Mundo,* 26 April 1930.

29. Francisco López Cruz, interview by author, Río Piedras, P. R., 6 December 1988.

30. Ayoroa Santaliz, "Manuel Jiménez Otero," 10.

31. López Cruz, interview, 6 December 1988.

32. For Handy's account of his discovery and use of the blues, see his *Father of the Blues: An Autobiography* (1941; reprint, New York: Collier, 1970).

33. "Order Blank and Advance List: New Victor International Records, September 1929," Box 1, File 1, Music Division, Harold D. Smith Collection, National Library of Canada, Ottawa.

34. Echevarría Alvarado, *La plena,* 152.

35. Richard Spottswood, "Ethnic Music on Records: A Discography of Ethnic Recordings Produced in the United States, 1894–1932" (Los Angeles: John Edwards Memorial Forum, 1984, computer printout), 1690–96.

36. Campos Parsi, *Música,* 74.

37. Echevarría Alvarado, *La plena,* 107.

38. Ibid.

39. Since in the original Spanish there are no pronouns before the verbs, the person arriving from China could be a man or a woman.

40. Ramón Cepeda, interview.

41. Echevarría Alvarado, *La plena,* 92.

42. Ibid., 152.

43. Monserrate Deliz, "Puerto Rican Music," *Present-Day American Literature* 4, no. 1 (1930): 12–16.

44. Tomás Blanco, "Elogio a la plena," *Ateneo Puertorriqueño* 1, no. 1 (1935): 98.

45. Juan Flores, *The Insular Vision: Pedreira's Interpretation of Puerto Rican Culture* (New York: Research Foundation of the City University of New York, 1978), 37.

46. Braulio Dueño Colón, "Estudio sobre la danza puertorriqueña," *Educación* 36 (March 1973): 116.

47. See John Storm Roberts, *Black Music of Two Worlds* (New York: Praeger, 1972); and Angel Quintero Rivera, "Music, Social Classes, and the National Question in Puerto Rico" (Río Piedras: Centro de Investigaciones Sociales, University of Puerto Rico, February 1987, photocopy).

48. Flores, "Bumbún," 23.

49. José Luis González, *El país de los cuatro pisos y otros ensayos* (Río Piedras, P.R.: Ediciones Huracán, 1987).

50. Margot Arce, "Puerto Rico en las canciones de Rafael Hernández," *Isla* 1, no. 4 (1939): 4–6; Augusto Rodríguez, "Rafael Hernández: El cantor puertorriqueño," in *Antología del pensamiento puertorriqueño*, ed. Eugenio Fernández Méndez (1935; reprint, Río Piedras: University of Puerto Rico, 1975), 985–91.

CONCLUSION

1. Cab Calloway and Brian Rollins, *Of Minnie the Moocher and Me* (New York: Thomas Y. Crowell, 1976), 81.

2. Nathan Glazer and Daniel Moynihan, *Beyond the Melting Pot: The Negroes, Puerto Ricans, Jews, Italians, and Irish of New York City* (Cambridge: MIT Press, 1963), 91–92.

3. By the 1940s the major record labels had changed their focus from selling phonographs to creating mammoth hit records for the widest possible audience. During this era independent labels arose among many of the ethnic groups previously recorded by Victor, Columbia, and Decca.

4. This debate clearly has relevance today, for example, in the cases of Native American societies fighting for recognition or debating over criteria for accepting people as members.

5. See Noel Allende Goitia, "Por la encendida calle antillana: Cultura musical y discurso histórico en la sociedad puertorriqueña en la década del treinta (1929–1939)" (master's thesis, University of Puerto Rico, 1992); and Leonardo Acosta, *Música y descolonización* (Havana: Editorial Arte y Literatura, 1982).

6. I am indebted to Edgardo Díaz Díaz for pointing out this particular subtlety.

7. See Acosta, *Música y descolonización*; Peter Manuel, ed., *Essays on Cuban Music: North American and Cuban Perspectives* (Lanham, Md.: University Press of America, 1991), 40; and Pedro Malavet Vega, *Historia de la canción popular en Puerto Rico (1493–1898)* (Santo Domingo: Editora Corripio, 1992), 42.

8. Juan Flores, with John Attinasi and Pedro Pedraza, Jr., "La Carreta Made a U-Turn: Puerto Rican Language and Culture in the United States," *Daedalus* 110, no. 2 (1981): 193–217.

9. Victor Greene, *A Passion for Polka: Old-time Ethnic Music in America* (Berkeley and Los Angeles: University of California Press, 1992), 2; James Robbins, "The Cuban *Son* as Form, Genre, and Symbol," *Latin American Music*

Review 11, no. 2 (1990): 182; Peter Manuel, *Popular Musics of the Non-Western World: An Introductory Survey* (New York: Oxford University Press, 1988), 33.

10. Langston Hughes, *The Big Sea* (1940; reprint, New York: Hill and Wang, 1963), 228. Gladys Bentley was an African-American pianist popular during the Harlem Renaissance.

11. David Whisnant, *All That Is Native and Fine: The Politics of Culture in an American Region* (Chapel Hill: University of North Carolina Press, 1983), 13.

12. Luis Muñoz Marín, *Memorias: 1898–1946* (San Juan: Inter American University of Puerto Rico, 1982), 179.

13. According to Josean Ramos, *Vengo a decirles adiós a los muchachos* (San Juan: Sociedad de Autores Libres, 1989), 37, Muñoz wanted to delete or change the words "todo está desierto y el pueblo está muerto de necesidad" (everything is deserted and the town is dead of necessity), presumably because it reflected badly on his own attempts to turn the Puerto Rican economy around. In *La-Le-Lo-Lai: Puerto Rican Music and Its Performers* (New York: Plus Ultra, 1973), 48, Peter Bloch suggests that Hernández was pressured to change or destroy "Lamento Borincano" but refused to do so.

Bibliography

MANUSCRIPT COLLECTIONS

Brooklyn Historical Society. Brooklyn, N. Y. Puerto Rican Settlers Collection.
Centro de Estudios Puertorriqueños. Hunter College. New York, N. Y. Jesús Colón Papers. Benigno Giboyeaux, for the Estate of Jesús Colón and the Communist Party of the United States of America.
———. Microfilm Collection.
Instituto de Cultura Puertorriqueña. San Juan. Oral Histories and Clippings Collection. Music Division.
Library of Congress. Washington, D.C. American Folklife Center. Discography Collection.
———. Broadcasting and Recorded Sound Division. Record Collection.
National Library of Canada. Ottawa. Harold D. Smith Collection. Music Division.
National Personnel Records Center. St. Louis, Mo. Military Records.
New York Municipal Archives. New York, N. Y. Historical Records Survey. Works Progress Administration.
New York Public Library. New York, N. Y. Lincoln Center Branch. Rodgers and Hammerstein Division. Record Catalogs Collection. Sound Recordings Collection.
———. Main Branch. Microfilm and Microfiche Collection.
———. Arthur A. Schomburg Center for Research in Black Culture. Manuscript Division.
Radio Corporation of America Archives. New York, N. Y. Victor Talking Machine Company Manuscript Recording Ledgers, 1910–1920.
Yale University. New Haven, Conn. Historical Sound Recordings Collection.
———. Beinecke Manuscript Library. James Weldon Johnson Collection.

INTERVIEWS

Acosta, Magda. Interview by J. Barreto, December 1974, interview 66. Transcript. Puerto Rican Settlers Collection, Brooklyn Historical Society, Brooklyn, N.Y.

Acosta, Ramón. Interview by John D. Vázquez, 5 November 1974, interview 20. Transcript. Puerto Rican Settlers Collection, Brooklyn Historical Society, Brooklyn, N.Y.

Amadeo, Mike. Interview by author. Bronx, N. Y., 31 May 1988.

Arvelo, Pepito. Interview by Edgardo Díaz Díaz. Tape recording, 7 May 1985.

———. Interview by author. Santurce, P. R., 30 November 1988.

———. Interview by author. Bayamón, P. R., 12 December 1988.

Bauzá, Mario. Interview by author. New York, 8 May 1989.

———. Interview by author. New York, 2 June 1989.

Capó, Bobby. Interview by author. New York, 22 April 1988.

———. Interview by author. New York, 23 February 1989.

Carrasquillo, Magdalena. Interview by John D. Vázquez, 15 November 1974, interview 38. Transcript. Puerto Rican Settlers Collection, Brooklyn Historical Society, Brooklyn, N.Y.

Cepeda, Ramón. Interview by author. Bronx, N. Y., 30 July 1990.

Coen, Petra. Interview with author. Río Piedras, P. R., 9 January 1989.

Coen, Ray. Interview by author. Río Piedras, P. R., 9 January 1989.

Colón, Ramón. Interview by Pedro Rivera and Thomas Rivera, 30 April 1973, interview 1. Transcript. Puerto Rican Settlers Collection, Brooklyn Historical Society, Brooklyn, N.Y.

Dávila, Ovidio. Interview by author. Vega Alta, P. R., 16 December 1992.

Dávila, Ramón. Interview by author. Levittown, P. R., 29 December 1988.

Delgado, Esperanza. Interview by author. New York, 21 October 1988.

Duchesne, Angélica. Interview by author. Caparra Heights, P. R., 5 January 1993.

Duchesne, Benjamin. Interview by author. Río Piedras, P. R., 21 December 1992.

Europe, James Reese, Jr. Interview by author. North Bellmore, N. Y., 11 July 1990.

Flores, Juan. Interview by author. Brooklyn, N. Y., 16 August 1990.

Guanill, Pedro. Interview by Monte Rivera, 18 June 1974, interview 47. Transcript. Puerto Rican Settlers Collection, Brooklyn Historical Society, Brooklyn, N.Y.

Gutiérrez, Juan. Interview by author. New York, 12 November 1990.

Henríquez, Tito. Interview by Gustavo Batista. Tape recording, 1985. Instituto de Cultura Puertorriqueña, San Juan.

———. Interview by author. San Juan, 26 November 1988.

Hernández, Victoria. Interview by Jorge Pérez. 25 January 1980. Sound recording, Centro de Estudios Puertorriqueños, New York.

———. Interview by author. New York, 27 March 1989.

———. Interview by author. New York, 11 May 1989.

Javariz, Jorge. Interview by author. Bayamón, P. R., 13 December 1988.

Loperena, Felix. Interview by John D. Vázquez, 22 November 1974, interview 18. Transcript. Puerto Rican Settlers Collection, Brooklyn Historical Society, Brooklyn, N.Y.

López Cruz, Francisco. Interview by author. San Juan, 4 December 1988.

———. Interview by author. Río Piedras, P. R., 6 December 1988.

López Vidal, Francisco. Interview by author. Río Piedras, P. R., 15 December 1988.

Marks, Edward B., Jr. Interview by author. New York, 5 June 1989.

Medina, Felipe. Interview by John D. Vázquez, 16 October 1974, interview 44. Transcript. Puerto Rican Settlers Collection, Brooklyn Historical Society, Brooklyn, N.Y.

Mendelsohn, Fred. Interview by author. Syosset, N. Y., 12 May 1989.

Miranda, Miguelito. Interview by Edgardo Díaz Díaz. Tape recording, 13 April 1984. Hato Rey, P.R.

Molina, José. Interview by author. Santurce, P. R., 6 December 1988.

Ortíz Dávila, Pedro. Interview by Gustavo Batista, 1985. Transcript. Instituto de Cultura Puertorriqueña, San Juan.

———. Interview by Edgardo Díaz Díaz. Cataño, P. R., 31 May 1985.

Palmieri, Charlie. Interview by Centro de Estudios Puertorriqueños, 19 June 1974. Transcript. Centro de Estudios Puertorriqueños, New York.

Peña, Manuel. Interview by author. Bayamón, P. R., 12 December 1988.

Plasencia, Gonzalo. Interview by Jaime Barreto, 4 November 1974, interview 26. Transcript. Puerto Rican Settlers Collection, Brooklyn Historical Society, Brooklyn, N.Y.

Portela, Rafael. Interview by author. Río Piedras, P. R., 3 December 1988.

Ramírez, Juanchin. Interview by Gustavo Batista. Tape recording, 2 February 1985. Instituto de Cultura Puertorriqueña, San Juan.

Reyes, Marcial. Interview by Centro de Estudios Puertorriqueños, 11 December 1974. Transcript. Centro de Estudios Puertorriqueños, New York.

Rivera, Cecilio. Interview by John D. Vázquez, 2 November 1974, interview 34. Transcript. Puerto Rican Settlers Collection, Brooklyn Historical Society, Brooklyn, N.Y.

Rodríguez, Johnny. Interview by Gustavo Batista and Juan Mora Bosch. 2 February 1985. Transcript. Instituto de Cultura Puertorriqueña, San Juan.

———. Interview by author. Santurce, P. R., 21 December 1988.

Rodríguez, Ramón. Interview by John D. Vázquez, 29 October 1974, interview 10. Transcript. Puerto Rican Settlers Collection, Brooklyn Historical Society, Brooklyn, N.Y.

Rolón, Catalino. Interview by René López and Jorge Pérez, 1979. Transcript, Centro de Estudios Puertorriqueños, New York.

Roqué, Teresa. Interview by author. Aguadilla, P. R., 31 December 1992.

Salinas, José. Interview by author. Aguadilla, P. R., 3 November 1988.

Sepúlveda, Ernesto. Interview by John D. Vázquez, 6 November 1974, interview 64. Transcript, Puerto Rican Settlers Collection, Brooklyn Historical Society, Brooklyn, N.Y.

Tejada, Gloria, Josephine Festa, and Luis Marrero. Interview by John D.

Vázquez, 24 June 1974, interview 8. Transcript, Puerto Rican Settlers Collection, Brooklyn Historical Society, Brooklyn, N.Y.

Tizol, Juan, and Rosebud Tizol. Interview by Brad Dechter, 30 July 1980, interview 562b. Transcript, Ellington Project, Oral History Collection, Yale School of Music, New Haven, Conn.

Toro de Usera, Irma. Interview by author. Isla Verde, P. R., 24 December 1992.

Torres, Clemente. Interview by John D. Vázquez, 18 November 1974, interview 19. Transcript, Puerto Rican Settlers Collection, Brooklyn Historical Society, Brooklyn, N.Y.

Vaz, Efraín. Interview by Edgardo Díaz Díaz. Tape recording, Villa Carolina, P. R., 30 May 1985.

―――. Interview by author. Río Piedras, P. R., 4 January 1989.

Velázquez, Carolina. Interview by Mayda Cortiella, 6 August 1973, interview 48. Transcript, Puerto Rican Settlers Collection, Brooklyn Historical Society, Brooklyn, N.Y..

Vigoreaux, Ernesto. Interview by Gustavo Batišta. 30 September 1980. Transcript, Instituto de Cultura Puertorriqueña, San Juan.

―――. Interview by Edgardo Díaz Díaz. Tape recording, Río Piedras, P. R., 10 April 1985.

―――. Interview by author. Río Piedras, P. R., 17 November 1988.

―――. Interview by author. Río Piedras, P. R., 26 December 1988.

Vizoso, Mandy. Interview by author. Santurce, P. R., 30 December 1988.

Webber Rodríguez, Juana. Interview by John D. Vázquez, 25 October 1974, interview 5. Transcript, Puerto Rican Settlers Collection, Brooklyn Historical Society, Brooklyn, N.Y.

GENERAL REFERENCES

Abbott, Lynn. "'Play That Barber Shop Chord': A Case for the African-American Origin of Barbershop Harmony." *American Music* 10, no. 3 (1992): 289–325.

Acevedo, Francisco. "Su majestad la plena." *El Nuevo Mundo,* 5 October 1929.

Acosta, Leonardo. *Música y descolonización.* Havana: Editorial Arte y Literatura, 1982.

Alberti, Luis. *De música y orquestas bailables dominicanas, 1910–1959.* Santo Domingo: Editora Taller, 1975.

Allende Goitia, Noel. "Por la encendida calle antillana: Cultura musical y discurso histórico en la sociedad puertorriqueña en la década del treinta (1929–1939)." Master's thesis, University of Puerto Rico, 1992.

American Folklife Center, ed. *Ethnic Recordings in America: A Neglected Heritage.* Washington, D.C.: Library of Congress, 1982.

American Social History Project. *Who Built America? Working People and the Nation's Economy, Politics, Culture, and Society.* Vol. 2. New York: Pantheon, 1992.

Aponte Ledée, Rafael. "Una fotografía y . . . unos chuscos." *El Nuevo Día* (San Juan) 7 January 1987.

Arce, Margot. "Puerto Rico en las canciones de Rafael Hernández." *Isla* 1, no. 4 (1939): 4–6.

Armas, Vasco de. "Pedro Flores y Cordova." *El Nuevo Día*, 8 August 1982.

Armes, Roy. *Third World Film Making and the West.* Berkeley and Los Angeles: University of California Press, 1987.

Arnaz, Desi. *A Book.* New York: William Morrow, 1976.

Aronowitz, Stanley. *The Crisis in Historical Materialism: Class, Politics, and Culture in Marxist Theory.* New York: Praeger, 1981.

"Around the World with Our Record Makers: In China." *Columbia Record* 6, no. 3 (1908): 3–6.

Arrieta, Rubén O. "Don Pedro Flores, genio y persona." *El Nuevo Día* (San Juan), 14 April 1978.

Arte y artistas (Federación de Músicos de Puerto Rico) 1, nos. 5–7 (1946).

"Así era Myrta Silva." *El Vocero,* 5 December 1987.

Austerlitz, Paul. "Dominican *Merengue* and the Politics of Identity." Paper presented at the annual meeting of the Society for Ethnomusicology, Cambridge, Mass., 1989.

Averill, Gage. "Haitian Dance Bands, 1915–1970: Class, Race, and Authenticity." *Latin American Music Review* 10, no. 2 (1989): 203–35.

Ayoroa Santaliz, José Enrique. "Manuel Jiménez Otero ('Canario')." *La canción popular* 4, no. 4 (1989): 3–12.

———. "Rafael Hernández." *El Reportero,* 24 October 1987.

———. "La trompeta mágica de Puerto Rico." *La canción popular* 5, no. 5 (1990): 57–63.

Badger, Reid. "The Conquests of Europe: The Remarkable Career of James Reese Europe." *Alabama Heritage* 1 (summer 1986): 34–49.

———. "James Reese Europe and the Prehistory of Jazz." *American Music* 7, no. 1 (1989): 49–67.

Balseiro, José A. "The Puerto Rican Danza." *Present-Day American Literature* 4, no. 1 (1930): 9–12.

Barradas, Efraín. "How to Read Bernardo Vega." In *The Commuter Nation: Perspectives on Puerto Rican Migration,* edited by Carlos Torre, Hugo Rodríguez-Vecchini, and William Burgos. Río Piedras: University of Puerto Rico Press, forthcoming.

Barth, Fredrik, ed. *Ethnic Groups and Boundaries.* Boston: Little, Brown, 1969.

Batista, Gustavo. "Rafael Duchesne." *El Reportero,* 24 May 1983, *Viva* section.

Bauza, Nydia. "Tributo póstumo para Davilita en el ICP." *El Reportero,* 9 July 1986.

Bechet, Sidney. *Treat It Gentle.* New York: Hill and Wang, 1960.

Becker, Howard. *Art Worlds.* Berkeley and Los Angeles: University of California Press, 1982.

Benson, Susan Porter, Stephen Brier, and Roy Rosenzweig, eds. *Presenting the Past.* Philadelphia: Temple University Press, 1985.

Bergad, Laird. *Coffee and the Growth of Agrarian Capitalism in Nineteenth Century Puerto Rico.* Princeton: Princeton University Press, 1983.

Berlin, Edward A. *Reflections and Research on Ragtime.* Brooklyn: Institute for Studies in American Music, Conservatory of Music, Brooklyn College of the City University of New York, 1987.

Betances, Samuel. "The Prejudice of Having No Prejudice in Puerto Rico." Parts 1 and 2. *The Rican* 2 (winter 1972): 41–54 and 3 (spring 1973): 22–37.

Betancourt, Ma Dhyan Elsa. *Hasta siempre Rafael Hernández.* Río Piedras, P.R.: Yaravi, 1981.

Black, Jan Knippers. *The Dominican Republic: Politics and Development in an Unsovereign State.* Boston: Allen and Unwin, 1986.

Blacking, John. *How Musical Is Man?* Seattle: University of Washington Press, 1973.

Blanco, Tomás. "Elogio a la plena." *Ateneo Puertorriqueño* 1, no. 1 (1935): 97–106.

Bloch, Peter. *La-Le-Lo-Lai: Puerto Rican Music and Its Performers.* New York: Plus Ultra, 1973.

Bodnar, John. *The Transplanted.* Bloomington: Indiana University Press, 1985.

Brecher, Jeremy. "A Report on Doing History from Below: The Brass Workers History Project." In *Presenting the Past,* edited by Susan Porter Benson, Stephen Brier, and Roy Rosenzweig. Philadelphia: Temple University Press, 1986.

Brecher, Jeremy, John Brown Childs, and Jill Cutler, eds. *Global Visions: Beyond the New World Order.* Boston: South End, 1993.

Brereton, Bridget. *Race Relations in Colonial Trinidad.* Cambridge: Cambridge University Press, 1979.

Brown, Scott E. *James P. Johnson: A Case of Mistaken Identity.* Metuchen, N.J.: Scarecrow Press and Institute of Jazz Studies, Rutgers University, 1986.

Bukowczyk, John. *And My Children Did Not Know Me: A History of the Polish-Americans.* Bloomington: Indiana University Press, 1987.

———. "The Transformation of Working-class Ethnicity: Corporate Control, Americanization, and the Polish Immigrant Middle Class in Bayonne, New Jersey 1915–1925." *Labor History* 25, no. 1 (winter 1984): 53–84.

Butler, Frank E. "How Wireless Came to Cuba." *Radio Broadcast* 6, no. 5 (1925): 916–25.

Calder, Bruce J. *The Impact of Intervention: The Dominican Republic during the U.S. Occupation of 1916–1924.* Austin: University of Texas Press, 1984.

Callejo, Fernando. *Música y músicos puertorriqueños.* 1915. Reprint. San Juan: Editorial Coqui, 1971.

Calloway, Cab, and Brian Rollins. *Of Minnie the Moocher and Me.* New York: Thomas Y. Crowell, 1976.

Campos Parsi, Héctor. *Música.* Vol. 7 of *La gran enciclopedia de Puerto Rico.* Madrid: Ediciones R, 1976.

———. "Unos bailan, otros lloran: Crónica de la música puertorriqueña durante la gran depresión (1928–1931)." Master's thesis, Centro de Estudios Avanzados de Puerto Rico y el Caribe, 1992.

La canción popular (Revista de la Asociación Puertorriqueña de Coleccionistas de Música Popular) 1–7. 1986–92.

Cantwell, Robert. *Bluegrass Breakdown.* Urbana: University of Illinois Press, 1984.

Carpentier, Alejo. *La música en Cuba.* Mexico: Fondo de Cultura Económica, 1946.

Castiel Jacobson, Gloria. "The Life and Music of Ernesto Lecuona: 1895–1963." Ph.D. diss., University of Florida, 1982.

Centro de Estudios de la Realidad Puertorriqueña. *La tercera raíz: Presencia africana en Puerto Rico.* San Juan: Instituto de Cultura Puertorriqueña, 1992.

Chanan, Michael. *The Cuban Image.* Bloomington: Indiana University Press, 1985.

Charters, Samuel B., and Leonard Kunstadt. *Jazz: A History of the New York Scene.* Garden City, N.Y.: Doubleday, 1962.

Chávez, Linda. *Out of the Barrio: Towards a New Politics of Hispanic Assimilation.* New York: Basic, 1991.

Chenault, Lawrence. *The Puerto Rican Migrant in New York City.* 1938. Reprint. New York: Russell and Russell, 1970.

Chilton, John. *McKinney's Music: A Biodiscography of McKinney's Cotton Pickers.* London: Bloomsbury Bookshop, 1978.

Colon, Jesús. "Editorial." *El Machete,* 24 April 1927.

———. *A Puerto Rican in New York and Other Sketches.* 1961. Reprint. New York: International Publishers, 1982.

Colón, Ramón. *Carlos Tapia: A Puerto Rican Hero in New York.* New York: Vantage, 1976.

Columbia Record. 1904–17.

Cooper, Patricia. "From Hand Craft to Mass Production: Men, Women, and Work Cultures in American Cigar Factories, 1900–1919." Ph.D. diss., University of Maryland, 1981.

La Correspondencia (Puerto Rico). 1917.

Cramer, Jo. "Forty Years on Broadway: E. B. Marks Looks Over His Four Decades of Song Publishing." *Metronome* 49, no. 10 (1933): 28–29.

Cruse, Harold. *The Crisis of the Negro Intellectual.* New York: William Morrow, 1967.

Cuchi Coll, Isabel. "Plácido Acevedo será invitado especial." *El Mundo,* 15 November 1968.

Cugat, Xavier. *Yo, Cugat: Mis primeros 80 años.* Palafrugell, Spain: Dasa Ediciones, 1981.

Curtis, Natalie. "The Negro's Contribution to the Music of America." *Craftsman,* February 1913. Reprinted in *Harlem on My Mind: Cultural Capital of Black America,* edited by Allen Schoener, 26–27. New York: Random House, 1968.

Dávila Hernández, Ovidio. "¿Quién fue el primer cantante puertorriqueño en grabar música popular?" *El Mundo,* 11 October 1981, *Telerevista* section.

Deliz, Monserrate. "Puerto Rican Music." *Present-Day American Literature* 4, no. 1 (1930): 12–16.

Díaz Ayala, Cristóbal. *Música cubana del areyto a nueva trova.* San Juan: Editorial Cubanacán, 1981.

Díaz Díaz, Edgardo. "El impacto del fonógrafo en la sociedad portorriqueña del siglo XIX." *La canción popular* 4, no. 4 (1989): 37–47.

———. "La música bailable de los carnets: Forma y significado de su repertorio en Puerto Rico (1877–1930)." *Revista musical puertorriqueña* 5 (January–June 1990): 2–21.

———. "Música para anunciar en la sociedad del siglo XIX." *Revista musical puertorriqueña* 1 (January–June 1987): 7–13.

———. "Social Meaning of the *Guaracha* in Two Puerto Rican Urban Contexts (1871–1926)." Paper, University of Texas, Austin, n.d.

Díaz Montero, Aníbal. *Mirando el mundo.* San Juan: Editorial Díaz Mont, 1979.

Dickey, Dan William. *The Kennedy Corridos: A Study of the Ballads of a Mexican-American Hero.* Austin: University of Texas Press, 1978.

Dietz, James. *Economic History of Puerto Rico: Institutional Change and Capitalist Development.* Princeton: Princeton University Press, 1986.

di Leonardo, Micaela. *The Varieties of Ethnic Experience: Kinship, Class, and Gender among California Italian-Americans.* Ithaca: Cornell University Press, 1984.

DiMeglio, John E. *Vaudeville U.S.A.* Bowling Green, Ohio: Bowling Green University Popular Press, 1973.

Directorio hispano de la ciudad de Nueva York. New York: Alpina, 1929.

Dixon, Robert M. W., and John Godrich. *Recording the Blues.* New York: Stein and Day, 1970.

Donahue, Frances Marie. "A Study of the Original Puerto Rican Colony in Brooklyn, 1938–1943." Master's thesis, Fordham University, 1945.

Dower, Catherine. *Puerto Rican Music following the Spanish American War.* Lanham, Md.: University Press of America, 1983.

Duany, Jorge. "After the Revolution: The Search for Roots in Afro-Cuban Culture." *Latin American Research Review* 23, no. 1 (1988): 244–55.

———. "Popular Music in Puerto Rico: Toward an Anthropology of *Salsa.*" *Latin American Music Review* 5, no. 2 (1984): 187–216.

Dueño Colón, Braulio. "Estudio sobre la danza puertorriqueña." *Educación* 36 (March 1973): 113–22.

Dufrasne, José Emanuel. "Los instrumentos musicales afroboricuas." In Centro de Estudios de la Realidad Puertorriqueña, *La tercera raíz: Presencia africana en Puerto Rico.* San Juan: Instituto de Cultura Puertorriqueña, 1992.

Echevarría Alvarado, Félix. *La plena: Origen, sentido y desarollo en el folklore puertorriqueño.* Santurce, P.R.: Express Offset and Printing, 1984.

"Edison Phonographs in Four Corners of the World: Instruments Entertaining and Educating Civilized People and Untutored Savages." *Talking Machine World* 24, no. 1 (1928): 42–43.

Elder, Jacob Delworth. "Evolution of the Traditional Calypso of Trinidad and Tobago: A Socio-Historical Analysis of Song Change." Ph.D. diss., University of Pennsylvania, 1966.

Ellington, Duke. *Music Is My Mistress.* Garden City, N.Y.: Doubleday, 1973.

Erenberg, Lewis A. *Steppin' Out: New York Nightlife and the Transformation of American Culture, 1890–1930.* Westport, Conn.: Greenwood, 1981.

Ewen, David. *All the Years of American Popular Music.* Englewood Cliffs, N.J.: Prentice-Hall, 1977.

Feather, Leonard. *The Encyclopedia of Jazz.* New York: Horizon, 1960.

Fernández Méndez, Eugenio. "Grandes valores de nuestro pueblo: Paquito López Cruz." *Avance,* 24 June 1974, 41–45.

——. *Historia cultural de Puerto Rico, 1493–1968.* San Juan: Ediciones "El Cemí," 1970.

Ferris, William, and Mary L. Hart, eds. *Folk Music and Modern Sound.* Jackson: University of Mississippi Press, 1982.

Figueroa, Pablo. *Hispanic Theater in New York City: 1920–1976.* New York: Off-Off Broadway Alliance and El Museo del Barrio, 1977.

Fletcher, Tom. *One Hundred Years of the Negro in Show Business.* New York: Burdge, 1954.

Flores, Juan. "Bumbún and the Beginnings of the Plena." *Centro de Estudios Puertorriqueños Bulletin* 2, no. 3 (1988): 16–25.

——. Foreword to *A Puerto Rican in New York and Other Sketches,* by Jesús Colón, ix–xvii. 1961. Reprint. New York: International Publishers, 1982.

——. *The Insular Vision: Pedreira's Interpretation of Puerto Rican Culture.* New York: Research Foundation of the City University of New York, 1981.

Flores, Juan, with John Attinasi and Pedro Pedraza, Jr. "La Carreta Made a U-Turn: Puerto Rican Language and Culture in the United States." *Daedalus* 110, no. 2 (1981): 193–217.

Fox, Ted. *Showtime at the Apollo.* New York: Holt, Rinehart and Winston, 1983.

"Fue en Ponce. . .Augusto Coen nos relata el origen de la plena." *Alma Latina,* 5 May 1951, 5.

Fuentes, Carlos. "Hispanic U.S.A.: A Mirror of the Other." *Nation,* 30 March 1992, 408–11.

Galvin, Miles. *The Organized Labor Movement in Puerto Rico.* London: Associated University Press, 1979.

García, Gervasio L. *Historia crítica, historia sin coartadas: Algunos problemas de la historia de Puerto Rico.* Río Piedras, P.R.: Ediciones Huracán, 1985.

García, Gervasio L., and A. G. Quintero Rivera. *Desafío y solidaridad.* Río Piedras, P.R.: Ediciones Huracán, 1982.

García, Kino. "Puerto Rico: Hacia un cine nacional." *Centro* 2, no. 8 (1990): 80–90.

Gautier, Antonio. *Laureles de Ponce.* San Juan: Instituto de Cultura Puertorriqueña, 1979.

Gelatt, Roland. *The Fabulous Phonograph, 1877–1977.* New York: Macmillan, 1977.

Gillett, Charlie. *Making Tracks: Atlantic Records and the Growth of a Multi-Billion Dollar Industry.* New York: E. P. Dutton, 1974.

Gitlin, Jay. "Lumpen Proletariat or Professional Artists? American Musicians and Their Unions: 1880–1900." Department of History, Yale University, 1981. Photocopy.

Glazer, Nathan, and Daniel Moynihan. *Beyond the Melting Pot: The Negroes, Puerto Ricans, Jews, Italians, and Irish of New York City.* Cambridge: MIT Press, 1963.

Goldman, Shifra, and Tomás Ybarra-Frausto. *Arte Chicano: A Comprehensive Annotated Bibliography of Chicano Art, 1965–1981.* Berkeley: Chicano Studies Library Publications Unit, 1985.

Goldsmith, Harry A. "The Buyer of Foreign Records." *Voice of the Victor* 13, no. 5 (1918): 87.

González, José Luis. *El país de los cuatro pisos y otros ensayos.* Río Piedras, P.R.: Ediciones Huracán, 1987.

———. "La protesta jíbara en el Lamento Borincano." *El Nuevo Día* (San Juan), 18 April 1982.

González Negrón, Máximo. "La Orquesta Happy Hills." *La canción popular* 3, no. 3 (1988): 27–31.

González Orta, Victoria. "Anécdotas sobre Davilita." *El Vocero,* 12 July 1986.

Gordon, Maxine. "Cultural Aspects of Puerto Rico's Race Problem." *American Sociological Review* 15, no. 3 (1950): 382–92.

Grame, Theodore. *America's Ethnic Music.* Tarpon Springs, Fla.: Cultural Maintenance Association, 1976.

Greene, Victor. *A Passion for Polka: Old-time Ethnic Music in America.* Berkeley and Los Angeles: University of California Press, 1992.

Gronow, Pekka. "Ethnic Recordings: An Introduction." In *Ethnic Recordings in America: A Neglected Heritage,* edited by the American Folklife Center, 1–49. Washington, D.C.: Library of Congress, 1982.

Guía Hispana. New York: Guía Hispana, 1934.

Gutman, Herbert. *Work, Culture, and Society in Industrializing America: Essays in American Working Class and Social History.* New York: Knopf, 1975.

Hammond, John [Henry Johnson, pseud.]. "Music: New Recordings." *The New Masses,* 31 March 1936, 27.

———. "The Negro in the Jazz Band." *The New Masses,* 17 November 1936, 15.

Hammond, John, with Irving Townsend. *John Hammond on Record: An Autobiography.* New York: Summit, 1977.

Handlin, Oscar. *The Uprooted.* New York: Grosset and Dunlap, 1951.

Handy, W. C. *Father of the Blues: An Autobiography.* 1941. Reprint. New York: Collier, 1970.

Harker, David. *One for the Money: Politics and Popular Song.* London: Hutchinson, 1980.

Hazen, Margaret Hindle, and Robert M. Hazen. *The Music Men: An Illustrated History of Brass Bands in America, 1800–1920.* Washington, D.C.: Smithsonian Institution Press, 1987.

Hennessey, Thomas. "From Jazz to Swing: Black Jazz Musicians and Their Music—1917–1935." Ph.D. diss., Northwestern University, 1973.

Henríquez Díaz, Tito. "Fragmentos de unas memorias." *Revista del Instituto de Cultura Puertorriqueña* 21, nos. 92–93 (1986): 3–12.

History Task Force, Centro de Estudios Puertorriqueños. *Labor Migration under Capitalism: The Puerto Rican Experience.* New York: Monthly Review, 1979.

Hobsbawm, Eric, and Terence Ranger, eds. *The Invention of Tradition.* New York: Cambridge University Press, 1983.

Huggins, Nathan Irvin. *Harlem Renaissance.* New York: Oxford University Press, 1971.

Hughes, Langston. *The Big Sea.* 1940. Reprint. New York: Hill and Wang, 1963.

Incháustegui, Arístides. *El disco en República Dominicana.* Santo Domingo: Amigo del Hogar, 1988.

"In Memoriam—Manuel Jiménez—'Canario.'" *Revista del Instituto de Cultura Puertorriqueña* 18, no. 69 (1975): 1.

Javariz, Jorge. "Cincuenta años de música en Puerto Rico." *La canción popular* 2, no. 2 (1987): 3–5.

———. "Rafael Hernández: El hombre y su música." WPR Radio, Puerto Rico. October 1992–January 1993.

———. "Trayectoria artística y discográfica de Rafael Hernández." In *El disco en Puerto Rico, 1892–1965,* 26–49. Ponce, P.R.: Museo del Arte, 1992.

Johnson, E. R. Fenmore. *His Master's Voice Was Eldridge Reeves Johnson.* Milford, Del.: State Media, 1974.

Johnson, James Weldon. *Black Manhattan.* 1930. Reprint. New York: Arno and New York Times, 1968.

Kanellos, Nicolás. *A History of Hispanic Theater in the United States: Origins to 1944.* Austin: University of Texas Press, 1990.

———, ed. *Hispanic Theater in the United States.* Houston: Arte Público, 1984.

Katz, Elihu, and George Wedell, with Michael Pilsworth and Dov Shindr. *Broadcasting in the Third World: Promise and Performance.* Cambridge: Harvard University Press, 1977.

Keil, Charles. "Slovenian Style in Milwaukee." In *Folk Music and Modern Sound,* edited by William Ferris and Mary L. Hart, 32–59. Jackson: University of Mississippi Press, 1982.

Kernfeld, Barry, ed. *The New Grove Dictionary of Jazz.* London: Macmillan, 1988.

Kimball, Robert, and William Bolcom. *Reminiscing with Sissle and Blake.* New York: Viking, 1973.

Knight, Franklin. *The Caribbean: The Genesis of a Fragmented Nationalism.* New York: Oxford University Press, 1990.

Leary, James P. "Old Time Music in Northern Wisconsin." *American Music* 2, no. 1 (spring 1984): 71–87.

Leiter, Robert D. *The Musicians and Petrillo.* New York: Bookman Associates, 1953.

León, Augusto. "La música de Puerto Rico en Nueva York." *Puerto Rico Ilustrado* 32 (September–October 1941): 6.

León Sánchez, Carmelo de. "Datos biográficos de Davilita." *Todo,* 27 November 1986.

Lewis, David Levering. *When Harlem Was in Vogue.* New York: Alfred A. Knopf, 1981.

Lewis, Gordon. *Puerto Rico: Freedom and Power in the Caribbean.* New York: Monthly Review, 1963.

Leymarie, Isabelle. "Salsa and Migration." In *The Commuter Nation: Perspectives on Puerto Rican Migration,* edited by Carlos Torre, Hugo

Rodríguez-Vecchini, and William Burgos. Río Piedras: University of Puerto Rico Press, forthcoming.

Lichty, Lawrence W., and Malachi C. Topping. *American Broadcasting: A Source Book on the History of Radio and Television.* New York: Hastings House, 1975.

Limón, José. "Folklore, Social Conflict, and the United States–Mexico Border." In *Handbook of American Folklore,* edited by Richard M. Dorson, 216–26. Bloomington: Indiana University Press, 1983.

———. "Mass Culture, Ethnicity, and the Concept of Symbolic Action: A Departure from Herbert Gans." Paper presented at the ninth biennial convention of the American Studies Association, November 1983.

———. "Western Marxism and Folklore." *Journal of American Folklore* 96, no. 379 (1983): 34–52.

Little, Arthur W. *From Harlem to the Rhine.* 1930. Reprint. New York: Haskell House, 1974.

López, Adalberto. "The Beginnings of Colonization: Puerto Rico, 1493–1800." In *Puerto Rico and Puerto Ricans: Studies in History and Society,* edited by Adalberto López and James Petras, 12–41. Cambridge, Mass.: Schenkman, 1974.

López, Adalberto, and James Petras, eds. *Puerto Rico and Puerto Ricans: Studies in History and Society.* Cambridge, Mass.: Schenkman, 1974.

López Cruz, Francisco. *La música folklórica de Puerto Rico.* Sharon, Conn.: Troutman, 1967.

López Martínez, Pío. *Historia de Cayey.* San Juan: Cooperativa de Artes Gráficas Romualdo Real, 1972.

"Making Records in Porto Rico." *Talking Machine World* 5, no. 6 (1909): 14.

Malavet Vega, Pedro. "Agenda del futuro en la canción popular." *Claridad,* 27 June–3 July 1986, *Suplemento en rojo* section.

———. *El tango y Gardel.* Barcelona: Zip Editora, 1975.

———. *Historia de la canción popular en Puerto Rico (1493–1898).* Santo Domingo: Editora Corripio, 1992.

———. *La vellonera está directa.* Santo Domingo: Editora Corripio, 1985.

Maldonado-Denis, Manuel. *The Emigration Dialectic.* Translated by Roberto Simón Crespi. New York: International Publishers, 1980. Originally published as *Puerto Rico y Estados Unidos: Emigración y colonialismo* (Mexico: Siglo Veintiuno Editores, 1976).

Malone, Bill. *Country Music U.S.A.* Austin: University of Texas Press, 1968.

Manhattan Address Telephone Directory. New York Telephone Company. Summer 1930.

Manuel, Peter. *Popular Musics of the Non-Western World: An Introductory Survey.* New York: Oxford University Press, 1988.

———, ed. *Essays on Cuban Music: North American and Cuban Perspectives.* Lanham, Md.: University Press of America, 1991.

Marcus, George E., and Michael M. J. Fischer. *Anthropology as Cultural Critique.* Chicago: University of Chicago Press, 1986.

Marks, Edward B., as told to Abbot J. Liebling. *They All Sang: From Tony Pastor to Rudy Vallee.* New York: Viking, 1934.

Mass Violence in America: The Complete Report of Mayor La Guardia's Commission on the Harlem Riot of March 19, 1935. 1935. Reprint. New York: Arno and New York Times, 1969.

McCoy, James. "The Bomba and Aguinaldo of Puerto Rico as They Have Evolved from Indigenous, African, and European Cultures." Ph.D. diss., Florida State University, 1968.

McDonald, J. Fred. *Don't Touch That Dial! Radio Programming in American Life 1920–1960.* Chicago: Nelson-Hall, 1979.

McKay, Claude. *Harlem: Negro Metropolis.* New York: E. P. Dutton, 1940.

———. *A Long Way from Home.* 1937. Reprint. London: Pluto, 1970.

Mintz, Sidney. *Caribbean Transformations.* 1974. Reprint. New York: Columbia University Press, 1989.

———. *Workers in the Cane: A Puerto Rican Life History.* 1960. Reprint. New York: W. W. Norton, 1974.

Morales Carrión, Arturo. *Puerto Rico: A Political and Cultural History.* New York: W. W. Norton, 1983.

Morawska, Ewa. "A Replica of the 'Old-Country' Relationship in the Ethnic Niche: East European Jews and Gentiles in Small-town Western Pennsylvania, 1880s–1930s." *American Jewish History* 75, no. 1 (1987): 27–87.

Moreno Caldero, Antonio. "El Cuarteto Mayarí." *La canción popular* 4, no. 4 (1989): 13–26.

———. "Don Plácido Acevedo Sosa." *La canción popular* 6, no. 6 (1991): 33–42.

Morris, Ronald L. *Wait until Dark: Jazz and the Underworld, 1880–1940.* Bowling Green, Ohio: Bowling Green University Popular Press, 1980.

Muñoz, María Luisa. *La música en Puerto Rico: Panorama histórico-cultural.* Sharon, Conn.: Troutman, 1966.

Muñoz Marín, Luis. *Memorias: 1898–1946.* San Juan: Inter American University of Puerto Rico, 1982.

La música en Aguadilla. Booklet of the Decimocuarto Festival de la Música de Rafael Hernández. N. p., 1988.

"Músico portorriqueño que triunfa en Nueva York." *El Mundo,* 24 November 1940.

Music-World Almanak (New York). September 1930, April 1931.

"Myrta Silva: Una leyenda viviente." *Tú,* 30 November 1974, 2–16.

Negrón, Hector Raul. "A Study of the Puerto Rican Employment Service Located in New York City." Master's thesis, Fordham University, 1940.

The New Masses. 1936–37.

El Nuevo Mundo (New York). 1928–30.

Olán, María A. "¿Dónde está el Cuarteto Mayarí?" *El Mundo,* 2 September 1973.

Orama Padilla, C. "En la muerte del plenero mayor 'Canario.'" *Revista del Instituto de Cultura Puertorriqueña* 18, no. 69 (1975): 1–3.

Orsi, Robert. *The Madonna of 115th Street: Faith and Community in Italian Harlem, 1880–1950.* New Haven: Yale University Press, 1985.

Ortíz Ramos, Pablo Marcial. *A tres voces y guitarras: Los tríos en Puerto Rico.* Santo Domingo: Editora Corripio, 1991.

Osofsky, Gilbert. *Harlem: The Making of a Ghetto: Negro New York, 1890–1930.* New York: Harper and Row, 1963.

Pacini Hernández, Deborah. "Music of Marginality: Social Identity and Class in Bachata." Ph.D. diss., Cornell University, 1989.

Padilla, Felix. *Latino Ethnic Consciousness.* Notre Dame, Ind.: University of Notre Dame Press, 1985.

———. *Puerto Rican Chicago.* Notre Dame, Ind.: University of Notre Dame Press, 1987.

Peiss, Kathy. *Cheap Amusements: Working Women and Leisure in Turn-of-the-Century New York.* Philadelphia: Temple University Press, 1986.

Peña, Manuel. *The Texas-Mexican Conjunto: History of a Working-class Music.* Austin: University of Texas Press, 1985.

Pérez, Louis A., Jr. *Cuba and the United States: Ties of Singular Intimacy.* Athens: University of Georgia Press, 1990.

———. *Cuba under the Platt Amendment, 1902–1934.* Pittsburgh: University of Pittsburgh Press, 1986.

Picó, Fernando. *Historia general de Puerto Rico.* Río Piedras, P.R.: Ediciones Huracán, 1988.

———. *Los gallos peleados.* Río Piedras, P.R.: Ediciones Huracán, 1983.

Picó de Hernández, Isabel. "The Quest for Race, Sex, and Ethnic Equality in Puerto Rico." *Caribbean Review* 14, no. 4 (1985): 127–41.

Plenas: Manuel "Canario" Jiménez y Su Conjunto Típico. Liner notes, L. P. ICP/MP-5, Instituto de Cultura Puertorriqueña, 1964.

Portela, Rafael. "Compositores del Viejo San Juan." *La canción popular* 5, no. 5 (1991): 53–54.

———. "La orquesta de Carmelo Díaz Soler." *Claridad,* 27 June–3 July 1986, *Suplemento en rojo* section.

Poyo, Gerald. *"With All, and for the Good of All": The Emergence of Popular Nationalism in the Cuban Communities of the United States, 1848–1898.* Durham, N.C.: Duke University Press, 1989.

La Prensa (New York). 1918–1940.

Quintero Rivera, Angel. "Music, Social Classes, and the National Question in Puerto Rico." Río Piedras: Centro de Investigaciones Sociales, University of Puerto Rico, February 1987. Photocopy.

———. *Patricios y plebeyos: Burgueses, hacendados, artesanos y obreros.* Río Piedras, P.R.: Ediciones Huracán, 1988.

———. "Socialist and Cigarmaker: Artisans' Proletarianization in the Making of the Working Class." *Latin American Perspectives* 10, nos. 2–3 (1983): 19–39.

Rafael Hernández vive. . .y siempre está en nosotros. Aguadilla, P.R.: Publicaciones Año Centenario, 1991.

Ramos, Josean. *Vengo a decirles adiós a los muchachos.* San Juan: Sociedad de Autores Libres, 1989.

"Recuerda composiciones grabadas Trío Borinquen." *El Mundo,* 18 January 1964, suppl.

Reichard de Cancio, Haydée E. *Memorias de mi pueblo. . .Aguadilla.* 1990. Reprint. Quebradillas, P.R.: San Rafael, 1991.

Revista Roqué. N. p., n.d. Personal collection of Rafael Portela, Río Piedras, P.R.

Reyes-Schramm, Adelaida. "The Role of Music in the Interaction of Black Americans and Hispanos in New York City's East Harlem." Ph.D. diss., Columbia University, 1975.

Rico Salazar, Jaime. *Cien años de boleros.* Bogotá: Centro de Estudios Musicales y La Academia de Guitarra Latinoamericana, 1987.

Rivera, Edward. *Family Installments: Memories of Growing Up Hispanic.* New York: Penguin, 1983.

Rivera Cabán, Rafael. *Aguadilla [la villa del ojo de agua]: Notas para su historia.* San Juan: Model Offset, 1985.

Robbins, James. "The Cuban *Son* as Form, Genre, and Symbol." *Latin American Music Review* 11, no. 2 (1990), 182–93.

Roberts, John Storm. *Black Music of Two Worlds.* New York: Praeger, 1972.

———. "The Latin Dimension in Popular Music." *BMI, The Many Worlds of Music* 3 (1976): 4–39.

———. *The Latin Tinge: The Impact of Latin American Music on the United States.* 1979. Reprint. Tivoli, N.Y.: Original Music, 1985.

Roberts Hernández, Wilson. *Eduardo Brito.* Santo Domingo: Ediciones de Taller, 1986.

Rodríguez, Augusto. "Rafael Hernández: El cantor puertorriqueño." In *Antología del pensamiento puertorriqueño,* edited by Eugenio Fernández Méndez, 985–91. 1935. Reprint. Río Piedras: University of Puerto Rico, 1975.

Rodríguez, Clara. *Puerto Ricans: Born in the U.S.A.* Boston: Unwin Hyman, 1989.

Rodríguez, Olavo Alén. *Géneros musicales de Cuba: De lo afrocubano a la salsa.* San Juan: Editorial Cubanacán, 1992.

Rodríguez Domínguez, Ezequiel. *Trío Matamoros: Treinta y cinco años de música popular cubana.* Havana: Editorial Arte y Literatura, 1978.

Rodríguez Escudero, Nestor A. *Hijos ilustres de Aguadilla.* Caparra Heights, P.R.: Centro Gráfico del Caribe, 1986.

Rogler, Charles. *Comerío: A Study of a Puerto Rican Town.* Lawrence: University of Kansas Press, 1940.

Roman, Ivan. "Outpouring of Emotion Marks Davilita's Funeral." *San Juan Star,* 11 July 1986.

Rosales, F. Arturo. "Spanish Language Theater and Early Mexican Immigration." In *Hispanic Theater in the United States,* edited by Nicolás Kanellos, 15–23. Houston: Arte Público, 1984.

Rosaly, Yolanda. "Me siento muy identificado con los pobres." *El Nuevo Día* (San Juan), 4 December 1987.

Roseberry, William. *Anthropologies and Histories.* New Brunswick, N.J.: Rutgers University Press, 1989.

Rosenzweig, Roy. *Eight Hours for What We Will: Workers and Leisure in an Industrial City, 1870–1920.* New York: Cambridge University Press, 1983.

Rust, Brian. *American Dance Band Discography, 1917–1942.* New Rochelle, N.Y.: Arlington House, 1975.

———. *The American Record Label Book.* New Rochelle, N.Y.: Arlington House, 1978.

———. *Jazz Records, 1897–1942.* Essex: Storyville, 1982.

———. *Victor Master Book, Vol. 2 (1925–1936).* Pinner, Middlesex: B. Rust, 1969.

Salazar, Max. "El Gran 'Federico': The Father of Dance Promotions." *Latin New York,* January 1973, 10–11.

———. "First in the Groove: Gabriel Oller, Aguinaldos to Salsa." Parts 1 and 2. *Latin New York,* February–March 1974, 1, 2.

———. "History of Afro-Cuban Music." *Sonido* 1, no. 1 (1981): 2–5.

———. "Machito: Frank Grillo 1909–1984." *Latin New York,* May 1984, 21–27.

———. "Machito: The Musician and the Roots of New York's Latin Music." *Latin New York,* April 1983, 23–28.

———. "The Quest for Recognition." *Latin New York,* June–July 1976, 37–38.

Sanabria, Carlos. "Labor Migration from Puerto Rico, 1900–1930, and the Origins of the Puerto Rican Community in New York City." Master's thesis, Hunter College, 1985.

Sánchez-Korrol, Virginia. *From Colonia to Community: The History of Puerto Ricans in New York City, 1917–1948.* Westport, Conn.: Greenwood, 1983.

Sanjek, Russell. *From Print to Plastic: Publishing and Promoting America's Popular Music (1900–1980).* Brooklyn: Institute for Studies in America's Popular Music, Brooklyn College of the City University of New York, 1983.

Santaliz, Coquí. "Aquí estoy todavía, querido pueblo." *El Reportero,* 14 May 1984.

Santiago, Javier. "Un tributo a Davilita." *El Nuevo Día* (San Juan), 20 July 1986.

Schafer, William J., with Richard B. Allen. *Brass Bands and New Orleans Jazz.* Baton Rouge: Louisiana State University Press, 1977.

Schafer, William J., and Johannes Reidel. *The Art of Ragtime.* 1973. Reprint. New York: Da Capo, 1977.

Schaffer, Alan. *Vito Marcantonio: Radical in Congress.* Syracuse: Syracuse University Press, 1966.

Schiffman, Jack. *Uptown: The Story of Harlem's Apollo Theater.* New York: Cowles, 1971.

Schoener, Allen, ed. *Harlem on My Mind: Cultural Capital of Black America, 1900–1968.* New York: Random House, 1968.

Scott, Emmett J. *Scott's Official History of the American Negro in the World War.* 1919. Reprint. New York: Arno and New York Times, 1969.

Seda Bonilla, Eduardo. *La cultura política de Puerto Rico.* Río Piedras, P.R.: Ediciones Amauta, 1976.

Sinnette, Elinor Des Verney. *Arthur Alphonso Schomburg: Black Bibliophile and Collector.* Detroit: New York Public Library and Wayne State University Press, 1989.

Sissle, Noble. "Happy in Hell: Memoirs of Lieutenant James 'Jim' Europe [October 1942]." Manuscript Division, Arthur A. Schomburg Center for Research in Black Culture, New York Public Library, New York City.

Sklar, Robert. *Movie-Made America: A Cultural History of the American Movies.* New York: Random House, 1975.

Slobin, Mark. *Tenement Songs: The Popular Music of the Jewish Immigrants.* Urbana: University of Illinois Press, 1982.

Slobin, Mark, and Richard Spottswood. "David Medoff: A Case Study in Inter-Ethnic Popular Culture." *American Music* 3, no. 3 (1985): 261–76.

Slonimsky, Nicholas. *Music of Latin America.* New York: Thomas Y. Crowell, 1945.

Smith, Harold. "Going After the Foreign Business." *Voice of the Victor* 12, no. 9 (1917): 173.

"Spanish Records: Mexican Specialties." *Columbia Record* 2, no. 1 (1904): 2.

Spottswood, Richard. "Commercial Ethnic Recordings in the United States." In *Ethnic Recordings in America: A Neglected Heritage,* edited by the American Folklife Center, 51–66. Washington, D.C.: Library of Congress, 1982.

———. "Ethnic and Popular Style in America." In *Folk Music and Modern Sound,* edited by William Ferris and Mary L. Hart, 60–70. Jackson: University of Mississippi Press, 1982.

———. "Ethnic Music on Records: A Discography of Ethnic Recordings Produced in the United States, 1894–1932." Los Angeles: John Edwards Memorial Forum, 1984. Computer printout. American Folklife Center, Library of Congress, Washington, D.C.

Starr, Frederick. "Making Graphophone Records in Central Africa." *Columbia Record* 7, no. 10 (1909): 10–13.

Stearns, Marshall. *The Story of Jazz.* New York: Oxford University Press, 1956.

Steinberg, Stephen. *The Ethnic Myth: Race, Ethnicity, and Class in America.* New York: Atheneum, 1981.

Tawa, Nicholas. *A Sound of Strangers.* Metuchen, N.J.: Scarecrow, 1982.

Thompson, Donald. "El ambiente musical en Puerto Rico en la década de 1880." *Cupey* 6, nos. 1–2 (1989): 120–39.

———. "A New World Mbira: The Caribbean Marímbula." *African Music Society Journal* 5, no. 4 (1975–76): 140–48.

Thompson, E. P. *The Poverty of Theory and Other Essays.* New York: Monthly Review, 1978.

Tiempos Viejos. WPR Radio, Puerto Rico. March 1963.

Toll, Robert. *The Entertainment Machine: American Show Business in the Twentieth Century.* New York: Oxford University Press, 1982.

Torre, Carlos, Hugo Rodríguez-Vecchini, and William Burgos, eds. *The Commuter Nation: Perspectives on Puerto Rican Migration.* Río Piedras: University of Puerto Rico Press, forthcoming.

Torregrosa, José Luis. *Historia de la radio en Puerto Rico.* Hato Rey, P.R.: Esmaco, 1991.

Tucci, Terig. *Gardel en Nueva York.* New York: Webb, 1969.

Ulanov, Barry. *Duke Ellington.* 1946. Reprint. New York: Da Capo, 1975.

Vecoli, Rudolph. "Contadini in Chicago: A Critique of the Uprooted." *Journal of American History* 51, no. 1 (1964): 404–17.

Vega, Bernardo. *Memoirs of Bernardo Vega.* Edited by César Andreu Iglesias. Translated by Juan Flores. New York: Monthly Review, 1984. Originally published as *Memorias de Bernardo Vega* (Río Piedras, P.R.: Ediciones Huracán, 1977).

Villar Roces, Mario. *Municipios.* Vol. 13 of *La gran enciclopedia de Puerto Rico.* Madrid: Ediciones R, 1976.

Voice of the Victor. 1911–18.

Walker, Leo. *The Big Band Almanac.* Pasadena: Ward Ritchie, 1989.

Waller, Maurice, and Anthony Calabrese. *Fats Waller.* New York: Schirmer, 1977.

Ware, Caroline. *Greenwich Village, 1920–1930: A Comment on American Civilization in the Post-War Years.* Boston: Houghton Mifflin, 1935.

"What International Department Is Doing." *Columbia Record* 15, no. 3 (1917): 5.

Whisnant, David. *All That Is Native and Fine: The Politics of Culture in an American Region.* Chapel Hill: University of North Carolina Press, 1983.

Williams, Raymond. "Base and Superstructure in Marxist Cultural Theory." In *Problems in Materialism and Culture,* 31–49. London: Verso, 1980.

———. *The Country and the City.* New York: Oxford University Press, 1973.

Wolf, Eric. *Europe and the People without History.* Berkeley and Los Angeles: University of California Press, 1982.

Yans-McLaughlin, Virginia. *Family and Community: Italian Immigrants in Buffalo, 1880–1930.* Ithaca: Cornell University Press, 1977.

Zervignon, Pedro. "Cantor que cante a los pobres, ni muerto se ha de callar." *El Reportero,* 10 July 1986.

———. "Rafael Hernández: Cuba y México en su vida." *El Nuevo Día* (San Juan), 24 October 1988.

Selected Discography

Note: Many of the recordings referred to in this book are no longer issued and are only available through private collections and special archives. Those interested in pursuing this area should consult the following:

Library of Congress. Washington, D. C. Broadcasting and Recorded Sound Division. Record Collection.

New York Public Library. New York, N. Y. Lincoln Center Branch. Rodgers and Hammerstein Division.

Syracuse University Library. Syracuse, N. Y. Diane and Arthur B. Belfer Audio Laboratory and Archive.

ANTHOLOGIES, INDIVIDUAL ARTISTS, AND GROUPS

Canario y Su Grupo. *Plenas.* Ansonia ALP 1232.

Capó, Bobby, with Cuarteto Marcano. *El eco y el carretero.* M&A 564.

Cuarteto Caney. *Cuarteto Caney.* Decca/Borinquen DG 1197.

Cuarteto Mayarí with Plácido Acevedo. *El cofre musical del recuerdo.* Guarani Record GLP-200.

The Cuban Danzon: Its Ancestors and Descendents. Ethnic Folkways FE 4066.

Gardel, Carlos. *Tangos.* BMG NK 90343.

Grupo Victoria. *Epoca de oro del Grupo Victoria con Davilita.* M&A 546.

Machín, Antonio, y Su Cuarteto. *Como Siempre.* BMG/RCA 3359-2-RL.

The Music of Puerto Rico, 1929–1946. Harlequin HQ 2075.

Ortíz Dávila, Pedro. *Davilita.* Island Records GLP-202.

Santos, Daniel. *El legendario Daniel Santos con el cuarteto original de Pedro Flores.* BMG/RCA 3363-2-RL.

Trío Borinquen. *Memorias del Trío Borinquen.* Memorias LP 583.

———. *Trío Borinquen.* Assia Records ALP-001.

Trío Matamoros. *Trío Matamoros.* RCA 05(0131)01081.

Index

247

Compositor:	Graphic Composition, Inc.
Text:	10/13 Sabon
Display:	Sabon
Printer and binder:	BookCrafters